In Rehearsal

In Rehearsal is a clear and accessible how-to approach to the rehearsal process. Author Gary Sloan brings more than thirty years' worth of acting experience to bear on the question of how to rehearse both as an individual actor and as part of the team of professionals that underpins any successful production. Interviews with acclaimed actors, directors, playwrights, and designers share a wealth of knowledge on dynamic collaboration.

The book is divided into three main stages, helping readers to refine their craft in as straightforward and accessible a manner as possible:

- *In the world*: A flexible rehearsal program that can be employed daily and over a typical four-week production rehearsal.
- *In the room*: Advice on working independently and productively with other members of a company, such as directors, playwrights, designers, and technical crew; how your personal creative process varies depending on the role, be it Shakespeare, musicals, film, television, or understudying.
- *On your own*: Creating your own rehearsal process, exploring original and famous rehearsal techniques, breaking through actor's block, and how to practice every day.

In Rehearsal breaks down the rehearsal process from the actor's perspective and equips its reader with the tools to become a generous and resourceful performer both inside and outside the studio. Its independent, creative, and daily rehearsal techniques are essential for any modern actor.

Gary Sloan is professor of acting at The Catholic University of America in Washington, DC. He has been a professional actor for thirty years, performing leading roles in major theater companies throughout the United States.

Laurence Maslon is an author, illustrator, and associate chair of New York University's graduate acting program.

In Rehearsal

In the world, in the room, and on your own

Gary Sloan

Illustrations by Laurence Maslon

LONDON AND NEW YORK

First published 2012
by Routledge
2 Park Square, Milton Park, Abingdon, Oxon OX14 4RN

Simultaneously published in the USA and Canada
by Routledge
711 Third Avenue, New York, NY 10017

Routledge is an imprint of the Taylor & Francis Group, an informa business

British Library Cataloguing in Publication Data
A catalogue record for this book is available from the British Library

Library of Congress Cataloging in Publication Data
Sloan, Gary, 1952-
In rehearsal : in the world, in the room and on your own / by Gary Sloan.
p. cm.
Includes bibliographical references and index.
1. Acting. I. Title.
PN2061.S56 2011
792.02′8--dc23 2011025865

ISBN: 978-0-415-67840-7(hbk)
ISBN: 978-0-415-67841-4(pbk)
ISBN: 978-0-203-14616-3(ebk)

Typeset in Times New Roman by
HWA Text and Data Management, London

Printed and bound in Great Britain by
TJ International Ltd, Padstow, Cornwall

To
My mentor, James Young
For my Journey with Jonah

"… the readiness is all."

William Shakespeare, *Hamlet*, Act V, scene 2

Contents

Acknowledgments

Determining whom to thank for the inspiration, experiences, and wherewithal to write this book is the kind of calculus equation that would take a person to the moon. Allow me a page to remember those who have recently and over the course of many years contributed to *In Rehearsal.*

First of all, my thanks to Talia Rodgers and Ben Piggott at Routledge Publishing and to John Hodgson at HWA Text and Data Management.

I want to thank Grant-in-Aid from the office of Graduate Studies at the Catholic University of America; also my CUA provost, James Brennan; dean Larry Poos and drama department chair Gail Beach for granting me a sabbatical in the spring of 2010, during which time I charted the course of this book.

I acknowledge Christopher Wheatley and David Krasner for their experienced advice during my maiden voyage into writing. And from earlier days of our lives: Dick Willis for giving me my first rehearsal; James Young, my mentor who baptized me into the theater; and Nigel Goodwin for his crucial direction at my crossroad. To my teachers: Charley Helfert, who introduced me to the creative process, and Jack Clay, who introduced me to William Shakespeare at Southern Methodist University. Thanks to the late Jerry Turner from the Oregon Shakespeare Festival, where I began my professional rehearsal life, and to Christopher Martin, founder of CSC Repertory, who brought this actor to rehearsal in New York. I am grateful to David Leong, Ed Gero, and Beth Turcotte for their guidance during my academic sojourn and to Karen Giombetti for her important questions and crucial introductions during this process. My thanks to Bob Butler and Flo Gibson at Audio Book Contractors, Emily Morse of New Dramatists and Andrea Anesi Indexing. Thank you to Jim Brown for his work analyzing the University Survey and to professors Janet Zarish (NYU), Catherine Weidner (DePaul), Elizabeth Van den Berg (McDaniel), Mark Lewis (Wheaton), Luis Perez (Roosevelt), Stephen Satta (Towson), Erica Tobolski

(USC), Elliot Wasserman (USI), Michael Tolaydo (St. Mary's), and Alan Wade (GW) and their students, for participating in the survey. To Marietta Hedges, my admired colleague, for her dedication and insights to the actor's process; Stephen Fried, for our rehearsal of *Haunted Prince, the Ghosts of Edwin Booth;* and to actors Hal Holbrook and the late Robert Prosky, with whom rehearsal was life-changing.

To Eric Conger for early editing advice, along with Sherman Howard, Donna Bullock, Cain Devore, Keith Hamilton Cobb, Dan Southern, Casey Biggs, Conrad Feininger, John Reid, Eugene Pressman, David Leong, Barry Mulholland, Juanita Rucker, Kelly and Jane Cronk, Brian Reddy, and my eternal second, Gregg Mitchell, for your friendship and inspiration. I want to acknowledge Carol Gottschall Pfund for being the first to support my life's calling; my brothers John, Bob, and Tony for your advice and confidence; Mom and Dad for your faith and work ethic, and Grandma Hoeflein for taking this little boy to see *The Guns of Navarone*.

Thank you to all of the artists who contributed their experiences and thoughts throughout this book. I am honored that Zelda Fichandler took such a keen interest in this work and agreed to contribute a few of her insights into rehearsal and the essence of good theatre.

I am deeply grateful to my children, Julia and Owen, for teaching me how to teach, how to love unconditionally, and how to realize the essence of life while I live it. Most of all, to my wife, Christie Brown, for your steadfast love, enlightened conversations, true partnership, and the spark that lit the fire to write *In Rehearsal*.

Foreword

Zelda Fichandler

Founding Artistic Director of Arena Stage, Washington, D.C.; Arts Professor Emeritus and Former Chair, Graduate Acting Program, Tisch School of the Arts, New York University

Beginning

I've now read *In Rehearsal*: *in the world, in the room, and on your own*, by Gary Sloan, twice—the first time when he invited me to join in with blurbs from others that are sprinkled through the book; remarks that respond to the actor's process in preparing a role, and the place she occupies in the arduous, joyous task of making an artwork—a production. Later, Sloan asked me whether I would write the Foreword. I wanted to prepare for that to be sure I hadn't missed anything, and I read the book again. He has so much to say that interests me.

I found the book transparent and clear, written with simplicity and deep thought. Sloan's capacity for empathy is admirable; as he himself is both a successful actor and teacher, he speaks with both experience and knowledge. He opens up to the young actor and to the mature professional and, perhaps, to a curious theatergoer, the process that begins as soon as the actor knows the part is hers. From there, the actor launches the work of private study at home and in the world, before moving into the rehearsal hall (usually ill-lit, cramped, and loaded with stored items that will never be used again!), where the life of the play, both internal and external, is explored. Finally, she arrives at her destination—the stage—and steps into an alternate reality, as the house lights dim and the stage lights go up.

Visitors love to watch the rehearsal process with its private work of discovering—*un*covering the stream of life hidden under the words of the play—but usually the actors and director prefer that the delicate work proceed among themselves until they have given form to the lives of the characters and are ready to be private-in-public. The process of work will continue, supporting the entire run of the play, as no performance is an exact repetition of the one before it but must be re-imagined, re-awakened, to live in a fresh way each time. Theater is an art of the moment and depends on so many factors, from the leading lady's headache to the temperature of the theater to an actor's spontaneous recognition of what that line in the text, which remained elusive in rehearsal, really means.

Sloan tells us early on that this is not "an acting book, which details the *craft* of acting." There are many of these already available, and you probably already have one or several of them. This is something quite different, and I believe the reader will find its perceptions, which illuminate a broader territory, complementary to the other books. Its emphasis on the hard work required of the actor in studying and preparing on her own and the detailing of that work will be important to every actor who takes her profession seriously.

The description of the nature of the collaboration between actor and director, varying greatly with each director and each production, is presented with insight by a number of working actors and directors who have written blurbs for the book. The success or failure of the collaboration, as every actor will recognize, will determine in large part the success or failure of the production as a whole.

My agreement with Sloan, as he speaks on behalf of the actor, is airtight:

> The revolution that I'm interested in seeing is the one where more of us take control of our process, come into rehearsal more prepared, speak honestly with authenticity during rehearsal, demand a freedom to explore and insist on ways to collaborate as much as possible while we find characterization under difficult or ideal situations.

All the work I have done in the theater has been actor-centered. At the same time, it has often been very difficult to convince even eager students that their place is at the very center of the art. Only gradually do they come to accept that theater is the most human of all the arts. And that because theater boomerangs back into the reality from which it came, they have the capacity, through their talent and expressivity, to change the world. It has given me great personal satisfaction to bring a number of them to this well of understanding. There is real need for this revolution as Sloan defines it.

Theater is a performance art, an experience between the actor and the audience. By the time the audience arrives to join in, the characters of the playwright have already been absorbed into the bodies of the actors. Inevitably, they become the primary figures with whom the audience identifies and through whom they are changed. Sloan is able to make us appreciate how this spiritual/physical transformation of self into another presence—the character—this walking in the shoes of another, comes about. And it gives credence to the revolution that needs to happen. Indeed, we must see the place of the actor differently, regarding her with greater respect and understanding that it takes decades, rather than a number of isolated productions, to make her a great artist. "Not-me, not *not*-me," this ultimately mysterious transformation, is expressed by an actor/author whose name I have unfortunately forgotten.

I have among my papers this note, and I share it with you to point to the scope of Sloan's thinking:

> Art brings life to life, and no art more than the art of the theater. Theater with its invented stories gives to the audience the opportunity to experience lives that they have never lived but might have, to see themselves in new ways. Theater with its many ways of looking at the world, engenders compassion, the highest human attribute, and, after all is said and done, reveals to us that we are all more simply human than otherwise.

In its essence, theater is actually very simple. It can take place in nothing more than a circle marked out by chalk on the floor. One person, the actor, crosses the "stage" for a reason particular to her, while another person, the audience, sits on a chair or squats on the ground and watches, identifying with the character and wondering where she is going and why. The actor has worked hard to be able to perform even this simple action specifically, with concentration and clear intention and with the ability to be interesting to the watcher.

Great acting, of course, takes deeper work—both while rehearsing for a production and continuing throughout the actor's life, whether she is in a production, or not. The world itself is the actor's ultimate school, and it's always in session. For to create a character with depth, ambivalence, layered thoughts and feelings, the required body and voice, in this historical period or another, able to really see and respond to the other characters, the actor must contain these possibilities within herself.

Mankind is *homo sapiens*, thinking man, but also *homo ludens,* playing man. Acting is a serious business, Sloan elaborates in the segment that is probably the key to his book, but it is also great fun (see his Hamlet story at the beginning of it and enjoy!).

There is much creative play in the actor's work. All ways of reaching the truth are explored in the rehearsal hall, one of the most joyous places in the world to be. Games, improvisation, trying something in various ways, sharing opinions and suggestions, seeing as courage an actor's perhaps-foolish attempt at something, inviting the unplanned-for and responding to it, are all pathways to theatrical truth. Abandoning the personal ego for the ego that wants to ferret out the truth of the play, is itself a high form of play—of freedom, which is another word for play.

Konstantin Stanislavsky, the legendary Russian actor and teacher, co-founder of the Moscow Art Theater, has reminded us to "love the art in oneself, not oneself in art." It falls to the theater community at large and to each individual actor, in rehearsal and onstage, to create an environment where all can do their work to their fullest capacity. There will be dissent. Again, the work is hard, and truth is variable, and there is often not just one "best way to do it." However, that is also fun: to accept the challenge of the clash of viewpoints and to resolve the discord. Isn't that our responsibility as creative people? Indeed, the creative process itself consists of overcoming the forces that contrive to inhibit it.

In Rehearsal is an intriguing book: practical/spiritual, serious/playful, dense in thought/light in expression. I'll read it yet again, I'm sure.

Prologue

Hoodwinking Hamlet

I played a practical joke on Cain DeVore. Cain is an actor and filmmaker who lives in Hollywood, California. We were doing some landscaping work on his property before a party he was throwing for members of the Filmmakers Alliance.

Every day we were digging and uprooting in different areas of his yard. One day, I decided that I would take a realistic prop skull from a production of *Hamlet* that I had done and bury it somewhere on his property. I thought it would be funny if I could fool him into thinking that we had found a dead body. I spent days scouting different locations and planting it in areas where he was working, but he would simply work around wherever I buried it. Besides, I began to worry that he might uncover it by smashing it with a shovel so I decided to "find it" myself.

Soon after, I was working beside his back patio and digging out a huge rose bush. This was the place. So, I began to tunnel my way under the patio to bury the skull as far in as might be findable.

He was an hour away from returning to his house after an errand when I suddenly began to worry. If I couldn't make him believe that I had found a rotting corpse on his property, my acting career was a sham! I began to doubt my abilities as an actor and actually became nervous. I was afraid that I just wouldn't be credible enough to *really* pull it off, because I didn't want it to be one of those jokes where you say something and then crack up ten seconds later. I wanted to see what he would do if he really believed it. However, this was outrageous stuff, and I feared he'd see through it immediately and that I wouldn't be able to stay focused and convince him otherwise. He wouldn't believe me at first, for sure, so how could I pull this off? How should I approach it? How should I tell him? I realized that I had never performed without some sort of rehearsal. So, I began at the beginning. Stanislavski, let's see what you've taught me when it counts!

"Okay, Sloan. What if you really found something in the ground underneath a back patio that you thought might be a real person's skull? What would you do? What would you *really* do?!"

I stopped and looked into the hole and began to imagine it. First, what are the given circumstances or, rather, what did they need to be to make them believable? The passing of time. I packed the skull with dirt and placed it underneath the patio in the hole I had already dug. I pushed it back into the hole underneath the patio so that only the top of the skull was showing. Then, privately, I started to reenact the situation.

I was on my hands and knees digging with a trowel and scraped the thing I had just buried. "Hey, what's this?" I improvised. I stopped, stared, slowly touched it, and stopped again. I examined it more closely, brushing away bits of dirt until I imagined that it would dawn on me that this could actually be a buried skull. It probably had the rest of its skeleton stretched out horizontally under the patio! "Don't touch it anymore, Sloan, this is a crime scene!"

"Okay, I've got to call Cain, but don't alarm him over the phone, just prepare him: I've found something and I don't know what it is but am very concerned, how soon will he be home?"

No answer.

"Okay, I gotta do this in person when he drives up." How would I tell him? If this had really happened, where should I—no, where *would* I—be when he drives up? "I'd be in the hole, staring and thinking." This makes it about the skull and not about my ability to lie. It takes the focus off my acting and puts it on the story itself.

What would I be doing? What do I want Cain to do? "I don't know, uh . . . I would want *him* to decide what to do, it's his house, after all, and the skull is buried under his patio. It's his problem!" So, I'd be concerned and want to help *him* decide what to do! I just found it. Hell, maybe *he* killed somebody! No, no, no . . . wrong direction . . . But, when you have an objective, you always have something stopping you from achieving it. You have an obstacle.. So, what's my obstacle? I'm worried, I'm amazed, because I've never touched a real skull before, never found a dead body, never even called the police in an emergency. So, I have to get him to help me see whether this is even the real thing! That's it. I don't know if this is real or not, and I need him to figure this out.

He pulls up.

I'm in the hole, focused on what I've found. Repeat to myself: "It's about the skull, not about the lie." And the thing is, it already looks so real (thanks to Chester Hardison in the props department), that I don't have to do a helluva lot. My objective is to determine what it is and then help Cain figure out what to do!

I had to keep thinking as if I'd found a skull, because my mind was starting to race and the tendency to overact is very strong. Stop. Think. Breathe. Concentrate. Be there.

Now, I've buried the skull horizontally beneath the patio and only left a little bit of it showing. It's hard and green looking. I had packed the insides with dirt, to make it heavier and give it the sense of time underground. (I wish I could've found some worms! Nah, that's overkill, would probably look staged. . . the worms might blow my cover and take focus!)

Anyway, he pulls up. I'm staring at the hole, look up, and motion for him to come over. I start to breathe heavier. Just breathe. This is the moment of truth (sort of). I stand up.

"What's up, buddy?" he said, walking toward me. Just breathe, Sloan. Shake your head and don't speak too fast. Breathe. Think: This could be burial ground. If it's a skull, then we've found a murder victim.

"I don't know, I think I found something." (Look at him and then quickly back into the ground—concerned, puzzled, and *not* playing that it's a skull, only *suspecting* that it might be!)

"What?"

Whatever nerves I still had I decided were a good thing. "Use them," I thought to myself. This could be a scary situation, after all.

"I, uh, (swallow) I don't know, but it feels like it could be a skull and I didn't want to dig it up until you got here. I don't know, it could be a skull." Just breathe, Sloan, just breathe and turn back toward the hole, look at Cain, now look in the hole, focus on the skull. Is it or isn't it? Kneel down. Less is more! Think the thoughts, not the result. *Is* it a skull? Think. Inner monologue time! (I don't know whether it is or whether it isn't, because if it is, we've got a problem, and my fingerprints are now on it . . . should we use gloves?) Good idea, put your gloves on, Sloan. Always good to find some sort of activity that supports your action! It's about the situation, not about his reaction and especially not my own performance. It's about the thing in the ground! Think of uncovering a bomb, carefully and slowly, without excitement, just one little move at a time.

"Let me see." Cain moves toward the hole.

He wipes away some dirt and feels the top of the prop. "Nah, that's, that feels like a, uh, like an old turnip or something."

(I have no lines. I don't want any lines. My career's at stake!)

He continues to wipe away the dirt and reveal the perfectly shaped top of the skull. Then, pushing dirt away from its side and reaching in, he suddenly jumps back.

"Holy shit, I felt the eye socket!"

My work was done!!! Done, done, done.

Cain was hooked. All I had to do was stay out of the way. Follow his lead, breathe, and assume the supporting role, not the lead anymore. I was now Horatio and he was Hamlet, driving the scene the way it had to go.

"You sure?" I said under my breath, shaking my head. Inner monologue time, because now the dialogue begins! . . . Think: This used to be someone. I bravely looked him squarely in the face for the first time, my own actor test. This turned out to be easy, because he was now all about the skull in the half-dug hole, and I wasn't even there.

His own inner monologue began to race. "We can't touch this, we can't move this . . . we've got to call the cops, we've got to do something, we've got to call the cops." Cain started to walk back and forth quickly, furiously thinking out loud.

At this point, I was just standing there, motionless and like holding a kite in the wind, he was going faster than I ever could have convinced him to go; blown by his own sweeping imagination.

"Oh my God!" he suddenly shouted, "I know who did this!"

This was the first time I almost broke out of the scene and had to literally clench my jaw to keep from laughing. Now Cain had the murderer, too!

"That son of a bitch! That son of a bitch! It's the guy who lived here when I bought the house! I bet this was his wife. We've got to call the cops."

I just nodded. I suddenly had a very small part, even though I was the one driving the scene, because I had the secret.

Cain sat down on the patio and put his hands over his face. "But I can't," he said, "Damn!"

I heard my cue. "Why?"

"I've got too many parking tickets!"

Too many parking tickets? Just breathe, Sloan, breathe, because even Neil Simon couldn't have written the parking ticket line. Hold for audience laughter, and stay in the scene! This isn't about you and laughing is not in the stage directions. You're acting career is on the line, remember? The stakes are still high.

"Ah fuck it—that doesn't matter." He headed in through his back door and I could hear him climbing the stairs.

"Cain!" I yelled.

"What?"

"There's something else! Come here for a second, will ya?"

Now, I had thought about the end of this scene when I buried the skull. I had actually played Hamlet with this skull at the Shakespeare Theater in Washington, DC, so I had a picture of myself holding the skull that I brought with me that day. I had buried it under the dirt close by, figuring it to be my revelation of the joke.

I could hear him rushing down the stairs and, as he came through the back door, I held up the black and white picture from the ground and handed it to him."

"This?"

He stared at it for a full three seconds until it dawned on him what it was and what I had done. You just can't describe the way a guy's face relaxes with a little embarrassment and a hint of admiration and then tenses with rage when he looks up at you having realized your prank.

My laugh was so deep and profound, that I don't even remember it being out loud. One of those intense deeply satisfying earthquakes inside your body that shakes everything until you have to slowly kneel to the ground holding your heart. I wasn't laughing because he had been fooled, but at the storyline he had created about the previous owners. I could finally let out my amusement of his personal and so very human crisis: whether to report a murder or pay his parking tickets. However, true to character, he'd leapt up and headed toward the phone.

Later, he confessed to me that when he saw the long-haired person in the picture that he initially thought that the murderer had buried a picture of his wife alongside the body! His mind was totally in the story.

Better than the prank, my acting career was saved, and I could hold my head up high, knowing that when it counted, I could hold it together, get out of the way, and act out a complete fiction as if it were true.

Dustin Hoffman on *Inside the Actor's Studio* quoted Jean Renoir:

> The film-maker [Jean] Renoir said a great thing; I saw an interview of his. He said as a director and as an actor, you don't have to know everything about it. You're not going to be able to do everything the script calls for. You do what you can, that's what you share, that's what you give. The audience, he says, is the co-author and the co-director and the collaborator. They will do the rest.

Cain found the skull, had the murderer, overcame his own obstacles, and was on his way to call the police. To this day, I'm still looking over my shoulder for him to exact his revenge. However, it was my thirty-minute rehearsal, backed up by twenty years of practice, that made all the difference: suggesting that actors have got to know what works for them and be ready to do it *anywhere!*

Part I
In the world

"It's a holy place," he said, referring to the dusty, dark, concrete, windowless freshman-dorm storage space, where we played theatre games, rehearsed scenes for class, and produced one show a semester. It had been cleared out and christened the Arena Theater by James Young, Wheaton College's first full-time theatre professor.

Twenty-eight years later, I came back to this room, long since returned to its original use, packed with mattresses, desks, and bed frames. It was a moment as I've imagined dying might be, seeing my life pass before me like a movie. All those theatres, faraway cities, productions, auditions, unemployment lines, relationships, survival jobs, and rehearsal rooms flashed through my mind and literally bent me over with emotion. It was here, here in this unlikely storage room, where my life's work was born.

Acting teacher Sanford Meisner is known to have said that it takes twenty years to become an actor.

Malcolm Gladwell, in his book *Outliers*, writes about the 10,000 hours it takes to become a success at anything.

Peter O'Toole, in an interview with Charlie Rose, said: "It's not just a question of learning your lines. The old fashioned word for it is study. You go alone, you have no observer, no interlocutor and unobserved, uninhibited, private study is the backbone of any fine actor or actress."

I want to make the case that your work is truly born and raised in the way that you approach rehearsing it. I want to make the case that the way you rehearse stems from the way you live, and however you approach life directly influences your creativity in rehearsal. This is not an acting book that details *the craft* of acting, though rehearsal, like practicing any skill, involves process and specific approaches. Let's look under the hood.

You may have the idea that the director is in charge of your rehearsal, much as your teachers are in charge of your classes. I hope you'll reconsider that.

What is an effective rehearsal process? How do *you* rehearse, similarly or differently from everyone else? How often? Are you entering tech rehearsal feeling as if you haven't even scratched the surface of the play? Do you feel you lose the character once you leave the rehearsal room? Are you frustrated by the amount of time that you're simply waiting around during rehearsal?

Most important, do you feel that you have a creative rehearsal process that you can depend on to stabilize your work in different plays, with difficult actors, controlling or inexperienced directors (or brilliant ones!)? While you're getting off-book, discovering the blocking, finding your characterization, and trying new things, are you worried about being judged by your peers?

What *is* the actor's job? What is the director's job? How do they work together, and what if they disagree? Should you have any input regarding your costume? How about your living room? What is your responsibility to the playwright? And how are you informing your artistic life with your regular life? Is there a difference?

I asked a friend of mine recently about his progress on a show he was doing, and he began lamenting a problem with another actor. "He doesn't know how to rehearse."

I think I know what he meant. His scene partner didn't have a process. He had no progression of exploring or trying different approaches to a scene: building his character layer by layer, beat by beat, finding a through-action and evolving a performance over time.

One of my graduate students at The Catholic University of America was studying the role of Laura in Tennessee Williams's *The Glass Menagerie*. She was very studious about it and read much about the history of the play's productions, the life of the author, the world of St. Louis during the time of the play, but when it came to step into Laura's shoes in the rehearsal room, she confessed, "Now what do I do? I have all this information, but I don't know how to play her. What do I do now?"

She had learned the blocking, memorized the lines, and put on Laura's costume, but she still felt as if she were faking it, playing only herself all dressed up as Laura.

In the book *How to Write*, Richard Rhodes describes his craft in this way: "Writing is a process not of inspired free association, but of concrete problem solving. Inspiration, if you will, comes out of the process of problem solving, not the other way around." An actor's rehearsal process is problem solving, too. You are Sherlock Holmes, constantly searching for clues to solve the problems inherent with creating life on stage. It is not making an instant cake; the character is made from scratch. It doesn't even look like a cake at first. It's egg yolks, confectioners' sugar, cups of milk, flour, and baking powder and teaspoons of salt. The first week of rehearsal doesn't resemble much of what the production will become, even though the pressure to perform at the very first reading is the actors' nemesis.

The rehearsal room is where you learn how to live in the story and *inhabit a role*. Laura waits in the words of the script until you study her world, her author's world, her given circumstances in the story, and then practice her by going back to basics; studying, reflecting, listening, reacting, making choices that occur to you without fear of criticism. You find her through-actions and pursuing her objectives one moment at a time. Laura *lives* when the actress tries to get what she wants.

Jerry Turner was the artistic director of the Oregon Shakespeare Festival in Ashland, Oregon, where I began my professional career. I will always remember finishing a final rehearsal of Shakespeare's *Coriolanus* and hearing him say how he hated to leave the rehearsal room, with all of its mocked-up clothing, taped floors, and the sweat it took to find the play. He said he had seen so many shows lose their guts when they left the rehearsal room for tech rehearsals and the performance. He lamented that it always took a long time to get the story back. From that moment on, I have always worked to take the rehearsal sweat right into tech, into opening night, and during the run of the show.

The rehearsal room is as big as your life. Acting is a 24/7 occupation where every day, every relationship, every job, every broken heart, every memory, every mistake, and every adventure is available to your character in *their* story.

Rehearsal is also a creative state that you need to develop every day, when you are in a show and when you are not.

> If you practice an art, be proud of it and make it proud of you. It may break your heart but it will fill your heart before it breaks it; it will make you a person in your own right.
>
> —Maxwell Anderson, *The Essence of Tragedy and Other Footnotes and Papers*, 1939

I want to make the case that you cannot become a great actor without learning how to *rehearse* your acting effectively and continually. You need techniques and discipline to know how to rehearse your craft, how to strengthen your artistic habits, how to increase your sense of exploration and self-confidence in life that directly affects the way you rehearse.

The room you enter to rehearse a particular play is also a world unto itself. It's whatever *you* make it and is as freeing or constricting as your habits and understanding of the rehearsal process. You can become someone who has ten ideas for every one idea of the director, assuming the responsibility for what you do in *your* rehearsal and in *your* performance.

As actors, we continue in 4,000 years of footprints. My mentor, James Young, used to *baptize* us into the world of theater as if it were a spiritual beginning. The storage room in the freshman dorm was where we played Viola Spolin theatre games and our lives were changed, but if we came unprepared for our scene, Jim turned on us like the Biblical hair-shirt Baptist himself and scolded, "You're offering shit to God!"

For more than thirty years, I have endeavored to offer something more acceptable. Learning *how* has been the challenge, and whatever I've learned has been at the feet and shoulder to shoulder with my directors, playwrights, teachers, designers, actors, and crew. So, necessarily, the voices in this book are more than mine. I will quote remarks from actors with whom I've either spoken directly, heard, or read. Quotes I've obtained personally are introduced as such, and quotes that I've read or heard on the media are referenced. Everyone I've quoted has at one time or another stepped into rehearsal hoping to be original and authentic, and all of them have discovered a creative process that works for them. Some of my friends are famous, most are not. However, they are all successful—having made a living, thriving and surviving a life in the theatre. This book is about finding *your own way of working* and *living* as an actor.

> There are not very many good actors, there are thousands who have so inscribed on their social security, or whatever it is … very few people can do it and you may think that is a mercy, but very few people can do it. And the ones who can have this extraordinary attitude that the words, the part is linked straight to one's own heart immediately, one feels it and knows it immediately, and one finds it, not easy, but eventually you will be able to express it, if you study, and by study the mechanical fact of study is you go alone, and you bang and bang and bang, you try different things, different whatever, yes, but to plug into one's emotion is the most important thing. Actors are people, only more so … "peopledom," lots of people in there.
>
> —Peter O'Toole, *The Charlie Rose Show*

The following chapters are not about the photosynthesis of good acting and how to do it but how to prepare the ground for it to happen. It is about productive *rehearsing* and growing into the actor you are meant to become, over time.

Many are called. Few are chosen.

And he spoke many things unto them in parables, saying, Behold, a sower went forth to sow;

And when he sowed, some seeds fell by the way side, and the fowls came and devoured them up:

Some fell upon the stony places, where they had not much earth: and forthwith they sprung up, because they had no deepness of earth:

And when the sun was up, they were scorched; and because they had no root, they withered away.

And some fell among thorns; and the thorns sprung up, and choked them:

But other fell into good ground, and brought forth fruit, some an hundredfold, some sixty-fold, some thirty-fold.

Who hath ears to hear, let him hear.

—Matthew, Chapter 13:3–9

1 The givens of rehearsal

Good ground

> I believe that we learn by practice. Whether it means to learn to dance by practicing dancing or to learn to live by practicing living, the principles are the same.... One becomes in some area an athlete of God.
>
> —Martha Graham, American dancer and choreographer, pioneer of modern dance, in a letter to Ted Shawn in 1923

Reporters are trained to ask basic life questions when they report a story; they are known as the 5 Ws (and 1 H), the *Given Circumstances*, also known as *the givens*, or the *who, what, where, when, why,* and *how* questions. Equally, actors need to know the given circumstances of their character to realistically live in the scene.

Who am I? What do I want? Where am I? When is this taking place? Why am I doing this? How do I get what I want?

However, you must ask these questions not only to discover your characters; *you need to ask and answer these same questions about your rehearsal process itself.* Too many students and professional actors alike are relying on directors to give them the answers and organize how they should rehearse. As actors, you need to form your own answers and your own creative rehearsal process if you want to fulfill your potential and originality.

Who?

You. Without you, the character is only words on a page. You are the role, cast because somebody saw something of the character in you and you in the character, or at least the knowledge that you could do it. Start positively, without second guessing: You are the best person for the role.

However, who are *you*? What would I have to know if I were going to play you?

You are bringing yourself to the process of rehearsal along with the riches of your life and stage experiences. You are bringing your imagination, your work ethic, your questions, your fears, your inhibitions, interests, and the way you look.

Actor Robert Prosky put it this way:

> As an artist, the main thing you offer is your individuality. We understand ourselves little enough. And we understand the character we're playing even less well. But the communication between the real individual and the fictional individual is so complex, that any diminution of that process is not paying full attention to what it is to be an actor.

What matters is authenticity of self: you're willing to commit all you are to the work at hand.

You are exploring your *self*, your connection with other actors, the script, *your* character and the best working relationship with your director, designers, dramaturgs, stage managers, crew, and staff. You must bring *yourself* to the table, with *your* questions, *your* research, and a belief that problems will present themselves as a good thing to deepen your understanding and performance.

It's also self-sacrifice at the same time: You need to get out of your own way. Self-consciousness should give way to telling the story of the play. The character will slowly begin to appear *as you* rehearse and then will start to dominate the action in the rehearsal room.

What?

What *is* rehearsal, and what do you want to achieve?

I asked this question of students at ten universities in the United States, and the answers often had to do with memorizing, blocking, and finding character. These are elements, of course, but I would add that rehearsal should be a much deeper experience than what lies at the surface of putting a show together. It's a little like asking, what is living? And the answers would include eating, drinking, sleeping, making love, and working, which begs the question, is that the essence of what living is? Is the *purpose* of rehearsal really to memorize lines and learn the blocking?

I was having my car worked on recently, and the mechanic asked me what I did for a living. I replied that I was an actor and a teacher. He said, "Oh, I took acting. It was the easiest 'A' I ever got … all you have to do is memorize!"

Rehearsal is like practicing on a flying trapeze, demanding complete commitment. It's also a playground, where spontaneity, impulses, and a childlike sense of play are encouraged. In Malcolm Gladwell's book *Blink*, he quotes a player from the improvisational group, *Mother,* "We think of what we're doing as a lot like basketball," he said. Malcolm continues the thought, "Basketball is an intricate, high speed game filled with split-second, spontaneous decisions. But that spontaneity is possible only when everyone first engages in hours of highly repetitive and structured practice."

My brother Tony assisted coach Bob Knight while a student at Indiana University. He reminded me recently of how player Steve Alford (Indiana's Mr. Basketball, 1983) was well known for the amount of free throw shots he would take every day. Now the head coach at the University of New Mexico, having had an extremely successful college, professional, and coaching career in his sport, Steve confirmed his method of practice. "I've been shooting all my life. I started shooting and charting 100 a day after my Freshman season."

It's the principle I want to emphasize. Do young actors believe that a successful career is based solely on talent or to be practiced only during the course of a production?

Rehearse stems from an old French word, *rehercier,* which translates to "rake over," to "go over again." It also stems from *repete*, meaning, "to repeat." It doesn't sound like a very artistic endeavor, but there is a secret in this word that those who rely solely on spontaneity and instinct will not discover. Repetition opens the door to character.

The definition of rehearsal includes other dynamic words, and each one could be its own chapter:

Review … study … prepare … trial … ground work … homework … training … dummy run … practice.

> Every rehearsal room reveals itself to itself.
>
> —Cate Blanchett, Australian stage and film actor,
> National Public Radio, *The Diane Rehm Show*

A rehearsal has its own life, growing out of the leadership of the director, organizational abilities of the stage manager, support of the producing theater but, most crucially, from the commitment, investment, ownership, and creativity of every single person in the cast. And not to be diminished, every play's story emanates a palpable energy from its characters and theme, which must be given weight. The 500-pound gorilla in this room is the play itself.

As Ken Jenkins, actor/director, said to us one day during a rehearsal of Patrick Meyer's *K-2* at the Actor's Theatre of Louisville, "There are three characters in this play; Harold, Taylor and the mountain. The mountain 'plays' and you have to let it."

The suspension of disbelief that the audience experiences during the course of the show has more to do with the story than your particular performance. So, during rehearsal, take some of the weight off *your* shoulders and join the party. The story is what drives the rehearsal where it's going.

Where?

The public space

Rehearsal spaces are usually not very grand. They have taped floors marking the parameters of the imagined set, sometimes a section in the corner for couches, tables, and coffee makers, with a big table hosting the director, stage manager, and assistant stage manager sitting ominously in front of the playing area. They could be considered your first audience but better to be considered your fellow players. Large, small, old, and new, this describes most every rehearsal room I have known in thirty years.

My first rehearsal space was a girls' high school gymnasium. At Hartford Stage, we rehearsed on the second floor of a car dealership. Arena Stage's rehearsal room used to be located in the back room of a shopping mall in southeast Washington. Rehearsals for a production of *Romeo and Juliet* at the Folger Theatre in Washington, D.C. were above a photo store on Capitol Hill. The Actors Theatre of Louisville rehearsal hall for *Cyrano de Bergerac* was in a local church's gymnasium. I've rehearsed in theatre lobbies, hotel ballrooms, classrooms, antique stores, courtyards, front yards, chapels, living rooms, subways, kindergarten rooms, kitchens, dance studios, back patios, black boxes, and basements. The rehearsal room is anywhere that an actor or a director chooses to work. There is also a private space, perhaps the most underrated and overlooked space in an actor's world.

The private space

In an interview on the Charlie Rose show, legendary Irish actor Peter O'Toole (*Lawrence of Arabia*) insists that an actor's primary rehearsal is time spent studying alone with the words of the script.

> Hundreds of years of tried, proven, professional practice … study, study, study, the more you study the more sense of meaning you can tease out of each sentence, the more you memorize it, something happens and you trust your unconscious mind … and it comes out.

Why, then, are actors often reluctant to study privately? It could be that you don't know what to do or how to go about it. I've sat alone with a script not really wanting to study it and not trusting my ideas. I've been afraid that my choices might interfere with the director's intentions.

And there was never enough time. The university experience makes demands on the student actor from every direction. A life in the theatre is often strangled by survival jobs and the intensity of paying bills. There just doesn't seem to be the time *outside of rehearsal* for personal study.

Hold on. Adjustment. There isn't *any* time spent with script that is *outside* of rehearsal! *Your* time with the script is the *heart* of your rehearsal. The first time you read it through, don't just look to see how big your part is! Read it for the story. Read it again, letting your thoughts and reactions roam. Take down some notes about whatever occurs to you. You've just started your prompt book! Then read your lines out loud, again and again, training your mouth and your ear to recognize them. They will be yours soon enough. Don't be afraid of questions: they're your best friends.

Early private rehearsal is like a first date. Get to know your character and their story a little at a time and be honest with them. There are things that you will immediately understand and things that are hidden to begin with. If you neglect this personal time with your role, whatever the reason, you will sacrifice confidence and depth.

Analyzing a script always sounded like writing a research paper to me, but a first date sounds like a walk in the park. Have fun, be yourself, follow what interests you, and take the time.

Mr. O'Toole is giving very tried and true advice. The more time spent alone with the script, the more you will develop your independent muscles and instincts. You'll learn to trust yourself. When you bring your revelations and explored ideas to the group rehearsal, you won't always know whether they're good or not. What matters is that you are exploring and becoming your own best director.

The consecrated space

> The Holy Theatre … the stage is a place where the invisible can appear and has a deep hold on our thoughts.
>
> —Peter Brook, *The Empty Space*

My first theatre teacher was Professor James Young, who was not interested in simply teaching theatre to the curious speech communication majors within our department. He was interested in revelation and christened us into a theatre of legends such as Stanislavski, Beckett, Brecht, Joseph Chaikin, Harold Pinter, Ingmar Bergman, and Peter Brook.

I was in his first class at Wheaton College, and he introduced us to an essential art form for anyone wanting to understand the human condition.

He saw acting as a spiritual undertaking, soulful enough to enter into life's mysteries and strong enough to withstand the heartbreak of rejection or the temptations of success.

The storage room in the freshman dorm was our church.

Actress Naomi Jacobson is a Woolly Mammoth Theatre Company member living in the Washington, D.C. area:

> I worked with Director Bill Alexander doing *Henry IV Part II* at The Shakespeare Theatre in Washington, D.C. One rehearsal protocol he used that I adored was that whoever was called for a particular rehearsal time was brought into the room by the stage manager and the door was closed. No one wandered in or out, no distractions, no one whispered or got coffee or did crossword puzzles. Anyone could observe any rehearsal they liked, but if you chose to be in the room, you were in the room, no leaving before that scene rehearsal was over. The focus, the concentration and honoring of the work was tremendous, as was the sense that the work was important, and those in the room were all vital to the process, whether acting or observing. I've never been in a more thrilling rehearsal room.

When?

A professional rehearsal is usually scheduled six days a week, for eight hours a day. Occasionally, a cast will vote to rehearse six hours straight without a lunch break and, most often, a director will choose to stagger a rehearsal call, meaning that only the actors working a particular scene will be called for that hour or day of rehearsal.

In the theatre, during the waiting time for their scene to begin, conscientious actors will study their role in preparation for that day's work. However, you can also justify relaxing, to keep yourself loose: reading a book, smoking a cigarette, shooting the breeze with other actors, or flirting with the theatre's staff. Whatever you do, make it a choice that supports the work you're about to begin.

Far too many actors bring their outside distractions, worries, stories, and cell phones into the rehearsal space. Instead of work, rehearsal becomes the cafeteria. Instead of church, it's turned into the mall. Shooting the breeze can be a warm-up but, before an audition, a film shoot, or a stage rehearsal, be careful to whom, why, where, when, and how you release your energy.

I spoke with the renowned Broadway legend Chita Rivera, who spoke about the immediate priorities when entering rehearsal:

> Listening, being on time, focusing, being exactly where you're supposed to be. If you're in that rehearsal hall, you're there, no place

else. I can't believe that people have phones that are on in rehearsal halls, it blows me away.

Be ready and single-minded during the formal rehearsal schedule. This is not a hobby or something you can live without, because if it is, you will live without it soon enough.

Equally, be ready, committed to, and protective of your private rehearsal time too. In other words, don't answer the phone. The interruption can easily throw you off track.

Like stage combat, if you don't practice the new moves at home the same night you've learned them, chances are they won't stick. It's *your job* to practice the sword fight, or the blocking, or the new character moments at night when you get home, and maybe the first thing the next morning when you get out of bed.

Why?

Why did you audition for this play? Why did you accept this role? Why do you want to be an actor in the first place? Try answering the question by asking another actor and then reciprocate. Say it aloud, because your reason will inform what you do in rehearsal and how you do it. Taking personal responsibility for your choice to become an actor or even to act in a particular role has a great underlying reason. It is the firepower you need to succeed in a role or in the ups and downs in the life as an actor.

Actors can be doctors for the heart and mind. Playwrights create the medicine, but we deliver it. It's one of the ways we grow as human beings. As Hamlet says, "*... the purpose of playing, whose end, both at the first and now, was and is, to hold, as 'twere, the mirror up to nature, to show virtue her own feature, scorn her own image, and the very age and body of the time his form and pressure.*"

When you walk into rehearsal as an actor, you are working to become the living embodiment of the story. You have been asked to do something very few people can do.

Remember, *"It takes twenty years to become an actor."*

In other words, you are *becoming*. You're learning the ropes, so give yourself the time it takes to really sail. It takes years. Mentally and emotionally, you need to see any given production as a piece of your puzzle, rather than an Olympic race. It's a four- or five-week experience that will become part of your twenty years, whether you become an actor *or* an accountant. It seems crucial, of course, and you worry that failing could derail your confidence and casting for the rest of the season, but that's out of your hands, isn't it? You cannot *force* this experience into a great success. You can only do your best and trust that it will fit in the larger scheme of things as it's supposed to fit. Worrying about the outcome will not hit the home run. Having faith and practicing could get you to first base, and that's what you want.

I believe in an *actor's independence*. Become an artist who takes ownership of your rehearsal process and characterization, hopefully in cooperation with your director, designers, and writers. However, they are not in charge of your work: you are.

The rehearsal room that my first acting teacher believed in is where your creative spirit is reborn, and you learn how to live in the story. This is the kind of work that can change your life, one rehearsal at a time.

How?

> The actor creates the whole length of a human soul's life on the stage every time he creates a part. This human soul must be visible in all its aspects, physical, mental, and emotional.
>
> —Richard Boleslavsky, *Acting, The First Six Lessons*

A tennis professional once called me and said that a lot of people had told him that he should look into acting. He asked me what he needed to know and how he could get started. I thought for a minute and said, "Well, if I wanted to become a tennis pro, what would *I* need to know, and how would *I* get started?"

Obviously, it takes years of commitment, love, practice, observation, training, and productions. It became clear during our conversation that he was not really talking about acting but more about headshots and agents. Of course, a person can win the lottery, and a good-looking tennis pro can step into a commercial and become famous. However, we're concerned with how to live a life in the theatre and how to inhabit a character through a rehearsal process.

There are many books on acting techniques, and no doubt you have had many classes and productions that have started you on your twenty-year road to learning the craft of acting. *However, how do you practice what you know? And how do you like to rehearse?*

You might be an actor who has learned to wait for the director to give you all the blocking and character suggestions. If you are, I want to suggest that you need to fly solo and begin taking more responsibility for your work. Of course, *some* directors will insist that they give you blocking instructions first, especially with regard to time pressures and, ultimately, a director's blocking can free you up to focus on the more emotional objectives in the scene rather than movement. Take them, but also stay open to your instincts. You always have the basics guiding the way—listening, reacting, making your own choices, finding the through-actions within the given circumstances, and following where they lead. Less *is* more. When acting in front of the camera, I have been directed to merely *think the thought* and the camera will see it. It's *also* the first thing to do in rehearsal. Think first, broaden later, and then deepen.

Wrap-up

The 5 Ws (and 1 H)

Remember *your* given circumstances as you continue *your* rehearsal process. *Who, what, where, when, why*, and *how?*

Who are you? You are an actor who has original ideas and ownership of your rehearsal, someone who takes responsibility for your preparation and is always ready to work. You are depending on yourself to make something positive out of this experience and take another step toward becoming the actor and the person you want to become.

What is rehearsal and what do you want to accomplish? It's like answering the question, what is life and what do you want from it? It is what you make it. In the public forum, it is learning and working the show while, at the same time, privately digging, exploring, and reviewing the discoveries that you've found.

Where does rehearsal happen? It happens in the structured setting and privately; as Mr. O'Toole suggests, during the "… alone, unobserved, uninhibited, private study" of your own. It happens anywhere and everywhere.

When does rehearsal happen? 24/7.

Why are you doing this show, and why do you want to be an actor? Your very personal and essential reasons are at the heart of it all and need to be acknowledged. They are buoyed by the fun of it, successful experiences in the past, and your mentors, which will all be tested by difficult roles, difficult directors, and not being cast at all.

How do you rehearse? There are emotional answers to this question: passionately, patiently. There are technical answers: follow direction, warm-up, private study, explore characterization by observing people. The rest of this book makes suggestions for how you can develop your own creative rehearsal process for any situation, every day and for any play.

Just practice

Sports writer Dan Wetzel wrote a memorable scenario of the 2010 USA National Collegiate football championship game between the Texas Longhorns and the Alabama Crimson Tides at the Rose Bowl in Pasadena, CA.

It was a game in which the Texas star quarterback, senior Colt McCoy, was hurt during the first quarter of the game and a shocked freshman backup,

Garrett Gilbert, entered the championship game like a Broadway understudy about to step into the leading role on opening night. In this story, however, the stage was too big, and Gilbert was too inexperienced. He returned to the locker room at halftime with his team trailing 24 to 6.
Mr. Wetzel continues,

> "Terrible," Gilbert said. "I felt terrible."
>
> There were the two quarterbacks in the halftime locker room … there was no commiserating. McCoy was in Gilbert's face; not shouting, just teaching.
>
> He needed Gilbert to remember a most important lesson—how to forget. The first half was done and gone. Nothing was going to change it.
>
> "You've got to forget everything," McCoy told him. "You've got nothing to gain. You've got nothing to lose. You've got nothing to prove. Just go out there and practice."

This is the word that caught my attention. During the toughest moment of his football career and maybe his life, he was exhorted to *practice*. He did, and brought his team back to within three points in the final quarter, one completion at a time.

> The two quarterbacks, both sons of Texas who dreamed of leading Texas to a championship, shared the same pain and disappointment. Yet where there was finality for the senior, there was a glimmer of hope for the freshman."
>
> "… this is something to build on," the freshman realized.

We're *always* in rehearsal. We *are* what we rehearse.

> If it be now, tis not to come, if it be not to come, it will be now, if it be not now, yet it will come … the readiness is all … let be."
>
> —William Shakespeare, *Hamlet*

2 The four-week gig Act 1: the first two weeks

In the work of a theatre, the playwright provides the scaffold of meaning and intention to which the other arts attach. In performance, it's the actor who is at the center. Theatre as a performing art is an art of experience between the actor and the audience. It's through the flesh and blood of the actor that the playwright comes alive, no matter when she actually lived. Playwright and actors are natural companions, creating in different ways but always symbiotically.

The great Russian playwright, Anton Chekhov, spoke to the Acting Company of the Moscow Art Theatre at the first rehearsal of his *The Seagull*—something like this: Never be afraid of an author. An actor is a free artist. You must create an image different from the author's. When the two images fuse into one, then an artistic work is created.

And sometimes, if she does her work well, the actor can show the playwright what he didn't even know was there!

Study, preparation, trying on your role in privacy, deep preoccupation with the task, belief in your creative self, contributing to the exploration of character and event at rehearsals, will make you an essential participant in the creation of an original piece of work that you will share with an audience.

—Zelda Fichandler, director/teacher

The four-week gig: an overview

In the United States, there has developed a traditional approach to mounting a contemporary or even a classical production that generally takes anywhere from three to six weeks. In this chapter, I want to suggest what you can expect and perhaps hope to accomplish during your study before the official start of rehearsal; the first day; the four weeks in the rehearsal room; and entering technical rehearsal and previews.

Preparing to play

The first thing to remember is that the standard amount of time given to rehearse a play professionally and in university is, generally, *not enough!* It's enough time to mount a production but, in the regional theater, four weeks is certainly not enough time to fully explore and exhaust all the possibilities that most stories deserve. Professionally, the actors are working up to eight hours a day, whereas in university, generally only four hours a night. So, you need to realize that when you're cast to play a role, you are already behind schedule and need to get going to have as good a shot as possible to do your best work. So, get motivated to start work immediately once you're cast, whether that's a week or six months before the official rehearsal is to begin. *Your* rehearsal begins the moment you get the part.

So what do you do?

One obvious suggestion is to plan out a personal rehearsal schedule between now and the start of the official rehearsal process. Show up on the first day with as much knowledge about the author, character, and given circumstances as you can.

Based in New York, Stephen Fried freelances in the regional theatre and also teaches directing at the New School for Drama in New York. I recently asked Stephen for his advice regarding an actor's preparation before rehearsal.

> In terms of the preparation I expect, there are of course the bare essentials of text analysis. I expect the actor to know the meaning of not just every word or phrase that he says, but also of every word or phrase that's said to him, or about him when he is offstage. And by "meaning," I don't just mean "what the words literally mean," but also what they might connote—what layers of meaning, be it via allusion, period-specific reference, or lyrical construction, do the words bring into the play? Assuming that the character could choose to express himself in any possible way, why did he choose this combination of words here? So I expect the actor to have spent time considering why he says the particular things that he says in the particular way that he says them at the particular moment in time when he says them. Thinking about this might also require research into the period of the play and production. Overall, I want the actor to come into rehearsals with an informed point of view on the role, and on the play. Hopefully, the combination of a thorough audition process and conversations with the director prior to the start of rehearsals will ensure that the actor's point of view is in line with the ideas of the production, though it's likely that the actor will need to remain flexible, and allow his point of view to evolve and even change to suit the development of the production. Still, what I

absolutely don't want is for the actor to enter as a blank slate, waiting to be written on. I want an actor to bring in ideas and convictions, born out of time spent methodically considering every inch of the play. In this way, the actor will be a true collaborator.

The first day

Meet and greet

The first day of rehearsal can be the most intimidating. There is a fear that whatever happens on this day will set the tone for the entire experience. Unless you are in a university setting where you know most everyone in the room, chances are you may not know anyone, and so the pressure to prove that you deserved the job is high. The tables for the first reading are sometimes in the background as you mingle over coffee, introducing yourself to those you bump into, and reconnecting with the director, whom you last saw at the audition. This process is pretty much the same whether you have been hired in a regional theatre and are a long way from home or off-Broadway and have just taken the subway to the gig. You may have a local theatre that you have finally broken into, or it could be the same room that you have often entered, because you are a company member at a theatre that often casts you.

Try to remember why you are there.

The play's the thing.

It is not opening night. It is the first day that you are meeting the people you are about to travel with. You're getting on the playground with these kids pretty soon, so just take it a moment at a time … as in a scene … no need to impress, to anticipate, or to charm the socks off everybody. Just keep your eyes and ears open, and listen to the best of your ability. Who are they? How are they? And what do they think of the play?

Remember, it's their first day, too. They're wanting to make a good first impression, so let them, by listening and being inquisitive or just by leaving them alone. The best first impression you can make is by encouraging your cohorts to make a good first impression. It's a four-way stop: watch, look, listen, and be generous. You're not in a hurry.

There are introductions all around. In the regions, you might meet some of the theatre supporters who have made special donations to meet the cast on the first day. You might be introduced to the volunteers of the theatre who have helped supply furnishings in your lodging. The house manager will probably be there, box office personnel, development officers, and publicity people.

Your antenna must be high. You never know who will offer a morsel of information or insight to the play that will enliven your own search. Your work on the role in collaboration with everyone else has officially begun but, most important, your work on the role is about to go public.

As F. Murray Abraham writes in *Actors on Shakespeare, A Midsummer Nights Dream*,

> On the first day of rehearsal, it's easy to anticipate and project a mixture of actor and role. In the playing of a character these two elements get confused and overlap, because the process of becoming a character begins long before that day. The process begins as soon as an actor reads a script, subconsciously selecting characteristics that might be suitable for the role. I suppose it's like the early stage of pregnancy: it might not show, but it's part of everything you do, gestating and nurturing even while you sleep.

Director and designer presentations

Often the first day continues with a presentation by the director, introducing him or herself to the cast and talking about why they're interested in this play. The director may offer insights that she or he discovered while working on the text over the past few months or even years.

This is also the time for questions and the beginning of your relationship with costumer, set designer, stage manager, production manager and, usually, the crew. Introduce yourself and, because you have been reading the play and beginning to imagine yourself in the story, it's a good time for early questions and observations, as time permits. Like a first date, you can't overwhelm your partners with too many questions or comments, as it's mostly a friendly chance to say hello. *However*, it may be a while before you see your set and costume designer again, and if you're really taking charge of your experience, you'll want to know how they arrived at their design and what they think of the play that you've been studying. Your conversation will show them that you take an interest and, if the time comes that you can't negotiate a set of stairs or have trouble with the length of sleeves on your costume, these conversations with the director and designer will serve you well. Be as knowledgeable as you can be about the play and as inquisitive as the occasion permits.

You have cast yourself at the center of your creative universe. Everybody else has more or less done the same thing with themselves, by the way. Like the famous joke about the spear carrier in *Hamlet*: when asked what the play is about, the actor replies, "Well, there's this guard . . ." You need to know what the costume designer has in mind for your clothes to begin imagining the character that fits in them, or at least chooses how to interact with regard to your suggestions. The director needs to sense that you take your character and the play as seriously as they will be doing.

The first week

You have most likely already experienced the basic sequence of the formal rehearsal. Up and down in four or five weeks and usually following a similar pattern:

- First week: Table reads and discussion.
- Second week: Begin blocking your way through the entire play.
- Third week: Reworking the scenes and run-throughs.
- Fourth week: Run-throughs and fixes, notes, leaving the rehearsal room and beginning technical rehearsals in the theatre; concluding with final dress rehearsals and possibly opening night.
- Fifth week: Previews begin and opening night; begin the run of the play.

When approaching a new play or even a film, actor and comedian, Robin Williams said to *The New York Times,* "It's the idea of going, relax, you got the gig, what do you want to do now?"

What *do* you want to do now? The mistake is often trying to do too much at once. As said earlier, the first week is not about opening night. It's about the first week: asking questions, getting to know the other actors, your playwright, your director and your character, one layer at a time.

Here are some suggestions:

Get to know the play through the players that have been cast. Accept them without judgment as you continue your own rehearsal process. They may not be the brother or love interest you imagined when you read it, but they are now!

The first week is usually around the table. Let the play reveal itself little by little, like layers of a cake. However, don't be afraid to let your instincts and impulses direct your reading and discussions.

First reads

This is your first chance to hear the world of this play and yourself in it. Listen and learn.

A neutral read is often suggested by the director. Neutral reads mean a reading without pressure to characterize or play as intensely as the scene may eventually need. It's a read for information, hearing the story and breaking in the words. I understand that you don't need to crawl on top of the table and kiss your leading lady in the love scene during the first read, but I can't imagine the benefit of staring down at the script and not including her during the exchange.

You are also making first connections and first impressions that begin to feed the relationship, actor to actor, character to character. You're taking your new car out for a spin.

Again, F. Murray Abraham speaks to the first read of his *A Midsummer Night's Dream* in the role of Bottom:

> The first read-through is usually a rambling, dry, almost inaudible affair, but there was nothing tentative about my approach—it was an all-out-attack. When I attack a text early on, I am challenging the others to be bold, to take a chance right now, at this moment, among colleagues. We should be able to trust one another. If I am willing to step up and fall on my face, then why can't they too? What is there to lose? In this way I break the ice for anyone willing to jump in with me. No one has to jump, but at least they have the choice … my choice was to play Bottom full out—but there's so much of him in me that I didn't know where to start. I decided to just jump in and see what came out.

Table reads are also the first and maybe the last opportunity to ask those embarrassing questions about what's going on. I say embarrassing because I once asked a director on the first day's rehearsal where the play was going to take place, and he said, "In the theater." Depending on the director, discussion and reading can last all week for everyone to get on the same page. This becomes a Sherlock Holmes murder mystery as everyone around the table begins to find the truths in the story. It's not a competition, however. Struggling to get attention and to ask the best questions or come up with the better answers is going to send things off track. Honest questions and revelations are the rules of the road. Keep your prompt book close at hand to record the ideas and questions.

Tyranny of mistrust

The tyranny during the first week is often a mistrust of the entire process. The first week is gathering the ingredients of the production.

In our production of *Dance of Death* at Arena Stage, director JoAnne Akalaitis used to refer to her process as making a stew, where all the ingredients of rehearsal discoveries were thrown in. It's all grist for the mill, as the old expression goes, giving yourself the freedom to suggest, ask, and imagine.

Mark Lewis, a veteran stage and televison actor, currently head of drama at Wheaton College in Illinois, suggests the need for a safe space:

> So much of what makes a good "room"—whether a rehearsal room, a learning room, a spiritual room—is that pains have been taken to make it a safe space in which to get it wrong. When we lack for this kind of an environment, we default to the one action that will kill acting 100% of the time—the impulse to work perfectly.

Give yourself the space to create, available for your muse or creativity itself to enter. Let yourself go down roads that may or may not lead to your final characterization. A puzzle can be a thousand pieces that are placed one at a time, revealing the picture in sections.

Continued reads

You're beginning to feel more comfortable with the group and your director. Hopefully you've lived with the text for many weeks before the official rehearsal began, so you're ahead of the game and you can also begin to feel freer to try things within your scenes. Slow the scene down, attack it, play the extremes, and have some fun rather than trying to impress or nail down the "right" way to do it. Surprise yourself and probably the cast, but don't marry any of your choices at this point. You're still dating, and most of the time, you're still sitting around the table.

Home work

Home work hasn't stopped now that you're in the middle of the first week and official work has begun. The ideas will have started to percolate, and you'll have additional questions that need follow-up. Your discussions will enliven your understanding of the character, leading you into additional areas to study during your time away from the scheduled rehearsal. For professionals, this is usually after dinner and before bed.

For students, you'll find free time late at night and during the day to review your notes. Review and reflection are crucial as you press forward.

Former artistic director of Arena Stage and head of directing at Temple University, Doug Wager:

> Prior to rehearsal every day, go through the script and write down all facts pertaining to your character, and write down all simple fact-based unanswered questions as they come up. Use the questions to guide your research into character backstory to more precisely refine the given circumstances. Work with the notion of identifying where you need to have clearly collaborative "shared character memories" between your character and any other characters they relate to in the

> play. You should KNOW the given circumstances inside out—from sublime to the ridiculous—is it early or late, is there a time issue, am I hungry, is it hot or cold, is it a public or private space, etc. This work continues and is refined as the process goes on—what your actions are or tactics are for getting what you want, are the result of a clear understanding of the given circumstances in the moment. Also to constantly assess the relationship of language to character—why this WORD NOW in this MOMENT?

Beats

At this point, you'll want to at least understand and perhaps have marked your script for beats, which are "thought changes," every time a new idea or intention is presented in the dialogue. There is a virus that attacks many actors, causing them to sound the same no matter what the intention or shift in the action implies. Understanding the beats in a scene can break up the monotonous reading.

Memorization

Subconsciously, if you have spent time with your words, to yourself and aloud, your brain has already started committing them to memory. You've prepared the soil for planting.

Many actors like to wait and learn their words *organically*, after they learn their initial blocking, so that associations aid their memory process. I have done it this way for more than twenty years, breaking the ice on the words and movement at the same time during the first blocking stages and then committing myself to *knowing* the scene the very next time we run it, which is usually a week later.

I still do this but have recently preferred to show up to first rehearsal, more or less "off book" or having the role totally memorized, to focus the short rehearsal process on characterization and actions, rather than remembering words. This preference can become more of a necessity with age, but even when I was younger, I found it to be freeing.

Once again, Zelda Fichandler, from her written memo to NYU actors, *Preparing to Rehearse:*

> It's very useful to come to the process with the words learned almost in a mechanical way (or if some living experience actually creeps in, welcome it and hold onto it, it may be useable). Learning the text separate from the moment-to-moment actions isn't going to hurt you; rather it gives you a tool (just like having a free voice and a relaxed and

ready body) so that you can concentrate on the deepest searches. The more one can short-cut the tedious matter of learning lines, the more time there is for uncovering the layers of the text.

The second week

On your feet

Script in hand, you step onto the rehearsal floor, which is marked with tape for doorways, levels, rooms, and stairs. Rehearsal furniture is placed according to the design, and the director is generally eager to block through the entire play to at least have a sense of its movement and workability. However, as your work (and your characters) find greater detail and authority, you might feel uncomfortable with the initial choices you and the director have made under pressure. Be open to changing it, and don't marry anything too early, but be extremely open to your own instincts and the director's evolving ideas as well.

Blocking

Lee Mikeska Gardner, professional actress and director in Washington, D.C., told me:

> Staging is the external manifestation of the internal objective. This is why I don't pre-block. I don't know what every character's objectives are every moment. And it's why staging changes, or evolves, as I prefer to say—because as the rehearsal period goes on the actor and director know more. As the objectives become deeper and more specific, the staging will evolve and usually simplify, to express that.

More often these days, a director will ask the actors to go with their flow and make up their own blocking the first few times through. The director is looking for ideas, giving you a chance to explore. So, try things! Or feel free to stand still and wait for the motivation to move.

Everyone has heard the cliché, "Don't just *stand* there, *do* something!" Forgive me, but I have to tell the old legend of the actress who changed positions so much during her speech that the director said, "Don't just *do* something, *stand* there!"

Stillness can often be the best choice, that is, until your needs, intentions, and motivations push you to go. Wandering around is often a sign of insecurity. Wait until you feel motivated and need to move.

A beat lasts as long as a particular thought or similar line of discussion continues, but when it changes, as in real life, our expression, delivery, and often a physical change occur.

Follow your actions and find activities. I believe that you should bring in many ideas and stay ahead of the director as often as possible. His or her job is to stage the play and bring all the artists together to tell the story. Your job is characterization. Make choices, back-story, and reasons for them. As Jim Young said, "Do your preparation and then be ready to go with the flow, responding to the instincts and ideas and actions of the other artists on stage."

As you try things, your thoughts will piggyback on one another, based on given circumstances. Who are you, what do you want, how are you going to get it, and what's in your way? Trust your instincts and *in-the-moment* ideas during early blocking choices and character questions, but stay open to the director's need to establish a movement template.

Remember that you don't need to inform the director ahead of time with ideas or impulses. Many actors, non-professional and professional alike, often ask permission to make a choice! "*Would it be okay if I moved to the chair on that line? Would it be okay if I cross down left during their monologue, because I feel like I wouldn't want to hear it and would rather stare out the window?*"

Show the other actors and director your choices and spontaneous discoveries rather than telling or telegraphing. Find out whether it works for *you!* There will be plenty of time to discuss whether it felt right, looked right, and worked. In the meantime, rehearsal is about exploring, so explore. It's your rehearsal.

Costume it

James Horan is a working stage and film actor based in Los Angeles:

> I work "from the outside in" as Olivier was fond of saying. I find that the clothes, especially, reveal a lot about the character for me, and I try to get a reasonable facsimile of the costume as early as possible in rehearsal. And of course, any prop I'm handling is crucial too, to have early on, so that I can develop behavior based on the character's handling of the prop, as well as his clothes. I do this to avoid those lapses of concentration that can occur when all of a sudden something unexpected happens with an article of clothing, or a prop, during the run. If you're wedded to these pieces, you just deal with whatever comes along. And behavior, of course, is the essence of all good acting.

The shoes are first. It's very important to begin walking in your character's shoes as soon as possible. Hard soles, heels, boots, find an approximation of whatever your character will end up with. You'll move differently from the bottom up. The shoes change your gait, stance, and physicality in dramatic ways. It's same with clothes. If the costume shop won't give you an approximation, find something on your own from your closet or the local charity/thrift store. Start to make choices and dress like your character in rehearsal.

Repeat it

Pressure yourself to do your scenes as many times as the director will allow during the day, and then always, *always* find a time later to run over what you just rehearsed. Run it in your apartment, dorm room, lounge, or a practice space.

I was cured of my own laziness during a production of *Cymbeline* at the Hartford Stage Company in Connecticut. One actor was reworking a scene with two others, and he couldn't remember where he was supposed to move on a particular line. The stage was going to be a clean, flat, raked surface without furniture and so, at one point, the actor stopped the scene, turned to the director, and asked, "Where did I go on that line?" The director exploded, "I don't know, I don't know, we did this days ago, why are you asking me? You're supposed to know where you go, I don't know!" The actor practically did a back hand-spring in retreat.

This was an unusual reaction from this director and in my experience with directors in general, but it got my attention! The stage manager or assistant stage manager always notes the blocking, and there isn't anything wrong with double checking your moves *before* rehearsal if you're uncertain about exactly what happened the last time you did it. Sometimes you'll just forget, and not all directors will blow a gasket, and there is a myth out there about blocking: *if you forget it, it probably wasn't organic enough, and the act of forgetting it means you should discover something else*. I suppose this could be true, but it's also a convenient excuse for not practicing it on your own. Practice it by walking through it at home while saying your lines, as opposed to sitting in a chair and trying to remember what you did.

During my graduate training, head of acting Jack Clay gave us great advice. We were studying Shakespeare, and he advised us to say it aloud anywhere and everywhere. He told us to put the script in our back pocket and refer to it off and on all day long. This was a revelation. From then on, I became "the *rehearser*," day and night; finding rooms, parks, pacing back and forth at a bus stop, or waiting on the subway platform. However, when you're repeating words, it is not simply a matter of making sure you know them but rather a continual investigation as to where they come from and why you're saying them in the scene. Repeating them for memory is a good inclination, but repeating them with intention, even quietly, is crucial. Otherwise, they might develop a particular delivery from mindless repetition. When you're discovering a role, inspiration and revelation come when you least expect them. It takes constant attention.

3 The four-week gig Act 2: weeks three and four

> … I had this problem too, where I was afraid to make a move, I have to feel it, and there was a teacher I had at Stellas [Adler]… and he would say, you gotta sometimes jump in, and that was true. If I just jumped in and did it and took the leap, you'd arrive at that place where you thought you had to go through all kinds of, you know … you'd just arrive there, and be there, believe it or not. So it's not to pamper yourself so much, you got to get out at the end of the day and you've got to do it, and if you make a mistake, you do it again, you try to do it again. …
>
> —Robert DeNiro, *Inside the Actor's Studio*

The third week

At this stage in rehearsal, you're beginning to gel. Sometimes, the most difficult part is expecting to be further along than you need to be. You're responsible for only one scene at a time, one line at a time, so continue working. Jump in, take the leap; if you make a mistake, you try to do it again.

The design run

Most often, after you have just blocked the entire play, the director will take a rehearsal to run through the play to show the designers. The set, costumes, and lighting designers are all working hard to create a look that supports the action of the story, so they need to see the first shape.

This run-through is not about you!

You will feel like performing because you're a thoroughbred and someone just opened the audience gate, but do your best just to rehearse during this run-through. You may not have your lines secure; you'll be remembering your blocking and discovering how to integrate some new activities in the space.

They are not watching you! They are looking at costume pieces, where and how the lighting should hang, which furniture to use or get rid of, and what shade to paint the wall. They will not be talking about your performance, they're professionals and understand the process. Their work is in process, too!

Do the run for information. What do you remember from the week's work and what don't you? What do you feel is working for your character and what not? Is there any blocking that feels especially awkward? Are there any new ideas about relationships or reasons for your character to do what he or she does?

Do not be judgmental of yourself or any of your fellow actors during this early run-through. Too much performing and you'll have to start over, because you've sprinted before you were ready. The designer run is a jog around the track.

Sizing it

Actors should just be speaking to each other during this third week. The intentions and thought-driven dialogue will take a more believable root in yourself if you're not shouting and looking for a performance level to fill the theater.

However, your director may disagree, and you may have to find a compromise that still keeps the integrity of your conversation with your fellow actors and also relieves any fears he or she may have about your vocal strengths and patterns. It's worthy of a personal conversation with the director if you're concerned that you're projecting unbelievably at this point in rehearsal.

Those with softer voices may need to begin increasing sound sooner rather than later to get used to the breath support and energy it takes to fill the auditorium. This takes some exercise, sizing the performance to fit the theater. There are directors who will insist on doing this much earlier, which can be good or bad, depending on the actor. If you're too concerned about volume early in the rehearsal, you may circumvent the subtle and thought-driven impulses, creating a semi-performance too early. Conversely, being too quiet for too long can equally create barriers when it's time to bring it up to the demands of a larger space.

One of my favorite actors was Lee J. Cobb. He became famous for originating the role of Willy Loman in Arthur Miller's *Death of a Salesman* on Broadway. I first became aware of him as the powerful and dangerous waterfront boss in Elia Kazan's film, *On the Waterfront*. His acting credits are legendary, but the reason I refer to his work in this context is because during his rehearsal period for *Salesman*, he was so private and slow-going during his discovery of the role, everyone was worried that he wouldn't have a performance. Miller explains this in his autobiography, *Timebends* (p. 187):

> Lee seemed to move about in a buffalo's stupefied trance, muttering his lines, plodding with deathly slowness from position to position, and behaving like a man who had been punched in the head. "He's just learning it" Kazan (the director) shakily reassured me after three or four days. I waited as a week went by and then ten days, and all that was emerging from Lee Cobb's throat was a bumpy hum. The other actors were nearing performance levels, but when they had to get a response from Lee all their rhythms slowed to near collapse. Kazan was no longer so sure and kept huddling with Lee, trying to pump him up. Nor did Lee offer any explanation, and I wondered whether he thought to actually play the part like a man with a foot in the grave. Between us, Kazan and I began referring to him as "the walrus."
>
> On about the twelfth day, in the afternoon … Lee stood up as usual from the bedroom chair and turned to Mildred Dunnock and bawled, "No, there's more people now … There's more people!" and, gesturing toward the empty upstage where the window was supposed to be, caused a block of apartment house to spring up in my brain, and the air became sour with the smell of kitchens where once there had been only the odors of earth, and he began to move frighteningly, with such ominous reality that my chest felt pressed down by an immense weight. After the scene had gone on for a few minutes, I glanced around to see if the others had my reaction. Jim Proctor had his head bent into his hands and was weeping. Eddie Kook was looking shocked, almost appalled, and tears were pouring over his cheeks, and Kazan, behind me was grinning like a fiend, gripping his temples with both hands, and we knew we had it—there was an unmistakable wave of life moving across the air of the empty theatre, a wave of Willy's pain and protest. I began to weep myself at some point that [was] not particularly sad, but it was as much, I think, out of pride in our art, in Lee's magical capacity to imagine, to collect within himself every mote of life since Genesis and to let it pour forth. He stood up there like a giant moving the Rocky Mountains into position.
>
> At the end of the act,… I ran up and kissed Lee, who pretended to be surprised, "But what did you expect, Arthur?" he said, his eyes full of his playful vanity. My God, I thought—he really is Willy!

I have always taken inspiration from this story. Early in my career, I thought that I needed to vocally project right away, in preparation for going on stage in a matter of weeks. I sacrificed thought, true feelings, simple talking, and listening by super-sizing too early.

In collaboration with your director, you'll be able to calibrate when and how to meet the vocal demands of the space you'll be performing in. However, don't be afraid to *take it off the stag*e in the beginning to play it for connections and thought-driven moments during early readings and rehearsal.

One of the beauties of the rehearsal room is that it affords you the time to warm into the story. Like dating, (isn't everything like dating?) you don't want to overwhelm your date with too much energy and enthusiasm before she or he knows you better.

Reworking

Here's your chance to really dig in and secure your words, intentions, obstacles, and relationships. This is the week to get your lines totally into your head and solidify them alongside the action. Have you got all the props you need? Work with real objects, never mime. Use substitute objects if necessary to get the feel of the timing and business. You need to be working with the real objects—watches, glasses with liquid, magazines—all the things your character would use and touch during the course of the scene.

Be jealous of your time with each scene and, while you're waiting to go, run through the scene in your head and the steps to get ready.

Secret: the scene often happens while the character is busy doing something else! So get busy doing that other thing, but let the scene keep interrupting it. The needs of all the characters are bursting into dialogue, even though everybody might be preoccupied with activities that belie their real intentions. You're finding the dual behavior now, trying to live an ordinary day, usually under extraordinary conditions.

There is much less talking this week. The discussions were around the table and when you were on your feet for the first time. *Just do it* without apology or permission from your director.

As you work through the play and possibly watch other sections of the play developing, you'll get a much clearer idea of the world, the director's concept, and what's yet to do.

At home alone

Repeat the work and the discoveries of that day that night!

Freelance director Eleanor Holdridge:

> Each day in rehearsal there will be huge amounts of new information coming at you. Your imaginative work at home will be (should be)

morphing into something different as input from your director and fellow actors influences your thoughts. Your homework should be to continue to ask yourself these questions: How do I change as I move throughout the play? What or who changes me? What do I want? How do I go after it? As you learn your lines, you should be re-thinking and imagining back-story, and identifying possible intentions to try out. Go over the work in rehearsal in your mind each night or morning after rehearsal. Were there moments where you were blocking impulse? Moments where you weren't playing a strong action? Are there unanswered questions that arose? Make a list of these, and next rehearsal see what happens if you can give in to the impulse, identify and play that action, answer those questions. As the rehearsals on each scene progresses, you should be able to identify a positive action and objective for every moment in the play. If you don't have one, identify one at home and try it next time in rehearsal. If things are still unclear, ask the director to help clarify the moment. Overall, you should be responding to the work in rehearsal and continually re-evaluating your past work. Beware of changing things drastically, of letting each new idea swing you away from your center, but find a way to let the work you've done get deeper and deeper as your character develops and finds expression in the world of the play.

Run-through

The end of the third week often contains another run of the show. This one is *go for broke!* Do what you do to the hilt to really see what you need to work on. Again, it's not a performance!—it's a run-through for even more information. You are still in process! The tendency is to believe that what you do is what it will be, but it's not. What you do is part of what it's becoming.

The fourth week

Run-throughs have arrived. Most directors use one day this week to run through the first half of the play and then fix. The next day you will probably run through the last half of the play and spend time reworking bits from it, too. Then you'll run the entire play. You're developing your long-distance emotional muscles.

Drill

Drill your lines before and after rehearsal if they are still the least bit uncertain. You cannot enter final run-throughs with any hesitation on the lines. If you do, the work will be all about *remembering* words, and that's the least important part. The words should be *rushing* at you like a wind, ready to be said in whatever way the inevitable new impulses hit you. *The work now is about following your character into her or his world.* You've done your preparation. You should be at the point where you don't even have to think about what move or which line comes next.

You're ready to fly, and this is when you really start behaving in character and begin to lose yourself in the story.

Becoming your character

Do you become or *get lost* in the character? No. You're always the actor in charge, aware of the technical aspects of the production, the audience's reactions, your scene partners, and new impulses. Are you influenced and perhaps changed as a person as a result of playing this character's story, emotions, words, and actions over and over?

Yes, I think you are.

Aristotle wrote, "*We are what we repeatedly do*." So, if you begin to personally react, engage, and respond—as your character would, in *your personal* life—it's because you're spending so much time focusing on your character's thoughts and objectives. The trick for the actor is practicing how to leave your character inside the theatre when the play is done.

Actor brain/character thoughts

I'll refer to the phenomenon of becoming your character without *becoming* your character by separating the realities and calling them "actor brain"/ "character thoughts." Your actor has the play's production in mind, while your character has their story in mind. And they talk to each other! They protect and guide each other. It is a dual consciousness.

Your actor brain keeps the character from rewriting him- or herself and making up words or actions that the writer never intended for him or her to do. Your actor brain is constantly reminding you of your responsibilities to other performers on stage, picking up the volume so your character can be heard and choosing to pick up the broken cup on the stage because you know it will be distracting during the rest of the scene.

Your actor brain tracks your character's thoughts and helps you stay in the story without letting outside worries and distractions interfere with the play. Your character is written in a way that tells the actor brain to fight for its objective, react more strongly to what's happening and find some preoccupied activities to fill the moment.

Nobody has said it better, in my opinion, than F. Murray Abraham about his relationship with Bottom, again in the *Actors on Shakespeare* series.

> Like most actors, I begin to assume the qualities of the character. If the character is allowed free rein, a sort of uncensored coursing, he'll lead you to places that only the unconscious can reveal. But you must trust your impulses, and that's the hardest part, because when they're off, you risk looking like a fool.
>
> Bottom couldn't wait to get to the theater; pulling me out of bed full of ideas for the performance that night … I had to keep telling him that he wasn't the whole play, only part of it. He told me that he was much more than I gave him credit for, and he was right.
>
> I never doubted that Bottom would live—so the task became a kind of game between him and me: how much freedom I would allow him, and how much he would chide me for my meekness.
>
> The internal battle is not uncommon. In order to achieve a living representation of life, the actor must believe in the importance of the character he is portraying.
>
> During rehearsal there is a sort of observing third eye that monitors what is being done. It then selects and records the successful attempts for future reference.

Super-size it

You're also finally ready to begin sharing this work with the audience, and so your actor brain will begin realizing that you need to reach the back of the house and prepare your characterization to enlarge itself beyond camera range and into the balcony. If you're in a small theater, your actor brain will know just how large the expression of your intentions and delivery needs to be.

Audiences also will be starting to form in the rehearsal room. By audiences, I mean those who have not been a part of your earlier blocking and run-throughs, those you have gotten used to seeing when you rehearse. Now, all of a sudden, strangers to your experience begin to enter. Designers, crew, producers, and possibly understudies begin to watch. Careful: you are still rehearsing! You are still practicing, finding, learning, and making mistakes. You're finding new moments by following your character's lead. Performing for your new guests is almost impossible not to do, so give yourself a break. It's just another step in learning how to focus on your scene and being watched at the same time. By the time I get around to first preview, I feel that I've already overcome the audience distraction in the rehearsal room or during technical rehearsals.

Take ownership of your process. Whoever is watching cannot help you or hurt your work. You're going for broke during the run-throughs, but that's for you to learn what works and what does not. *Performing* for anyone in particular at this point will only turn you to the safer and surer choices, distracted by trying to impress rather than simply listening to your scene partner and reacting full out.

The fifth week

Technical rehearsals

By the end of the fourth week and into a possible fifth, you'll be starting your technical rehearsals. Many actors dread this work, because it seems to put their own work on hold while the director and designers secure the overall production.

This is their rehearsal.

The fact that suddenly rehearsals are not about you is always an adjustment, but that's exactly what's happening. Rehearsal is suddenly more about the clothes, the set, and the lighting design, which are taking all the attention and conversation. There is much waiting around in the green room or dressing room while lighting cues are called and fixed. Finishing touches on the set take time, and the actor is asked to be ready at a moment's notice.

John Conklin is an internationally known costume and set designer with whom I recently spoke about the actor and designer's collaboration.

> John: Actors, in the rehearsal process grow and develop—organically and complexly over a period of focused time. Perhaps one productive way for everyone to think about tech rehearsals is to think of them as a corresponding and equivalent time for the visual elements to try to grow, develop and focus. The actors sometimes feel that the rehearsal process has been taken away from them; they're just pawns at the hands of the designers working with a director whose attention has turned away from the performers during tech—and to a certain extent, they are. But they have had three weeks or whatever in rehearsal to attempt new things, to go in new directions, to try things and accept or reject them An actor usually can come in to a room rehearsal and say—we've been working on this scene in one direction , I just thought today maybe I should trying play this whole scene angry—and then the director can say, well I don't know immediately where you're going but sure, let's do it, let's see what happens. The same kind of thing should be able to happen in tech—it is the designers' and director's time for visual rehearsal and experiment—not just an assigned period to make what they've envisioned, six months or two months before, come to actuality.
>
> Gary: I never thought of tech as your rehearsal.
>
> John: It's very helpful for actors to think of it that way—we see what you're accomplishing, let us build our work on what you're doing.

Techspectations

Remember, you have your own work to continue doing, and this can be a very valuable few days when the attention is *not* on you, so that you can continue letting your character lead you into new territory. Consider your character as the writer often does: a person separate from him- or herself to whom they are merely listening as they follow them through their story. Only now, their environment is beginning to appear. You're wearing their clothes, and their (your) world is finally more than the imaginary fluorescent-lighted rehearsal room.

Of course, you'll be encountering awkward staging changes, bits of the costume that don't work, and lighting that can throw you off at first. So, take notes on the difficulties to explain them during a note session (*not* always on stage during the playing of the scene). The director and designer are encountering a hundred choices and changes to consider. However, if something is dangerous, bring it up immediately. Remember that the designers and director are furiously taking notes on what works and what needs fixing. However this is really additional time for you to secure your confidence, comfort, familiarity, and even working through new realizations and ideas that come with this new world.

Breakthrough tech-through

I personally have always been what's known as a closer horse, someone who finds major discoveries and breakthrough in the final stretch or late rehearsals and especially a tech run-through. Maybe because of some personal reluctance to bare all at the beginning, shyness, or fear, I don't know. However, I have come to depend on real progress and confidence in the characterization right around the time of technical rehearsals. I'm finally left totally alone and given an entire set to play on in my new clothes! Maybe the very fact that my work is *not* the center of attention gives me sudden freedom to jump off the proverbial cliff.

Previews

A paying audience is about to see your show. I didn't say your performance; they are not coming to see your *performance*, they are coming to see the *production,* to experience the story. The playwright and director/designers are as much on the line as you. You give it everything tonight, seeing what still needs work and ironing out the wrinkles, discovering how the audience reacts and what adjustments may need to happen as a result. In other words, they are coming to a preview to have a special place in the creation of the work. Their reaction will make a difference.

Also, you may be faced with real performer anxieties that are common among us all. Stage fright rears its ugly head during these first few shows, and you wonder why you put yourself through this anxiety at all.

In an article entitled *Petrified* by John Lahr in the *New Yorker*, he quotes acting coach Susan Batson, who

> advises her students to try to displace the fear onto the role they're playing, to make it part of the performance, part of what she calls the 'previous circumstances' of the character. Her response is, "Can we use this?… the people who survive it are the ones who can take control of the situation and override it."

Warm-up

Dressing room rituals and created environment

Most athletes have developed a particular routine during the day of their event to maximize their spirit, mind, and body in preparation. It continues as they arrive at the arena. Rituals can include what you eat; when you shower, vocalize, physical warm up; music you listen to; people you allow into your circle; and problems that you avoid. It can be a specific order of doing things or whatever you have developed that works for you. You've set up your dressing table as your home away from home and maybe adorned it with motivating pictures alongside the character's accoutrement. You've arrived and begun turning your face toward what you love to do, in a place that only you and your fellow actors understand. Ever have family come to one of your shows? "Can you take us backstage?" they often ask. It's the inner sanctum and, now that you've left the rehearsal room, you're ready for church.

Touching every seat

I was very struck once before first preview of a show when an actor walked up and down the aisle and in-between every row of seats in the theatre, touching every one. I didn't want him to know I had seen him do it, and I didn't dare ask him why. I was so intrigued that, at another theatre many months after, I was feeling nervous about a performance and remembered my fellow player's ritual. I tried it, and the more seats I touched, the more I began to feel that my spirit—and even a cell from my body—were reaching out to every stranger about to sit in her or his seat. I would have actually been everywhere in the theatre by the time I stepped onto the stage. It made me feel as if I were more at one with what many actors feel is "the enemy." Instead, I had a secret. I had already reached out to them. My spirit as well as my physical being had occupied every seat in a very large space, bringing it closer to me as I performed. I would never ask the actor why he did it, but I've been doing it ever since on the night of the first preview.

You will succeed because there is no wrong that can be done. You'll learn from whatever you do, and that's the purpose of a preview, so take off the pressure and keep working. Previews are for rehearsing your performance.

Opening night

Recalling the locker room conversation between Texas Longhorn quarterback and his sudden replacement: "You've got to forget everything," McCoy told him. "You've got nothing to gain. You've got nothing to lose. You've got nothing to prove. Just go out there and practice."

The gifts arrive in front of your dressing room mirror, everybody has been telling you to "break a leg" all day, and you begin to feel as if tonight is something extremely important.

Most often, even experienced professionals will be glad this night is behind them to get back to the business of telling the story. The hoopla of an opening night is a celebration and can be exciting, but it can also become the event, as opposed to the play and your job in it.

Opening night is not the play, and the play is not opening night. They are two distinctive events. You can absolutely celebrate the fun of opening, giving and receiving gifts, well wishes, and the nerves of knowing that the critics are probably in the audience. After the show, you can join everyone in the celebration of the hard work, the experiences shared over time and, hopefully, the positive response of the audience. Positive or otherwise, however, your job remains in the play. Openings can feel like Christmas, but the play needs your full attention, separate from the opening night buzz.

Get there early, give and receive your gifts early, acknowledge the strange ritual of first night, and then begin your warm-up routine. Focus on it as just another night stepping into your character's shoes to live his or her story once again.

Go out there with nothing to gain, nothing to lose, and nothing to prove. Just continue practicing what you've learned over the past four weeks.

The run

For university, this amount of time can be much too short and a matter of one or two long weekends only. Often in the states regionally, it is only three to six weeks. A showcase in New York can run for a series of weekends, while off-Broadway can run only about four weeks. Broadway runs can begin out of town for months, during reworking of the script, and land in town for anywhere from one night to many years of eight shows a week.

Pre-show routine

Regardless of a short run or long one, the routine you create to maximize your experience is crucial.

During a production of *King Lear*, veteran actor Hal Holbrook (famous for his expansive television and movie career but in particular his one-person show, *Mark Twain Tonight!*) always arrived at the theatre very early. I remember him rushing down the hallway toward his dressing room and asked him whether everything was alright. "I'm running late," he told me. It was 4:15, and the show was at 8:00!

Of course, in this case, Hal, who was well known as a make-up expert in his portrayal of Twain, was equally committed to his make-up and warm-up routine for his Lear. He needed four hours for his routine. Actress, Gloria Biegler, was there at the time and told me that she also liked to hang out in the theater for hours before a show, preparing her body and soul for the evening's event. I interpreted this to mean that she wanted to be fully there and not rushing around before arriving at the theater just in time for the performance.

What is your preparation? Whatever helps you to get a head start and walk on stage ready to be there, fully engaged in your character's world.

I can tell when I'm watching actors *warming up* during the first few scenes of their show, because after fifteen minutes, they're different persons on stage; vocally and physically different. Don't do it. You could pull an actor hamstring if you try to race without doing your preparation.

Checking your props is a necessary ritual for all actors. The assistant stage manager or the props person could make a mistake but, more important, checking on them reinforces your own memory. I was playing Puck in *A Midsummer Night's Dream* in Ashland, Oregon. One night, I forgot "the flower." There just isn't a feeling like swinging into the scene in front of 1,500 people as the scampering merry wanderer of the night, having just "put a girdle round the earth in 40 minutes" to find a flower and then not have it when Oberon says, "I pray thee, give it me!"

Oops. I turned poor Oberon and all of us into mimes for the rest of the night whenever the flower was needed.

Check your props. It becomes a calming part of your ritual and an introduction to the world and work you're about to walk into.

As I've repeatedly said, the theater is the actor's church, different from the gym, the student lounge, Starbucks coffee house, the bar, or your house; so enter it with mindfulness, respect, and mystery. Your theatre has history.

PS: Your performance doesn't need any outside news or distractions to prepare. Turn off your cell phone (not even on vibrate), you can't be reached. You're doing something that not many people can do or understand, so treat it as such. Friends will learn not to try to reach you after "half hour," or whenever your preparation begins ... and they'll respect you for it. If you want to get in the zone tonight, eliminate all the distractions. It's not automatic.

Evolve and maintain

There are many schools of thought regarding how to keep the production alive, consistent with what you rehearsed and evolving at the same time. F. Murray Abraham as Bottom in *Actors on Shakespeare*:

> A performance has nothing to do with watching oneself. Standing in the wings waiting for an entrance should be like preparing to step off into space: you've no idea what will happen … the artist must be aware of the world he is part of, yet not completely controlling: he must be open to whatever possibility. The work continues to evolve, particularly with an audience in front of you; the creative process is one of the reasons they have come to the theater. Where else can they actually watch an artist creating something? That will never happen if the actor plays it safe.

Maintaining

Your character will begin to lead you in new directions, and you will want to follow them. The stage manager's job includes keeping the show from losing its original strengths and maintaining the director's work. Avoid leaping over balconies that wasn't rehearsed, even though you feel it's a great idea … wait until you've discussed it with your partners and stage manager. If it still seems in line with the entrance of your Musketeer, a rehearsal will be called to make sure you won't break your leg.

Martha Knight, long-time stage manager at Arena Stage and the Kennedy Center in Washington, D.C., says:

> And there again, please try to keep an open mind, when the stage manager comes and says "you know, there's something wrong with this moment, I don't know if you're stepping on his line or if he's jumping on your line, or what it is, but there's something wrong. Talk to me, help me, think about this," or sometimes I can just go and say "you know, you're not throwing the focus in the right place" and then half of the time, [actors] get their back up and say, "well I thought I had the right to go over there and look this way because I'm feeling this moment," "well, yeah but it changes it.…"

So, basically, as the production is a symphony of sights and sounds, it will not drastically change, and the challenge will be to maintain a freshness and sense of newness in the performance.

This is part of your practice: *finding* something that's already been found.

Keeping the work like new and deepening as you go is your challenge, your fun, and your job. People are paying to see you! You are building your life's work on every role you play. Every role is not only broadening your perspective on life and increasing your abilities but preparing the way for tougher challenges and roles to follow.

During a production of Shaw's *Arms and the Man*, a fellow actor commented in the dressing room that now that the show was open, his work was done, and he was already anxious about what his next job was going to be.

I remember thinking, *are you kidding?* We had three weeks of shows in front of us, and every one of those was like climbing to another advance camp up the mountain. I was not only going to relish the experience of playing Bluntschli but I needed the chance to strengthen my chops eight times a week and deepen my characterization in the process. This was George Bernard Shaw, after all. It would take me twenty years of doing Shaw to master it, like most any playwright's work. Did he say *done*?

The run of the show is the real beginning. Opening night is like going through a doorway into your new living space. It's playing the game you have practiced. In that playing, you practice deepening your performance by increasing the amount of time your actor brain gives in to your character's thinking while maintaining the integrity of the production everyone has built. You practice the amount of time you're thinking character thoughts that drive your action and less time worrying about how you're doing or how dreadful your scene partner is. You begin spending more time *in the zone*—listening, reacting, following a new impulse and, like the perfect golf shot in the middle of so many mediocre attempts, you feel as if you were born to do this, because you're learning how to concentrate, relax, and imagine realities on stage. The more you do it, *if* you focus and continue living in the role, the better actor you will become.

You can't take a single performance for granted.

Evolving

> How do I bring the everyday world that I live in and what's important to me in that world into my characterization of Bottom without warping the play or ignoring a responsibility to my fellow actors? By trusting the words completely."
>
> —F. Murray Abraham, *Actors on Shakespeare*

The show needs to both evolve and maintain at the same time. The structure of the house remains the same, but the furniture can get moved around a bit, and places that you tend to occupy within it will change. Any renovation of a scene needs to get the required *permit* license from the stage manager and/or director.

However, what's happening to you as a performer is evolving. Your work ethic, preparation discipline, routines, and commitment to your characterization and the well-being of the production gathers momentum and strength with every performance.

Not everyone approaches the work this way. But, all have to be concerned with their own "life in art and art in their own life."

If you want to do a few shows and have some fun, your routines and rituals and daily focus are not as necessary as it is for those of you who are looking at the mountain of becoming a working actor and preparing your work ethic for a long and arduous climb.

Audience

> … when you're an audience member of a piece of theater, you're responsible for the evening. You're asked to participate. Your life is being reflected back to you and you can immediately comment on it through your response and the actors really can feel that and shift and change according to the audiences.
>
> Cate Blanchett—*Iconoclasts*, The Sundance Channel

During the run, you have the luxury of a different audience every night, which gives you not only incentive and energy but feedback as the show moves along. Are they with it, are they bored, asleep, responsive, quiet, or sneezing the night away?

You will not have to adjust your intentions and character work as you perform every night, but your actor brain will often struggle with how to reinvest in the work to surf these particular waves of people, not to mention your own personal ups and downs during the course of the run. The audience is part of the trinity and has direct impact and responsibility. Give them that.

Exiting rituals

As discussed, obviously an actor does not become the character, but it is equally foolish to think that the work of characterization does not influence you.

You need to devise an exit strategy that will bring you back to yourself before entering the real world once again. Obviously, some roles will just fall away from you as you exit the last scene and take your curtain call, but others have demanded such an emotional cost for you to play them that the effects of having lived their life for two-and-a-half hours might prey upon your psyche to the point that you still feel the feelings of the character or are exhausted from their upheaval immediately after.

Develop dressing room and post-show rituals that will help you to de-program your way back into your world, such as imagining taking off your character with your clothes and makeup … washing off the character and revealing yourself to yourself once again. Utilize cast conversations, music, meditating on the event that has just occurred before rushing out into the night or, as we ritually performed in Robert Prosky's production of Arthur Miller's *The Price* in Vienna, a toast of Jameson and then a slow unwind while we discussed the audience, the mistakes, the surprises and almost always had a compliment or two for what happened in the adventure. It was never boring.

Closing

In practical terms, you are either sorry to see the show close or possibly thrilled, if it has been a disappointment. Let's focus on the good show closing.

The final performance has always been the most difficult for me. I am worried that if I make a mistake, it will be the one thing I remember, and that has the potential to spoil a good memory of the experience, which puts undo pressure on the show. I've since tried to look at it as just another performance. However, it's hard not to be emotional about having to say goodbye to the people with whom you have shared the high wire act.

Once again, first things first. Pre-show preparation will cue you into your duty, which is the story, your character, and your job. With every scene, you're saying goodbye, so stay forward-thinking on the next moment and the next scene, not the one that will never happen again.

You'll have plenty of time for a postmortem after the show at the closing night party.

This is not the last show—it's a show. The audience did not come to see the last show, they came to see the show. This is not your character's last time to enter this story. It's her or his first time, so if you fully engage in their experience, you won't be as prone to dwell on your own.

The prompt book

This has been your map and becomes your time capsule.

I have kept my prompt books, and they're not only a diary of shows gone by, but the notes in the margins and back pages have served as a life diary of my artistic thinking at the time and about life events. (There are also inevitably phone numbers, contact sheets, and a calendar listing parties and appointments, auditions, and daily events alongside the rehearsal schedule and notes about the play.)

> An actor is a sculptor who carves in snow.
>
> —Lawrence Barrett, actor

Our work on stage is almost always lost to the memories of those who saw it and the artistic muscles we've developed doing it. We're in good company after thousands of years of having only reviews and pictures of the brilliant performances that came before us.

But remember, we're continuing their footprints as we make our own.

4 A creative process

Six approaches

> The making of any art is problem solving.
>
> —Stephen Soderbergh, filmmaker, NPR *Studio 360*

The creative process

When I was considering graduate training schools, James Young recommended that I study with Charley Helfert at Southern Methodist University because he taught *a creative process*.

I had no idea what he was talking about until I took a class with Charley. We unpacked what it means by asking questions; brainstorming; trying different approaches; piggybacking on our original ideas with new ones; responding positively to other actors' ideas; and always trying something regardless of whether we thought it was going to work. Try it. Do it. What *else* is possible? Hey, what if . . . ?

In his creative dramatics class, he set up improvisational problems and ways to approach them.

Ways of thinking

- Fluency: lots of different answers for a solution.
- Flexibility: looking at a problem from different perspectives; pliable.
- Originality: trainable through practice, pushing oneself beyond the "expected" and cliché; independent; inventiveness.
- Elaboration: expanding and embellishing an idea, adding details.

The creative process is usually experienced through intense observation, being *open* to anything and being *spontaneous*. As Charley would put it, "An idea swells, becomes pregnant, then explodes out—usually from irritation and struggle, like a pearl."

When brainstorming solutions to the conflict in your play and characterization: throw out as many ideas as possible, the more and the wilder, the better. It's part of the process to build on other ideas (piggyback).

What if … ?

This simple question can become a mantra in the actor's rehearsal thinking.

What if we tried it this way? What if my character has a headache, is drunk, didn't get much sleep last night, starts to take off his clothes because it's so hot? You've got to be willing to try anything without asking permission of your director. Just do it, and see whether it works. You may want to warn somebody if you're going to try something that would potentially shock them or disrupt the previous rehearsed version of the scene. For instance, I had an impulse to spit at another character once. However, I waited and asked Tom Hulce, who was playing Romeo, whether he minded my character (Tybalt) spitting at him. He agreed to let me do it, as long as it was a spray and not "gloppy!" Otherwise, everybody's job is to *react*, and the more unpredictable the impulses during rehearsal, the better … not for unpredictability's sake but from your impulses as the character.

"What if" becomes a powerful way of thinking during rehearsal. Organically, ideas will occur to you in the moment of a scene, and you must have the courage to try them, *just try them r*ather than assessing whether they will be *good ideas* or whether they *will work.*

You won't know until you do it whether it works and, for that matter, the director won't know until he or she sees it.

What if you tried *everything* that occurred to you during a scene? That's what you should be doing! That's what rehearsal is for—one impulse at a time and fully.

Playwright, actor, and director, Keith Glover (*Coming of the Hurricane*) put it best I think:

> Be willing to make mistakes and if you make a mistake, make it LOUD! I've made a habit of saying that. I truly believe in it. It was said to me early and it was freeing. I always believe that an actor should be open to the experience of discovery beyond what they know.
>
> Be willing to crash a bit. Don't rush to get a performance together, even if the rehearsal period seems short. Don't try to get it right or craft a performance that takes the place of truly rehearsing. Discover. It's a journey that the cast and production team are going on together. They should have ideas, but also be willing to be surprised by something about the play that they were not aware of and therefore be willing to let go of preconceptions, initial ideas.

You must insist on your freedom to explore and try things. You might actually become an instinctive and problem-solving actor who knows how to bring your character to life through trial and error. It takes practice … practice … practice.

Be patient

In an off-Broadway showcase production of *A Hatful of Rain* by Michael Gazzo, several alumni of Wheaton College asked Jim Young whether he would direct. We performed the play in a lower-Manhattan loft space. I was acting my heart out in a scene when my character, Johnny, was suffering the effects of heroin addiction. Jim gave me a transforming piece of advice.

> You are trying to show me how addicted you are to heroin. But, your character wants to hide this fact, so try to hide the pain. Johnny doesn't want to admit he's addicted and will do everything he can do to not show it, even though he's in agony.

However, vintage Jim, he had to really bum me out by continuing, "The things I'm telling you now, you may not understand or even be able to do for another few years." What?!

I was opening my first play in New York in two weeks, and I knew that agents and casting directors were going to be there. What good was direction that I wouldn't understand for a couple of years do me?! My character, Johnny, was addicted to heroin, and I was going to show it if I had to make myself vomit blood! *This was New York, man!*

The lesson to try to *hide the pain* has stayed with me for thirty years, because I knew he was right, even though it was very hard to trust any form of subtlety during those early days. I was definitely of the "bigger is better" school of acting back then.

Outside ourselves

Elizabeth Gilbert (*Eat, Pray, Love*) appeared on the Internet program *TED Talks* and discussed an ancient perspective on creativity. She said that in the Greek and Roman cultures, society accepted the belief that creative inspiration came from outside ourselves. The Greeks called it *Daemons* and the Romans, *genius*. They were visiting entities who brought ideas for the ancient cultures to capture and bring into the world.

However, she continues, with the advent of the Renaissance, we began to put ourselves at the center of the universe and took full credit for our innovations:

> … people started to believe that creativity came completely from the self of the individual. And for the first time in history you start to hear people referring to this or that artist as being a genius, rather than having a genius. And I gotta tell you, I think that was a huge error.

She then relates a striking story about American poet Ruth Stone and her recognition of a powerful creative force that brought her poetry:

> … she would be out working in the fields and she said she would feel and hear a poem coming at her from over the landscape, like a thunderous train of air and it would come barreling down at her over the landscape and when she felt it coming, it would shake the earth under her feet. She knew that she had only one thing to do at that point and that was to, in her words, run like hell—and she would run like hell to the house and she would be getting chased by this poem—and the whole deal was she had to get to a pencil and paper fast enough so that when it thundered through her she could collect it and grab it on the page.
>
> Other times, she wouldn't be fast enough, and she'd be running and running and running and she wouldn't get to the house and the poem would barrel through her and she would miss it, and she said it would continue on across the landscape and, as she put it, look for another poet.

Elizabeth concludes by relating how she accepts the premise that a creative spirit aids us, rather informs us of insights and creative impulse, but we must be ready.

The path to becoming an actor and increasing our awareness of our muse and creative impulses—and creativity itself—happens in stages, like the rehearsal process. Week one is for week one's work. Similarly, year one as an actor is for year one's foundational work. You cannot rush it or skip it to get to the good stuff. It's *all* good stuff, especially the tough stuff. Otherwise you might as well package your characterization in a box … it'll *look* like cake, but *instant* cake won't ever be as rich as the real thing.

Obstacles will present themselves immediately, and they're supposed to. The story itself may hold on to its secrets, and you find that you can't figure out how to make the scenes live. The table work could be a laugh a minute but, once you get on your feet, it feels like you're under water and you've forgotten how to move. Or the opposite is true. The scenes are quickly staged but turn to stone, and you feel trapped. You might find significant moments very early in rehearsal and grow to mistrust them once your character begins finding your feet in the later scenes. Actors and directors may prove difficult and oppose your ideas or launch into a direction you sense will be disastrous.

You have time and you have the talent, which have brought you to the theatre in the first place. You are *becoming*, entering a rehearsal room that deserves your sense of play, trust, inhibition, honesty, patience, an open mind and, most of all, taking responsibility for your work as you practice, again and again, rehearsing to fulfill your potential as an actor.

However, there is an emerging and dangerous distraction to an actor's availability and focus.

Digital discipline

"Digital natives" is a term I saw Gary Small (UCLA) and co-author of *IBrain* explain on the PBS *NewsHour* program: "Digital natives are young people who grow up with the technology, 24/7, whose brains are wired to use it effectively." He says that the technology is creating a generation of addicts to technology. "It is so seductive to our brains."

It is the mindset and distraction from your creative process that I want to address as you are challenged more and more by texting, calls, tweets, e-mails, and constant interference from the outside as you focus on your role.

Your imagination and free association are under siege and will take infinitely more discipline than my generation, who had only radio, television, and the telephone as potential distractions from our private musings and personal rehearsals. We certainly couldn't be reached during walks or even in certain areas of the house! Now we can, of course, but I think having established years of private rehearsal and concentration, it is easier for us to turn things off while we focus. Conversely, it may be easier for younger actors to multi-task. However, do you lose anything, even though you're proficient and used to constant interruption?

Digital distractions

There is a popular habit building that increases our need and abilities to do everything all at once—not unusual to be on e-mail chat, Facebook chat, texts, plus three different kinds of homework … or for our purposes, memorizing lines or reviewing blocking.

What happens to teenage brains in a multi-tasking digital age or any of us for that matter?

Correspondent Miles O'Brien reported on the PBS *NewsHour*: "For most kids these days, it's second nature to be online, on air, typing, texting, posting, perusing, constantly connected, well informed … perpetually tempted and to my eyes, distracted … " Addictive?

Multi-tasking

> We can do it but at tremendous cost. You can't do two tasks as well as you can do each one separately.
>
> There's only so much brain capability at any one time. Through-put. You can divide it down as much as you want, but the price will be even higher then.
>
> Multi-tasking without a cost is a myth.
>
> —Marcel Juste, neuro-scientist, Carnegie Mellon University

It appears that we're building different brains … wiring our brains differently.

Hamlet's BlackBerry

As William Powers writes about our conundrum in his book, *Hamlet's BlackBerry*:

> Our screens … deliver the world to us, bringing all kinds of convenience and pleasure. But as we connect more and more, they're changing the nature of everyday life, making it more frantic and rushed. And we're losing something of great value, a way of thinking and moving though time that can be summed up in a single word, depth. Depth of thought and feeling, depth in our relationships, or work and everything we do. Since depth is what makes life fulfilling and meaningful, it's astounding that we're allowing this to happen.

What to do?

> These challenges were as real two millennia ago as they are today, and throughout history, people have been grappling with them and looking for creative ways to manage life in the crowd.
>
> The goal is no longer to be "in touch" but to erase the possibility of ever being out of touch.
>
> The simple act of going out for a walk is completely different today from what it was fifteen years ago. Whether you're walking down a big-city street or in the woods outside a country town, if you're carrying a mobile device with you, the global crowd comes along.
>
> This is not a small matter. It's a struggle that's taking place at the center of our lives. It's a struggle *for* the center of our lives, for control of how we think and feel. When you're scrambling all the time, that's what your inner life becomes, scrambled.
>
> Over and over in history, new technologies arrive that play to our natural maximalist tendencies. At the same time, quietly but

persistently, there's need to find balance. The best solutions serve as a kind of bridge to the tech future, one that ensures that we'll arrive with our sanity intact.

Digital dependency issues

"Technology free introspection is taking hold and balancing the overwhelming influence and need to connect."

Insisting on this balance is essential for the actor who is not only studying and marinating on a role … but open and hands-free enough to witness the world that is his or her classroom.

Permission, power and protection

My father-in-law, Jim Brown, worked for General Electric and has sometimes referred to "The three Ps" that were taught in GE's management school: "You've got to have the three Ps in order to do a job. Permission to do it, the power to get it done and the protection from anyone trying to end-run around you in the process."

As you accept a role, there is an unspoken rule with regard to everyone's job, but you have to make sure that there exists a personal contract, first and foremost with yourself and then with your director for permission, power, and protection during rehearsal.

The permission

Giving yourself the permission to create and take responsibility for your work is a commitment to yourself and a necessary contract with your director, playwright, and designers as you begin work on inhabiting your role. In the business world, the executive in charge puts the job in your hands to complete on time.

During the creation of your character during *your* rehearsal and performance, you have the ultimate responsibility and the final decisions regarding its completion. You may or may not agree with your director's idea and/or your designer's clothes, which have to be worked out, but it is an *agreement* that takes it to the next step. I always follow the artistic instincts of my director immediately to play out the idea and find out whether it's working. Again, it's the playwright's character that *I'm* fleshing out. The costume designer has worked out his or her artistic vision with the director and is bringing an entire concept to the world of the clothes to fit the production. Your particular sphere of influence here will most likely be with regard to pockets and colors as opposed to design, which has been determined beforehand. That is, unless it interferes with your concept, at which point, it is open for discussion, but you'll need strong reasoning and textual justification.

The reviews never blame the director for your conflicted performance, and you shouldn't either. Just as you have given yourself charge of your life, you are in charge of your characterization and must give yourself permission to create it. Now, where and how the character moves on stage is all a part of the negotiation and collaboration with your director and fellow actors.

However, the permission to try things, to own and to develop, is something that many young actors are afraid to give themselves. You might think it's better to hold back and see what the director wants you to do before venturing out there on your own. And as they are more experienced, they obviously should know more. Yes, that's true, but they have cast *you* because *you* struck them as being best for the role; now it's your turn to take that trust and run with it into someone that you want to play. Give yourself permission to do it; the director gave it to you when you were cast.

The power

Will I have the authority to do this job the way I think it should be done? Without the personal power, you are still answering to someone who has the final decision. Now, in the case of the actor, yes, the director has many final decisions on behalf of the production; otherwise there would be chaos and a different production for every actor in the show.

However, only you have the power to create your character and how she or he inhabits the world of the production. It is a God-like power *to make the words flesh*, as Mr. O'Toole put it, and that's what you're about. You're Dr. Frankenstein, and your character is the monster. You give yourself the permission and the power to do it when you begin creating. The audience gives you this power when they pay to see you perform.

The protection

One fear is: if I venture out there on my own, I could very well fall down and get lost. I might take one of those less-than-traveled roads and forget exactly where I'm going. It's both the risk and the triumph of the creative process. So, you need to know that you have the protection of those who hired you when you are experimenting and rehearsing. This is established quite early in rehearsals and, like dating, it's part of establishing a mutual trust with your fellow artists. Commit to them as you want them to commit to you. First of all, give it to yourself. Protect yourself from those who want you to only travel down safe and sure roads toward a predictable outcome.

Protect yourself from too much self-doubt along the way. Protect yourself by practicing the day's work over and over until you are certain you can remember and reproduce what was accomplished in rehearsal.

You need this protection from yourself for yourself, but you also need it from your director and designers. Work to get it by paying close attention to *their* goals and direction and then if you feel deserted by them because you don't seem to be fulfilling their vision for the character, protect yourself further by speaking with them about the freedoms you need to create and how you can possibly achieve both your goals and theirs. All you can do is to do your best to accommodate but, in the end, it's your character, and it's your choice.

I've recently discovered a simple sequence of studying the play that you can practice on your own, before and during the rehearsal process.

The practice of lectio divina: sacred reading

The four actions

This is an ancient monastic practice in Christianity that approaches the Scriptures in four actions: read, reflect, respond, and rest.

1 Read: Listen with the "ear of one's heart." Be attentive to a phrase or word.
2 Reflect: Hold on to the phrase or word that captures your heart and imagination; daydream.
3 Respond: Spontaneously respond with a prayer, a thought or a question.
4 Rest: Live with it for a while, and just let it be in your mind as you go about your day; sleep on it.

To make the most of the experience, study in the same place in a particular room to train your mind and body that this is the time it will begin to *focus*.

The spiritual methodology of *Lectio* is accomplished through four phases of study. For our purposes, I'll use rehearsal terminology.

A time

A consistent time for your private rehearsal is important. The morning is always a great time for concentration. The mind is rested and acts like a sponge. The end of the day is another good time. Although the brain is tired, you can get a head start on new material or solidify your day's work on rehearsed material. The key is to pre-select the time that will be devoted to study and to keep it. This leads to a habit that trains the mind and body for what it's about to do, which increases the effectiveness of the time.

A place

Free from distractions, isolated from other people, cell phones, computers, Facebooking, tweeting, texting, and television. Using the same place increases a familiarity that also trains the mind and body in what it's about to do.

Preparation

For private rehearsal, a short physical warm-down, breathing exercises, and meditating will transition you from the daily hubbub of activities and thoughts and focus your mind and body on the script.

Application

The goal of lectio divina is to enable its practitioners to obtain a deeper knowledge of scripture, thereby increasing their light of faith. For us, entering into the mystery of the playwright's world and our character's mindset, desires, and very soul takes no less focus and time.

Read, reflect, respond, and rest

Should actors be any less devoted or responsive to their author's words? It is a technique that can organize your time of study into a productive and repeatable sequence.

Devotion to one's art is only a word without method, and here is a method 2,000 years old created by very serious practitioners … monks! They ought to know something about study; they passed 10,000 hours of practice a long time ago!

The Four Agreements

Actress Kathryn Kelley told me that many actors carry around a little book entitled *The Four Agreements*. Curious, I looked into it and found that the contents of the book serve as an excellent approach to rehearsal attitudes and even characterization.

The following is an edited overview obtained from the website *Human Potential Unlimited*, which describes the meaning of each of *The Four Agreements*, by Don Miguel Ruiz.

1. Be impeccable with your word.
Speak with integrity. Say only what you mean. Avoid using the word to speak against yourself or to gossip about others. Use the power of your word in the direction of truth and love.

Impeccable means not speaking against yourself, either to yourself or to others. It means not rejecting yourself. To be impeccable means to take responsibility for yourself, to not participate in "the blame game." What you put out energetically will return to you. Proper use of the word creates proper use of energy; putting out love and gratitude perpetuates the same in the universe. The converse is also true.

2. Don't take anything personally.
Nothing others do is because of you. What others say and do is a projection of their own dream. When you are immune to the opinions and actions of others, you won't be the victim of needless suffering.

We take things personally when we agree with what others have said. If we didn't agree, the things that others say would not affect us emotionally. If we did not care about what others think about us, their words or behavior could not affect us.

Even if someone yells at you, gossips about you, harms you or yours, it still is not about you! Their actions and words are based on what they believe in their personal dream.

3. Don't make assumptions.
Find the courage to ask questions and to express what you really want. Communicate with others as clearly as you can to avoid misunderstandings, sadness, and drama. With just this one agreement, you can completely transform your life.

When we make assumptions, it is because we believe we know what others are thinking and feeling. We believe we know their point of view, their dream. We forget that our beliefs are just our point of view based on our belief system and personal experiences and have nothing to do with what others think and feel.

We make the assumption that everybody judges us, abuses us, victimizes us, and blames us the way we do ourselves. As a result, we reject ourselves before others have the chance to reject us. When we think this way, it becomes difficult to be ourselves in the world. Take action and be clear to others about what you want or do not want; do not gossip and make assumptions about things others tell you. Respect other points of view and avoid arguing just to be right. Stop expecting the people around you to know what is in your head.

4. Always do your best.

Your best is going to change from moment to moment. Under any circumstance, simply do your best, and you will avoid self-judgment, self-abuse, and regret.

Doing your best means enjoying the action without expecting a reward. The pleasure comes from doing what you like in life and having fun, not from how much you get paid. Enjoy the path traveled, and the destination will take care of itself. Living in the moment and releasing the past helps us to do the best we can in the moment. It allows us to be fully alive right now, enjoying what is present, not worrying about the past or the future. Have patience with yourself. Take action. Practice forgiveness. If you do your best always, transformation will happen as a matter of course.

If asked, I would suggest adding a fifth agreement to the previous four:

5. Say thank you.

It has been documented that one of the main reasons people change employment is from a feeling of being unappreciated, not recognized for their work and taken for granted. In rehearsal, you have daily opportunities to tell your colleagues how you have appreciated and benefited from their work. *Being* thankful is one of most powerful and enabling qualities you possess as an artist. You are grateful for your own gifts: the gifts and efforts of those around you and to those who have inspired, taught, and directed your paths.

Take the time to express your appreciation, and you'll become not only more aware of everyone else's contribution but become someone whom people are inclined to work with again.

Never take people for granted: what they do, who they are, or how they do their job.

It could be the most important approach of all as it opens you up to everyone's positive energy and creative input.

> And in the end, the love you take is equal to the love you make.
>
> —Paul McCartney, The Beatles, "The End" from *Abbey Road*

5 Get serious

Seven ways

> The art of living rightly is like all arts: It must be learned and practiced with incessant care.
>
> —Johann Wolfgang von Goethe, *Scientific Studies*, vol. 12

Many people are depending on you to be very serious in the way that you approach your rehearsal. Not just the director but your fellow actors, the producer or university, and the audience who will eventually take the time to see you and pay for it! As an acronym, the word *serious* could help you remember seven important approaches.

S-E-R-I-O-U-S: *Study, Explore, Repeat, Independently,* with *Ownership,* in an *Uninhibited* and *Spiritual* approach.

Private *study* is the beginning of the work, accomplished alone and open to your muse. *Exploring* is at the essence of rehearsal, so don't be too worried about getting it right as you are in trying things many different ways, every day. *Repetition* solidifies the work and opens the door to your creative spirit. Developing a sense of *independence* gives you confidence as you make yourself the primary partner in the process of discovering your character. You are totally responsible for your work and behavior throughout the rehearsal process, taking *ownership* of what you do and what you don't do is as much about your life as it is about your acting. *Uninhibited* means unrestrained, candid, open, natural, and abandoned to the work, which is really the only kind of actor anybody wants to pay to see. And *spiritual*, because you are exploring the human condition in a place where games are played and lives are changed.

But how? These are only words unless you know *how* to study. How do you *explore* or *repeat*? How do you adopt independence in a collaborative art? How do you take ownership and work in an *uninhibited* manner? How do you increase your sense of spirituality?

Study

This is your private rehearsal.

Repeating what Peter O'Toole has said,

> It's not just a question of learning your lines. The old fashioned word for it is study. You go alone, you have no observer, no interlocutor and unobserved, uninhibited, private study is the backbone of any fine actor or actress.

The very word denotes something boring to most of us. For most of our lives, the only practice that we've had studying is the *have-to* kind for class. It has negative connotations, like the words *research* or *analysis*. It all sounds very academic. We haven't adopted the meaning of study for ourselves or practiced it in an interesting way of living and working more effectively. It's not as much fun, until you start seeing the results of having done it.

To study and to consider: according to Merriam Webster's *Dictionary*, it is to *think about carefully*—to think of especially with regard to *taking some action*—to *gaze on steadily* or *reflectively* to *meditate, reflect endeavor* to *read in detail* especially with the intention of learning—*to engage*—to plot, to design.

You are at the beginning of *your* creative process with this play. Give it weight, give it time, give it all you've got.

Freelance director Stephen Fried:

> I think an actor needs time to marinate with a role—to consider his views on it, and what he has to bring to the role that no other actor can. This process of consideration and 'marinating' as I call it takes time, and it can't be rushed. You can't force yourself to have ideas about a role—they come to you when you're in the shower, or at the gym—not when you're at a desk trying to "think about the role."

The time and the place are essential for your private rehearsal. Your brain is most alert after it's rested. Morning time or after a nap is a great time for studying your role. However, the most important thing is finding an uninterrupted amount of time and a place where you feel free to think out loud, pace, practice, to be quiet, to read, take notes, and reflect.

So, how do you begin, and how do you continue studying throughout the rehearsal process?

Before rehearsal begins

Hopefully, you have months of consideration, reading, and traveling to obtain firsthand knowledge about your play and character. However, if you don't, you'll at least have a week before the official start of rehearsal, and it's all you. Block out a minimum of two hours a night for five nights for your own work. This is the beginning of devotion, taking ownership of and responsibility for your work on the play. Consider it *your* rehearsal where you begin to develop *your* ideas about the script. Your questions will start to emerge and, best of all, you'll begin rehearsal with the rest of the cast ready to continue working, rather than knowing very little about the play or what you think of it.

Your first read

Ed Herendeen, artistic director of the American Contemporary Play Festival, told me:

> I encourage actors to read the script out loud by themselves. I think that's an important first step to trust their intuition … and to ask the key questions; what do I say about myself, in terms of the character … what do other characters say about me, who I am, and you find that in the script, all the answers I believe in a good play are in the script … it's really the actor's job to know the script.

Eleanor Holdridge, freelance director and head of MFA Directing at The Catholic University of America, expands on this even further:

> Everything is about preparing for your presence in rehearsal, where you should be part of the collaborative environment yet open and flexible to receive input from the director and the other actors. The goal is to bring strong yet flexible choices about who your character is, how they see the world, and even the beginnings of what drives them throughout their journey within the play.

Begin your prompt book

The prompt book includes the script with room in the margins to note your ideas, blocking, and questions but also is the place where you'll bring any and every piece of research or dramaturgy, pictures, reviews of previous productions, or playwright information. My friend Cain Devore ("Hoodwinking Hamlet"), cofounder of Filmmakers Alliance in Los Angeles, calls this book, your *Bucket,* a place for every idea, "to do" lists, shot sequences, and contacts.

The amount of time you spend with your character and his or her story is directly related to the amount of confidence and authority you bring to the public rehearsal. There will always be distractions. There are always a hundred other things to accomplish during the day. However, if you want to be good, you will make your study a priority. Your subconscious may think you can "wing it," and maybe you *can* get away with an acceptable performance. However, you will never grow into what you are capable of doing without increasing the amount of private study on your role.

The prompt book is the perfect place to store biographical or historical material that illuminates your character's given circumstances.

Mr. Herendeen continues:

> And depending on if your script is about history or a period in history or about a specific geographical location then it's your job as the actor to—if you're doing *A Streetcar named Desire*, then you need to understand the French Quarter. You need to look up—and there are resources available to you as an actor to understand the climate of the geographical location, the political climate of what's going on in a particular period of history … if a play is written in a certain period then it's your job as the actor to understand that period, that geo-location, the social, political and religious climate of that particular period and place, and that's all research and that kind of research is actor research.

How to explore

I find that characterizations are discovered in three primary areas: the text; your self; and other people in the world that you may know or seek out. It's a 24/7 focus during your rehearsal period.

Last year, I was listening to an interview with novelist and playwright A.E. Hotchner on the *Diane Rehm* show (NPR). Hotchner was one of actor Paul Newman's best friends who told the story of how Newman explored the difficult characterization of a fighter. Hotchner was producing a live television show, starring James Dean, who was tragically killed just before shooting was to begin.

> Arthur Penn suggested using Paul for the role, whom he had worked with at Actors Studio. Paul came in and said that he didn't think he could replace his friend, James Dean and couldn't perform the difficult part of this fighter. But he was talked into doing it.
>
> The interesting thing was, at the first rehearsals, he was simply awful. He didn't at all, perform like that character, and he knew it! One day, because they ran out of room at NBC, we were rehearsing

> in a funeral parlor … where the back room had been stripped of its familiar [stuff], and there we were, but the ante-room was still full of caskets. So one day I'm leaving rehearsal and out of a coffin I hear, "Hutch!" and I nearly jumped out of my skin, and I went over and there's Newman in the coffin. And he said, "Batten down the hatch, I'm checking out." I said, "Oh come on, let's go have a beer;" and we did, and he said, "I'm just terrible in this role." Well not too long after, maybe a week later because we rehearsed for two weeks, Paul suddenly began a wonderful delineation of this character, and I said, "Where did this come from?" and he said, "Well, I went to downtown Los Angeles to a grubby gym where boxers hang out, and I met this sort of beat up boxer who was a little bit addle brained who walked around with kind of a shuffle, and I got to know him well." And that began to infuse his character and he doted on it, and it became a really extraordinary performance.

Newman told him, "But you know, what's difficult about it is, you can't be an imitation, you've got to take it as a kind of an infusion of that character, and to build on it and make it your own."

Exploring different approaches in rehearsal requires an understanding that it doesn't all come together at once. Week one is for asking questions. The second thrust is not only staging the play but exploring different approaches to your character, having practiced them at home, and open to changing your ideas when the inspiration hits. Or, like Mr. Newman, going out and finding your person.

Encountering a difficulty can be essential to the solution.

How to repeat

Repetition deepens the discoveries and opens new doors, too. Ask to go back over a scene as often as the director will agree to it. Can we do it again? If it's an exhausting scene: mark it. But repeat it, at least once and then again at home later the *same day!*

Repetition doesn't mean to try to do it exactly as it was done before but means with an eye on remembering the blocking, the intentions, the lines, so that when you return to the scene, you won't be concerned with where to sit but with what your character wants to happen.

Practicing and securing your discoveries is extremely important. Reacting, listening, and building on what others give you in the room bring your person to life. By repeating your discoveries, they will deepen and evolve, as long as you continue to search and attend to your repetition with openness and concentration.

The important thing to realize is that you are never merely repeating a scene for the sake of remembering it but to reinvestigate it from a more secure place. You are moving forward, always forward in your process … not merely maintaining but deepening and available to inspirations.

How to rehearse independently

Rehearsal happens in concert with directors, designers, and other actors, so what do I mean by independently? There is much that must be accomplished on your own for collaboration to be effective. Studying happens on your own, ideas for scenes and character and even the overall direction of the play itself come from trusting yourself to express ideas and act on them. Independence can also be defined by what it is not … relying on someone else, controlled by others, looking to other people for validation.

Independence is self-governing and shows a desire for *freedom*.

Asking questions is not a sign of weakness as long as they don't come from a dependent place, as in asking permission or "is this all right?" "Can I try it this way?" Try to practice saying, "I want you to watch this" or "tell me what you think of this."

It is most often too early to decide whether something works or doesn't. Live with choices for a while, and you'll know whether they work or don't.

You *are* the character and have the inside track to his or her motives and needs. Yes, guidance and suggestions are essential in the process, but they are helpful to *your* process, not the other way around. I like the example of Brian Reddy, a New York-based actor who has worked extensively on both coasts.

> I was doing Iago downtown [off-Broadway] at the Classic Stage Company and I made a choice during rehearsal one day to which the director responded, "Why did you do that?" And I said (half jokingly), "Because I'm Iago." The director replied, "Well, I don't think Iago would do that." So, I told him, "He just did."

Brian explained that even though they had had a rocky beginning, everything was in much better humor by this time and so he felt free to say whatever was on his mind.

The point is that you deserve life, liberty, and the pursuit of happiness as you create and rehearse, but it is often up to you to claim it for yourself.

How to take ownership

Ultimately, your performance has your stamp of approval, and you not only will be judged by it but, more important, you have to live with the performance that *YOU* have created. Directors can't create performance, they direct yours. You should have much to say about your costume (within the scope of the costumer's design concept and time restraints), your shoes, your blocking, your props, makeup and, most important of course, your characterization.

As a member of John Andrew's *The Shakespeare Guild*, I attended what is known as the *Gielgud Award* ceremony in honor of actor Kevin Kline many years ago. To the best of my memory, actor and clown Bill Irwin roasted his friend by saying that during the filming of a movie they were in, Kline told the director that his character wouldn't have a bedroom painted in that particular color!

Kevin Kline can get away with it, but for most of us, simply realizing that we have a voice in these matters is a start toward a meaningful conversation with all of our collaborators as we strive to do *our job* to the best of our ability.

How to be uninhibited

My first production at Wheaton College was a freshman orientation show entitled *Wheatonella,* a collegiate send-up of the musical version of Cinderella, with altered lyrics appropriate for a freshman introduction to the school. The audition was for a walk-on part who constantly intruded himself into the scenes with some contemporary Wheaton College reference point, such as a security guard separating loving couples on a bench or bringing in the local pizza at the end of a romantic song, whatever. The director, David Hale, asked me to do one specific thing, which was to stage my own death. He referenced Mortimer in the musical *The Fantastics*, saying that he was the character who was always asked to die, *Die Mortimer, die*. So he wanted me to do it, and I was totally frozen as to what to do. David then said something I have never forgotten. *"Anyone who is afraid of looking like a fool on stage, probably will, but if you go ahead and brave the foolish attempt, you won't."*

It worked for me as I leapt onto the stage and grabbed an imaginary dagger from the air and pummeled myself with it.

Stupid maybe, but it got me the part and, once again, began an improbable life in the theater. Twenty years later, I clutched at another imaginary dagger in the air while playing *Macbeth* at the Folger Theater in Washington, D.C. much less afraid of looking like a fool but much more aware of how foolish a half-hearted attempt would appear.

Actress Kate Eastwood Norris:

> We are not completely devastated when we come up with an idea that gets rejected while talking about it so why should we become so if

it gets rejected while showing it? We are actors, not debaters. Rush toward embarrassment, it saves a lot of time and takes all its power away.

What's spiritual about it?

According to Merriam Webster:

> *spiritualis,* from Latin, *of breathing, of wind.—Of, relating to, consisting of, or affecting the spirit.*

Breathing is a good place to begin. In other words, relax, check into yourself, be yourself and breathe! Not to belabor the point that most of your acting teachers have been preaching to you for years, but sometimes, when you're stuck, struggling, or nervous, the best thing to do is to stop and breathe. I have found that emotional scenes have arrived when I stop long enough in the middle of the scene to think, breathe, and then boom—tears, passion, stillness, or fire comes into the moment. It's all in the breath; your spirit, your true self and your connection to the earth. There is freedom in simply breathing and waiting.

Whatever spirituality means to you—be it passion, love, hard work, devotion, or a faith in God that inspires and guides you—include it in your rehearsal/life process. The essential belief system that you honor and follow in life is equally essential in your acting.

Actor Ted Van Griethuysen:

> A question I like to begin with in acting classes is this: Do you like the way you see people? Because, even though the artist in the person is usually ahead of the person, perceptually speaking, still you cannot really see a character in a play much better than the way you see people in life.
>
> Rembrandt, for example, probably saw his wife Saskia better when he painted her than he did in ordinary Dutch life. How you see is the most important equipment in an ordinary life, and it has everything to do with how you deal with the relation of art and life.
>
> Every actor has experienced that dichotomy. For two or more hours a night, you feel you are yourself, you are free, you can show what you feel and say what you feel. Then there are the larger number of hours a day when you just muddle through, without grand emotions and iambic pentameter. Sometimes that difference can be too much for the artist to bear.
>
> After a performance, the famous ballet dancer Vaslav Nijinsky would stay on the stage, leaping and leaping until exhausted, and the big old

> Russian peasant who looked after him would come and take him away to his dressing room. Then there was Nijinsky's famous grand jete, in which he would appear to leap into the air and simply stay there for a while and then come down. Apparently he felt, in that leap, a freedom, a profound joy that he could not feel in the everyday hours of his life.
>
> The teacher with whom I studied for many years, Eli Siegel, said that he thought that unbridgeable difference may have had something to do with why Nijinsky went mad. I mention this only to emphasize the importance of the question: Do you like the way you see people?

As actors, I personally believe that we are fulfilling, illuminating, and unveiling the very purpose of our existence when we create characters and story.

Zelda Fichandler:

> The fish dwell in the depths of the ocean,
> The eagle on the sides of Heaven.
> The one, though high, can be reached with an arrow;
> The other, though deep, with a hook.
> But the heart of man, at a foot's distance,
> Cannot be known.
>
> —A Burmese saying
>
> The actor, fully alive through her character, aims to cross that foot. Behind the veil of everyday life and the masks we wear there, is the character, emotionally open and free, for the person in the audience to see, to see *into*, and to see himself. *Teatron*—a theater—a place for seeing.

On the grounds of Tudor Hall, (Edwin Booth's homestead), architect Julie Gabrielli said, *"There is power in place."* The rehearsal room, wherever it may be at the time we lift our soul to practice, is our place to welcome power, be powerful, and access the power of life. The sherpas believe that there is a spirit inherent in the mountain that makes climbing it a spirit-filled experience. It is to be honored and respected or, according to the sherpas, suffer the consequences of the mountain's retribution.

Having fun is also one of the essentials of life … and a common reason to pursue acting. The art of pretending is something we are born to do and, as actors, we tap into a childlike sense of play. We practice a process that directs our sense of play into living works of art.

6 Living rehearsal

A 24/7 gig

> Emily: Do any human beings ever realize life while they live it? Every, every minute?
> Stage Manager: No. (Pause.) The saints and poets, maybe—they do some.
>
> —Thornton Wilder, *Our Town*

To realize life

I'm always interested in what the first impulse is for someone to pursue acting. I was lured into my first audition by the prospect of impressing girls. When I was only nine years old, I saw my older brother, John, kissing a girl in a high school play. This had to be in the back of my mind the first time I auditioned for a play entitled *The Little Moon of Alban,* directed by Dick Willis in high school. I didn't get the part of the guy who kisses the girl, but I got the part of the guy who gets a big laugh, and that was even better. I was sold. I got the kiss *after* the show.

The creative state

> Not only must your love of art, a love that is without fear or reproach, be the foundation of your life's career, but you must also be in love with something or somebody every day, with a picture, a flower, a song, a woman, a profile you saw by chance … a football match which produced in you a feeling of energy—with anything you like so long as your spirit is always in a state of exhilaration, so that the ordinary everyday life that surrounds you has always the power to light a spark in you.
>
> —Konstantin Stanislavski,
> Moscow Art Theatre actor, director, author, 1889

The rehearsal room is as big as your life. Being an actor is to be fully alert to the small and the significant everyday moments. Acting is a 24/7 gig, always on call, 24 hours a day and 7 days a week. Deepening your appreciation of life's little moments will deepen your approach to acting and give you more tools in rehearsal. It's vital to your life and your life's work to *practice* seeing, experiencing, and remembering. As actors, we are always *at work* and, at best, we are in a *creative state* of being as we go through the day and as we enter rehearsals for a production. As artists, what might otherwise simply be a misfortune or an exhilarating experience in life has the potential to be used in your work as well.

> I remember seeing Dustin Hoffman on a television talk show talking about his old room-mate, Bobby (Duval) walking up the street in New York, when a pigeon got hit by a car. He said that the pigeon struggled to make it to the curb, climbed up, and keeled over. "… and then Bobby said, 'I'm gonna play that someday.'"

What is the one driving force in your life that lives in your heart and mind twenty-four hours a day and seven days a week?

What do you need? What do you love? Survival would normally be one of the basic answers to the question, although finding shelter, food, and companionship and avoiding whatever can kill us is not as obvious in today's world as it once was (that is, until you move to New York City and begin a life in the theatre!). Survival jobs are aptly named when you're trying to make a living as an artist of any persuasion.

I performed in Shakespeare's *King Lear* with Hal Holbrook. He had the Pacific Ocean in his eyes. Hal sailed solo from California to Hawaii, and that experience was in his Lear … a boldness, fear, anger, and humility.

Rehearsing is a way of life, existing not just in the context of a production. As I worked on breathing when I first began training as an actor, so too, learning how to rehearse starts with the understanding that you're working on your craft every day, whether you're in a show or not.

If we are to mirror life, we have to be intensely aware of it as we live in it. Every feeling and experience we have had is on our palate when we create a character. And more important, such an awareness and respect for every little thing that happens to us will open our soul to life and, as Stanislavski says, strengthen the foundation of our work.

As he is often quoted, "Love the art in yourself more than yourself in the art."

Staying serious about your career

How to live in constant readiness to capture an element of your life for rehearsal? It is a muscle needing daily practice. Specifically, with regard to acting, you could be studying other roles that you hope to play someday or the simple act of observing someone on a subway that you can use in a later characterization. Explore new audition material, repeat audition material that you already have and the daily vocal and movement work to stay in shape. Take a more independent approach by calling a casting director and taking daily ownership of what you have to do to advance your art *and* your career. Say what you really feel in a group conversation for a change. See plays, movies, concerts, art exhibits, dance performances, lectures on the planets, whatever awakens your spirituality.

Studying roles

Piggyback principle

Rehearsing one role prepares you for another one, which is why practicing any role will strengthen your ability and confidence in rehearsal. Working on various monologues has obvious advantages because they can be used for auditions. Working on various texts outside the parameters of a given production will increase your knowledge and preparation for them specifically and the way you work on texts that you've been hired to do.

You're an actor: you've got to work at it … like a professional tennis player, or boxer, or musician. You practice by memorizing texts, working up scenes, taking classes, finding survival gigs that increase your performance abilities.

How do you work on roles that you may never be cast in, realistically? Keep them by your bed for starters. Take them on vacation with you and to Starbucks. Take one hour a day away from Facebook and read a play, a monologue, a poem that you want to memorize. This could be your life's work after all.

I was always impressed by an interview with Al Pacino, written by Lawrence Grobel for *Playboy* magazine. It was the first time I learned of his love for Shakespeare.

> Shakespeare is one of the reasons I've stayed an actor. Sometimes I spend full days doing Shakespeare by myself, just for the joy of reading it, saying those words.... I do Shakespeare when I am feeling a certain way. Sometimes I will sit here for a day and a night, acting out parts. I can go for ten hours straight. Maybe it goes back to the way I worked things out in my subconscious when I was very small, when I went

> home and acted all the parts in the movies I'd seen. People are always asking me to do Shakespeare—at home, at colleges, on film locations, in restaurants. It's like playing a piece of music, getting all the notes. It's great therapy.

I was equally instructed by an older actor who played an amazing Malvolio during my first professional production of *Twelfth Night* in Dallas, Texas. Once, I visited Dimo Condos in his New York apartment and saw that he had a copy of *Romeo and Juliet* by his bed. "What are you studying, Dimo?"

"Mercutio," he replied, "I've always wanted to play Mercutio."

"Dimo!" I think I blurted out, "you're too old for Mercutio. What is your interpretation, some kind of child molester?!"

"Heyyy" he said, "he can be older than those boys, kind of like the guy who still hangs out around your school after he's graduated. You know."

I thought, poor Dimo—just can't let go and accept his age and the roles he's right for. Only now do I realize how he felt. At fifty-eight—which I'm pretty sure is older than Dimo was when we had this conversation—I still feel like Mercutio, too. I played him 24 years ago, which seems like yesterday. He's in me, but Lord Capulet is in the wings—or the Prince—or maybe the Nurse! That would be a good role for an aging Mercutio, wouldn't it?

Dimo is a consummate actor, through and through, always studying and dreaming of roles yet to play. He could be a wild man in rehearsal, too. As Malvolio, Dimo could be seen dusting off the rehearsal furniture before his entrance; getting into the role as Olivia's servant. It was Dimo who invited me to the Actor's Studio in New York to see his work as Shylock in a scene with Ed Setrakian, who played Antonio. At one point, Dimo went up on his lines and started singing "Some Enchanted Evening" or another totally inappropriate tune. The audience of actors laughed, and he started cursing at us, seemingly still in character. Then, finally turning back to Ed, he re-entered the scene, at which point all manner of spitting and wrestling ensued until Dimo crashed onto the floor, a humiliated Shylock, still being asked by Antonio to lend him the money.

Rehearsing and performing it in class at the same time: this was alive. Would they ultimately perform it this way? No. But, did they find useful moments and act out the inner hatred while at the same time muscling through any performer anxieties too? Absolutely.

Lend a hand

There is an organization called Lend a Hand that represents actors, finding them temporary employment between gigs. As an actor living in Los Angeles and New York City for twenty years, sometimes I had to take survival jobs just to pay my bills. Over the years I accepted work as a receptionist in an investment firm; house cleaner; mover; caterer; bar tender; closet organizer; party entertainer; house painter; advertising coordinator; telemarketer; actor management; landscaping; dog walking; house sitting; and paint stripping. Every job you take is an acting class, full of interesting people and jobs that you might play someday. It's the only thing that kept me sane, telling myself, "I can play this someday, and if not this, at least my *feeling* about it!" It creates empathy. Empathy opens your heart, and it takes heart to rehearse.

Studying people

> I use the subway all the time. It's my form of transportation … my job is about playing people. And I think once you lose touch with people, what do you play? So, I'm here, and it's the best people watching in the world, you know.
>
> —Hilary Swank, "Oscar Gold" 2005 interview, CBS *60 Minutes*

Acting doesn't always broaden your horizons; living does. There are summers between semesters at school when all you want to do is act in a production, but the better choice could be traveling, working somewhere where you can observe people and make some money at the same time.

Your life bucket (journal)

Whether you're working on a play or aren't, the bucket is the thing because it gives you a place to write down what you've discovered, dreamed, or experienced. Again, you're practicing the art of observing by writing down experiences, feelings, and moments that you might someday refer to in a role. It's not that you'll necessarily remember to look back a few years at your bucket book and find exactly the experience that you wrote down but, somewhere in the back of your mind, you paid attention, and it will return to you.

A chronicle of your life observations also keeps the magic alive. It's unbelievable the things that people do and say, and you'll increase your habit of noticing the more you take notes. Learning how you tick is a lifelong process and will enable your work to translate into anything you do.

> For me, inspiration comes in the moment you might be watching television or you could be making scrambled eggs and have an idea,

> it's so random. I never thought that I would be so inspired by just the regular slow pacing of everyday living.
>
> —Nelly Furtado, singer/songwriter

Volunteering

Get out and put yourself into situations that you wouldn't normally see. I've done relief work in Bangladesh, worked in soup kitchens for the homeless, volunteered at hospitals for the mentally ill and, recently, I went door to door for the first time in the 2008 presidential campaign and felt my heart leap to my throat every time I knocked on someone's door. I had to improvise every conversation, not knowing whether I would encounter anger, agreement, or a conversation about something totally different. My personal stage deepened that day, because the unknown encounters gave me humility, presence, focus, and overcoming fear. Finding the time to devote yourself to causes larger than your own will expand your magnanimous spirit, which has a direct impact on your rehearsal and characterization. Your characters won't have to fight you as much for the space to do what *they* need to do, because you've practiced getting out of the way!

Legitimate jobs are not throwing in the towel. You must see them as increasing your knowledge of the world and how people behave. You need to walk in other professions' shoes to play them more effectively. Yes, you can also use your imagination and interview people, do research, and trail others as they do the jobs you might get the opportunity to play. A detective once told me that he had actors follow him around all the time to watch how he did his job. That's fine, but there is also something to be said to actually taking as many jobs as you can to understand them more fully, such as travel—better to live somewhere for a while if you really want to know the country.

Between gigs

You are building heart, empathy, and a perspective with whatever you do to survive until your next gig.

Practical benefits

The lessons you learn about approaching rehearsal seriously could influence the way you approach other jobs in your life, too. I was recently speaking with Laura Brown, who majored in theatre and journalism at the University of Maryland and then became a very successful fundraiser (she's presently the assistant dean of development for the University of Maryland's College of Arts and Humanities). According to Laura, she uses her acting skills "every day" as a fundraiser.

> Acting taught me how to listen; it taught me how to understand a character's—another person's—objective. Being able to listen carefully, and understand a prospective donor's interests and passions, are both essential skills for a fundraiser.

Heart and soul

Hamlet says, "See the players well bestowed. Do you hear? Let them be well used, for they are the abstract and brief chronicles of the time."

You have 4,000 years of actor footprints leading up to you as you "tread the boards." They have paved the way and are passing you the baton. Run with it, or don't take it at all.

Why do you want to become an actor?

You need a personal perspective that will see you through the tough times, the tough directors, the bad reviews, the agents and casting directors who can all too often become dismissive. You need a reason that will endure the long tours, the time away from home, low income, and the great roles, adulation, and what sometimes feels like a schizophrenic occupation.

It wasn't that long ago that an actor couldn't get a bank account in New York City, because our employment record was so scattered and uncertain. When I worked in Ashland, Oregon at The Oregon Shakespeare Festival, we were highly esteemed as performers, conducting tours and signing autographs after the shows. But, it wasn't until I led one particular tour around the theater, taking some questions from the patrons, that I realized what kind of life I had chosen. "I love actors," one older woman said, "I just wouldn't want my daughter to marry one."

It wasn't until film and television that *famous* actors became society's nobility. It has always been far from a respectable station in life—becoming an actor, a gypsy, a strolling player, following the wagon from one town to another, like the players in Hamlet.

Mr. Pacino once again from the *Playboy* interview:

> Actors are always outsiders. It's necessary to be able to interpret—and that gets distorted when you become famous. Our roots were always outside—we're wayward vagabonds, minstrels, outcasts. And that may explain why so many of us want to be accepted in the mainstream of life. …

It takes heart and soul to become an actor, valuing one's own personal experiences as our teachers and techniques, our memories and motivations.

Heartbreaks teach heart. Accidents, homeruns, and standing up for oneself or someone else teaches heart. Add some text to the essence of these experiences plus empathy and imagination and you've got life on stage.

Pacino:

> I used to walk from 92nd Street and Broadway right to the Village and back again, bopping along the street, thinking of parts. I worked out a lot of my role in "Godfather I" that way. I still get out there in the streets as much as I can. Watch a guy put 40 packs of crackers in his soup.

But *why* do you want to become an actor?

Your super objective

To further root you into your purposeful enterprise, examine your own personal given circumstances. What *is* your objective and *your* super objective? This objective, apart from your character's, is *your* personal and immediate goal in the scene or play that you're currently doing. The super objective, according to Stanislavski and, more recently, Uta Hagen in *Respect for Acting*, considers what your character—or in this case, *you*—want to accomplish overall, in the grand scheme of things, which is your life, present and future.

Too often we take the scene-by-scene, moment-by-moment events in our life totally for granted, as if we'll live forever or, in this case, as if this scene or production doesn't really matter that much in the great scheme of things. Think again.

This is *exactly* the scene or the moment or the production that *does* matter, especially if you're not fully engaged. This is when it counts the most *if* you want to do well. You can tell whether something is truly important to you by your actions. Like your character: it's her or his actions that tell us what he or she wants, sometimes spoken, sometimes not.

As a teacher, I never cease to be astonished at how little homework goes into the preparation of a scene from a student who says she or he wants to become a professional actor. Everything else seems to take precedent over their personal rehearsal and commitment to the assignment or scene.

I don't understand this, other than the fact that at twenty-something years of age, they are under tremendous pressure to do well in other classes, haven't learned how to organize their time and, possibly, believe that acting is something they can get away with by *winging it,* as a result of being talented.

If it's really what you are considering doing as a career, why don't you make it a priority of preparation and get all you can from the training at this stage of your dream?

For argument's sake, let's say that it's my teaching. Maybe I don't motivate or frighten or inspire everyone as I should. However, your director may not be up to your expectations either. Really, what do we have to do with it in the long run? You are the only one who can ultimately motivate, frighten, and inspire yourself into accomplishing your goals in acting. We should be the ones who feel pressure to do our directing and teaching better because of how seriously we know *you're* taking it!

I asked Emery Battis, a ninety-six-year-old actor and a professional for some seventy years, what his advice would be to a young actor. He repeated an old familiar adage: "A tourist in New York asked a passer-by how to get to Carnegie Hall. The New Yorker replied … practice … practice … practice."

You wouldn't imagine playing a musical solo in an orchestra without constant practice. You wouldn't imagine wanting to become the star player on your soccer team without daily practice and taking care of your body. You wouldn't imagine becoming a writer, painter, auto mechanic, or cook without constant and *daily* attention to the skills necessary to become the best.

Like the tennis player who asked me what he would have to do to become a professional, the answer is similar to what I would have to do to become a champion tennis player.

Unfortunately, actor training is often taken for granted, undervalued, and the sense of spontaneity or "*winging it*" has become an acceptable approach to scene study, auditions, characterization, and a young actor's approach to rehearsal and his or her life.

I often ponder the question, if an actor were transported over the centuries from AD 1600 into today's world, we would be amazed at the entire repertoire of entire texts that the actor could recite from his day. Transport any one of us back into the seventeenth century, and the people would say, "What do you do in the twenty-first century?"

"I'm an actor."

"Ah, please tell us your stories, recite us some plays, books, poems, and songs."

They would be amazed at how little our actors could recite from our own authors.

As you begin or continue your career as an actor, you need to rehearse both the art of living and commit yourself to a life of observation and studying roles that you hope to play someday, every day.

> Emily: Do any human beings ever realize life while they live it?—every, every minute?

Students of acting should try. For we are students of the world, "holding the mirror up to nature …"

Part II

In the room

If *you* wrote the play, how would you want the actor to approach it? If *you* were directing the play, how would you want your actors to work on their roles and take part in rehearsal? If *you* designed the set or the costumes, how would *you* want the actors to work in your space, find their light, wear your clothes, and discuss it with you?

As it is, you *are* the actor, so begin to work with these artists as you imagine they *hope* you will. What *are* their expectations? I asked them. I asked professional playwrights, directors, designers, dramaturgs, and stage managers what they do and how they want to work with you. Linguistically, "collaboration" implies more or less *equal* partners who work together.

There is a trinity of power here, thousands of years old. The triple spiral, found on the tomb at New Grange in Ireland and older than the pyramids, is a haunting and beautiful symbol of existence. It's carved in stone in the sacred place of an ancestral tomb, which was so constructed that the light from the sun fully enters the tomb only on the winter solstice, December 21, the darkest day of the year

Is it a symbol of life, death, and rebirth? Is it father, mother, and child; sun, moon, and earth; body, mind, and spirit? Whatever it means, it is a powerful, interconnected symbol of trinity.

The holy trinity of theatre is the story, the performer, and the audience.

Christopher Martin, founding artistic director of CSC Repertory in New York said,

> The author writes for the audience. The actor is the author's medium through which to reach the audience. The actor's reward comes from reaching the audience with the author. It is only then that the sides of the triangle are complete.

The director is a very recent but essential participant. Think of the three-legged stool as an appropriate symbol for the playwright, the actor, and the director. It's a perfect balance, upon which the audience sits to receive the play. All legs are equal in the production process or the experience is askew.

Casey Biggs, actor, director, and instructor for the New School in New York, put it this way:

> When each player, director and actor, are open to being led by the other and the actor has the ability to be present, sensitive and vulnerable to the forces of the story that is working on them both, then you have a good environment to create.

Triple Spiral image courtesy of World Heritage Ireland

7 Actor and playwright

The words made flesh

> The script sits in front of you. The writer has translated into ink what is in his spirit, in his soul, in his mind. Boom. I come along, I pick it up and the ink goes into my eyes, into my mind, into my body, blows around and that part begins to inhabit me … and one's job really, is to make the words flesh.
>
> —Peter O'Toole, *The Charlie Rose Show*

Actor/playwright collaboration

> I was surprised that the actors had so few questions about my play when they had the chance to ask me.

This was playwright and film and television writer Jacquelyn Reingold's (*String Fever*, *Girl Gone,* among others; HBO's *In Treatment*) reaction after a run through rehearsal of her play, *String Fever,* being produced by Theatre J in Washington, D.C. I wanted to know where my scenes came from in her mind and experience. However according to her, only one other actor approached her in this way during rehearsal.

There are many reasons for our reluctance in speaking with a playwright. A majority of us rarely meet the playwright, as the plays that we perform have had their premiere already or we're working on a classic, and the author is long gone.

However, whether they are living or aren't, there they are, in our hands as we turn the pages. We must embrace the playwright's every word and recognize them as living collaborators, rather than as literature.

Again, Al Pacino:

> The relationships that we have with writers are quite a thing; they're different from the ones we have with actors or musicians or composers

or politicians. Everything for me is the writer; without him, I don't exist.

Thanks to an organization in New York called *New Dramatists*, a sixty-year-old arts organization with a singular mission—to give playwrights time and space within an inspired and inspiring creative community to realize their artistic potential and create work that invigorates the American theatre—and to my wife, Christie Brown, who worked with so many of their writers, I was able to reach out to a few highly esteemed playwrights for their advice to actors who are about to do their play.

Research

Playwright and Obie Award-winning actor David Greenspan (*Dead Mother or Shirley Not All in Vain*, *She Stoops to Comedy*, among others):

> Each actor's process is different—so I wouldn't presume to advise him or her. I can speak, however, from my perspective as an actor. I once played a morphine addict—and spent a few hours in a needle exchange facility observing the clients. If the play is set in the past, I might do some advance reading about relevant aspects of the period—or speak to someone familiar with that era. If the play is an adaptation, I will have a look at the source material. And if the play is a revival, I will check to see if there is film or video documentation of a prior significant production—ideally the original production. Unless there are time constraints, I will not do too much work—or memorization—until rehearsals begin... so as to be in concert with the director and playwright's vision of the play.

Pretend the play is perfect

Playwright and librettist Karen Hartman (*Gum* and *Goldie*, *Max and Milk*, among others):

> Read the play many times. Read something else I've written. Look up words that are in a foreign language. If the play takes place in another time or place, learn a bit about that other time and place … just show up knowing the script, rested, open. Pretend the play is perfect.

Karen mentions being physically rested, and I think this is an aspect worth highlighting. Your physical condition when you approach the work can make a big difference. This can be a challenge whether you are in university and subject to sleep deprivation or in the profession and challenged by survival employment and family obligations that take a great deal of your time.

Plumb the text

Playwright, librettist, and translator Catherine Filloux (*Eyes of the Heart*, *Lemkin's House*, among others):

> It's all there in the text. Plumb the text. Every production I've had of a play, is with a play that has undergone so many rewrites and considerations, and been vetted by a collaborative team of actors and directors, that the text stands on its own, and I would start there.

An encounter

Playwright, contemporary theatre theorist, and activist Erik Ehn (*The Saint Plays*, adaptation of *The Sound and the Fury,* among others):

> Watch your sleep and nutrition, exercise patience, and expect that the answer will be more in your body than in your head, and more in your hearing than through any other sense. Encounter it like a natural object—like a condition of the weather, like a bad rain; maybe talk to some people who have been through the same distress, but otherwise—get wet.

They say it takes an entire village to raise a child, and I think that the same is true of a play. All of us are working to illuminate and interpret what is really going on.

Realizing the play

Playwright, librettist, and screenwriter Doug Wright (*Quills*, *I Am My Own Wife*, among others; *Quills* screenplay):

> There's an unfortunate tendency in the theater today for everyone in rehearsal for a new play to presume that they are there to "help" the writer draft a final version of his script. In some small way, this is true; no playwright can bring a piece to true completion without that first, crucial production. But it has created an excess of over-enthusiastic dramaturgs; cast, director and designers alike too often start by

> questioning the play, rather than attempting to truly REALIZE it. All too often, actors ask, "What could be better?" as opposed to "What's already here for me to excavate?" I tell actors, "Don't ask me to change something without trying it first, and not just one way: show me nine or ten versions of a particular line reading or a particular scene. I'll learn more in charting your efforts to make it work than I will in your arm-chair criticism of it." I learn so much more by watching actors on their feet than I do from hearing them expound around a table. After all, some of our greatest plays must've seemed inscrutable in the first few days of rehearsal; imagine what damage unwitting folk might have visited upon Pinter's *The Homecoming* or Beckett's *Happy Days* by demanding those works be more readily explicable.

Just do it, find it, experiment with it, give yourself time to discover it. This is not only a story but the writer's baby put in your care. Nurture it.

Asking the playwright questions is a rare privilege; when it presents itself, jump at it. However, there are also some unwritten codes of conduct when it comes to actor/playwright collaboration.

Unexpected choices

Playwright and screenwriter Jon Klein (*T Bone N Weasel*, *Dimly Perceived Threats to the System*, among others):

> First of all, is the director standing nearby? If so, draw him or her directly into the conversation. It can become problematic when a playwright makes suggestions to an actor that might contradict the director's concept of the character. Secondly, while it may be helpful to provide some further information regarding a character, that is still mainly the actor's job—to flesh out what is implied or suggested by the dialogue, in order to achieve a more fully realized background and motivation for the character. This is not only important for the actor's development, but often for the development of the play itself.

Do your homework

Playwright Arlene Hutton (*Last Train to Nibroc, As It Is in Heaven*, among others):

> The best actors I know prepare for their roles long before they learn their blocking and lines by getting familiar with my work. Reading other plays that I've written helps performers and directors grasp the

> themes and language and enables them to delve more deeply into the characters and story. Many of my plays are period pieces and it's essential to study the time and place in order to put the work in an historical context. So I think the best advice I can give actors is to do their own homework.

A vision defined

David Greenspan:

> Skilled directors, I've found, solicit the playwright's opinions and thoughts—and do not interfere in the relationship between playwright and actors—with the understanding that anything the playwright may communicate to the actors is or has been communicated to the director. The knowledgeable playwright incorporates the talents of his collaborators in service of realizing his or her vision. The actor and director do the same: like the playwright, they too have a vision. The only difference, as far I'm concerned, is that director and actor are interpreting the work of the playwright—and their vision must be defined in the context of as clear an understanding of the playwright's intentions as possible.

As the actor, you have your job, your vision of how to accomplish characterization and fulfill the playwright's intentions, usually working in intense day-to-day rehearsal with the director and the rest of the cast. Even though you may not have access to the playwright in person, you have access to their work; their characters, scenes, and plot, which are no less dynamic than if they were there in person.

Hands off

Playwright, actor, musician, and director Keith Glover (*Coming of the Hurricane, In Walks Ed,* among others):

> I prefer a room that has balance of respect between the various disciplines, which in turn will create trust. I hope an environment is created where all ideas are on the table, but the roles of the creation of the project are defined but fluid. I think problems occur when the participants lose sight of their responsibilities and start hedging in on the other creators' turf, which creates suspicion and lack of trust. Nothing then gets accomplished. The scene isn't working, so the actor wants to improvise lines rather than working through the text. The

director starts tossing out line readings instead of instilling patience to the actor's process, or the writer starts giving notes in the corner to the actors on break. When balance and respect are there you can take your hands off of it and let the magic happen.

Openness

Jon Klein:

> I believe in total openness. No one should be shut out of the exploratory process during rehearsals. No sitting in the corner of the room until you're called. I do generally believe in going through the director as a conduit to express my concerns, as should the actor. Not out of deference to a director's "authority;" it's just the most efficient way to communicate within a group of people. But I also don't believe in "secret" consultations. In terms of the script, there is nothing said during the course of a rehearsal that shouldn't be available for all to hear.

Channeling questions

Karen Hartman:

> I think it can be useful to speak directly to actors at the table, especially to clear up factual or back story questions. When the [actor] questions are larger ('What do I want most from my mother?') I don't answer them.

Equal voices

Playwright Lee Blessing (*A Walk in the Woods, Eleemosynary, Cobb*, among others):

> If we're speaking about a new production … then I prefer the traditional relationship which places the director in the middle of things, as the clearing house for all communications among playwright/director/actor. During rehearsals for a full production, I like to sit quietly and watch. I prefer to whisper thoughts to the director and let she or he decide what should be transmitted to the actor—and how it should be transmitted.
>
> If we're talking about a reading or a staged-reading of a play (sadly, by far the more common experience for a new play these days),

> then I've noticed a new relationship has evolved, in which the actor, director and playwright tend to have much more equal voices and speak without much regard for the above-mentioned traditional relationships. Directors often ask me (usually because there's so little rehearsal time) to speak up whenever I have a note or can add perspective to what's being discussed, and they encourage me to speak directly to the actors.

Healthy debate

Playwright, television writer, and activist Kia Corthron (*Breath Boom, A Cool Dip in the Barren Saharan Crick*, among others; episodes for *The Wire* and *The Jury*):

> I have found the work seems to be most successful when directors are not uncomfortable with me speaking directly with the actors (though my talk time is still always exponentially less than that of the director). Marion McClinton told me once that he didn't mind at all when I spoke directly with actors as long as he was there so that we didn't contradict each other later, and I transferred that wise advice in my work with other directors. That doesn't mean directors and actors and I agree on everything. I'm always up for healthy debate. What I find problematic is close-minded resistance. These are the actors and directors with whom I have to part ways.

I want to repeat that the debate continues whether you have the privilege of working with the playwright in person or don't. There they are, at your fingertips and soon occupying your every thinking moment during the rehearsal period, asking you to find a way in and back out again to bring their story to the audience in your own enlivening interpretation.

Experience

Doug Wright:

> If an actor makes a discovery about your play on his own, it's a victory he'll carry onstage with him every night. If he's simply trying to execute your instructions, he'll never feel as confident, and his performance will suffer. It's better to watch actors flounder through your text, then offer premature help. You have to know when to intercede, and when to let the rehearsal process proceed organically on its own. And nothing teaches that delicate balance of intervention and abstention but experience.

Actor's space

Erik Ehn:

> I like us to all have access to the dream-materials (the same adventures, crises, toil and trouble) and then go off a bit on our own to have the dreams we will. Actors have to have space in which to write the plays in their own medium.

Outstanding examples of actor/writer

So there you are, standing in the rehearsal room with an exciting new play in your hands and a director in charge of how the rehearsal is conducted. The playwright may even be in the room, adding additional pressure to fulfill everyone's expectations. How does the playwright feel about an actor's responsibility in this moment, and what are some examples of how they felt particular actors contributed to their work?

Commitment

David Greenspan:

> Certain actors are particularly inspired or remarkably gifted—there's no two ways around it—and their contributions are unforgettable. They bring a probing intelligence to the work. They ask questions or latch on to aspects of the script that illuminate the play—and at times, their work might inspire the playwright to reconsider elements of his or her play. I will say that the thing I find most welcome in the process is commitment. When an actor commits him or herself to the work wholeheartedly. When an actor doesn't do that, it can be a real bummer! Nothing is more disheartening than knowing an actor doesn't really care about the work. Even when a play has shortcomings, showing up every day—rehearsal or performance—to give it your best shot—is what makes the work rewarding.

Smart questions

Lee Blessing:

> Long ago I worked with Laura Linney on the world premiere of my play, *Fortinbras* at La Jolla Playhouse.
>
> Laura played the ghost of Ophelia, and what I noticed about her process was something I was more used to seeing in the work

of older, more established actors. What impressed me was pretty straightforward, I thought. She knew her lines. She knew where the commas were and sat with the text until she felt she knew why the commas were there. Her role was largely comic, but she built an extremely reliable, serious foundation for everything she did and said. She asked a lot of questions and they were smart questions.

When Laura got satisfying answers to her questions, she set about applying those answers to the role she was evolving. She trusted in my intelligence as it related to understanding what I'd written, and she trusted that her director (Des McAnuff) would help her to an extraordinary and consistent performance, which he did. In short, she gave us both the power to help her do her work.

The play was new, and it changed during the rehearsal process. Laura was not thrown by that. She used the same, reliable process to internalize changes and make them as solid and justified as every other aspect of her characterization. Her work on the play helped improve more than a few key aspects of it. She was also reliable at getting the biggest—and most grounded—laugh of the evening.

Jon Klein:

A few years before his sudden and unexpected death, I had the chance to work with the great actor J.T. Walsh, who was cast at Sundance to perform the title role in *The Einstein Project*. J.T. would be absolutely no one's immediate idea to play Albert Einstein; often cast as a "heavy" in his film roles, he was brusque, strong and more than a little intimidating. Exactly the qualities that we were looking for in our unorthodox characterization of Einstein! J.T.'s passion and commitment to the role resulted in more streamlined, brutally frank dialogue. Flowery and charming speeches evaporated, as he helped us realize that one or two powerful lines of dialogue would be more to the point, and create a stronger character. Even after Sundance, every subsequent revision in the play would continue to be inspired by J.T.'s amazing performance.

And, finally, Doug Wright speaks about his amazing collaboration with actor Jefferson Mays:

The actor Jefferson Mays was key to the evolution of my play *I Am My Own Wife*. I'd bring in reams of material, and he'd leap to the task at hand, committing himself fully to each half-baked draft. He spent very little time chatting about it, table-side. He'd hop up, adopt a new

> posture, pull a new accent from his considerable arsenal, and introduce me to a character I'd created the night before. It was exhilarating. In watching his struggle to realize scenes on my behalf, I could readily discern when they merely needed more rehearsal time and when I urgently needed to take them back to my proverbial typewriter.
>
> I wrote the play especially for Jefferson and his myriad talents; as an actor, I know him incredibly well because he'd already performed in two of my previous plays. So I knew the heights that he could scale. In an early incarnation of the play, I also had the privilege of directing him. Together, we were able to formulate an acting vocabulary—an economy of gesture, a sense of scale, and a behavioral vocabulary—that served the play. Later, the gifted Moises Kaufman would bring the production to glorious completion on Broadway. But I'll always treasure those rehearsals with Jefferson because—in those heady, delicious moments—I had the rare privilege of creating a play in three dimensions, with a real flesh-and-blood actor, instead of merely on the page.

It is to authors such as these and to the audience that you owe your primary concern. Your self and the director are dedicated to illuminating the author's intent for the *audience's* enlightenment. The relationship between actor and director is unmistakably a crucial one in the realization of the production. However, you work together, committed to revealing the story.

One can obviously make the case that Shakespeare directed his plays with intentional meter changes in the verse and punctuation and inserting prose. We can also make the case that authors continue to direct the action of their work with their flow of scenes, the way the dialogue occurs and when, punctuation, stage directions, pause instructions, and repetitive interjections.

Trust the text

Kia Corthron:

> One thing that my actors must keep in mind is to trust the text, to trust that the playwright was once a professional proofreader so typos are very very few: If I've left out a word I meant it, if I made a sentence run on for several lines without a period I meant it. I often have characters change emotion on a dime, and the actors have to go with that. A journalist interviewing me years ago remarked that my writing was said to "live in the subtext." At first I laughed, and then realized she was right. It's why my plays tend to be disastrous on cold reads. So much unsaid—and the actor needs to find all that or it doesn't make sense.

I asked New York actor John Tillotsen if he had any memorable incidents with regard to playwrights and directors. He wrote me from Vienna, Austria where he was playing Big Daddy in Tennessee Williams's *Cat On A Hot Tin Roof* at the Viennese English Theater.

> I did a play called *Mary Barnes* off Broadway in 1982. The whole cast was finding the play daunting and there were rewrites going on by the director and sometimes the cast. At one rehearsal it seemed everybody had an opinion about how to fix a particular scene … and after about an hour of discussion through which I had been very quiet, I piped up (I was probably the youngest and least experienced) and said, "Why don't we just do the scene? Isn't our job to illuminate what is given us not the other way around?"
>
> There was a big pause. I was sure I'd be fired or voted off the island. Miraculously everyone sort of nodded and agreed that was our job and we should do what was written. The scene became a highpoint of the production.

Your playwright is your best friend as you learn your role. Get to know him or her, read other plays by her or him, and begin to understand his or her paintings, brush strokes, and themes. It comes from within her or him, and that's where you have to go.

Enter: The director.

Elia Kazan, Lee J. Cobb, and Arthur Miller—director, actor, and playwright sharing the load

8 Actor and director

In the trenches

> When the director did finally appear toward the end of the nineteenth century, he filled so pressing a need that he quickly pre-empted the hegemony that had rested for centuries with playwrights and actors. The appearance of the director ushered in a new and original theatrical epoch. His experiments, his failures, and his triumphs set and sustained the stage …
>
> —Helen Krich Chinoy, *Directors on Directing*

However, where the director has become the star, "publicized, lionized and unionized" (*Directors on Directing*), particularly in the United States, the tendency is for the actor to become a passive participant in the creation of the director's vision of the playwright's creation. The truth of the matter is that we all have specific jobs in the process, and it's our own fault when we elevate the director as someone of greater import than ourselves in telling the story.

The mind and heart of the play are the playwright. The movement and physical life of the play are the actor. The choreographer, sculptor, coach, and conductor of the production are the director.

Directing has by definition a leadership role that does not subordinate the player.

It can feel like Christmas when we are offered a role. It can feel like a gift or, in some cases, a dream come true. It can also mean the difference between paying the rent by doing something you love, and a boring temp job. However, regardless of how much it means to *get the part*, a collaborative mindset is crucial to your sense of independence and ownership of the job when you enter rehearsal. Directors don't usually want to work with grateful kids, but we have often treated directors as benefactors, saving our existence and giving us permission to play.

The audition—hire

Auditioning is not an agreement. It's a first date. Auditioning does not mean that you will do the role. *(Unless you have been requested not to audition unless you will accept it, which occasionally happens, though rare.)* There are terms to be reached, getting your own sense of the director and even his or her concept of the play before you decide whether to commit. Even though you are the one being interviewed, auditioned, and chosen, it is still a two-way bargain, a two-way audition, and a two-way agreement. You are *agreeing* to collaborate on this project. She or he believes that you are right for the role and, by accepting the offer made by the producer, you are agreeing to work *with* the director, joining forces, essentially to interpret the play for the audience.

Once you are out of training, it is a business arrangement and needs to be approached professionally. In the world of supply and demand, the director has an early advantage in selecting from many auditions that psychologically can tilt the weight of the operation. However, once you are chosen, the weight shifts again.

As actors, our personal authority over our career and choices has become topsy-turvy through the years, especially with the addition of agents and casting directors coupled with the historically recent popular attraction of more people wanting to become actors.

Until this century, and especially before the advent of film, the acting profession was considered a lowly one and not widely respected. *Famous* actors have always been admired. However, today, with a surplus of people wanting to become actors, our stock has cheapened in the market place but *not inside the rehearsal room*!

Student questions

My student survey revealed more questions about how to work with a director than any other category.

"Should you go into a rehearsal with multiple takes on a character even though you're going to perform what the director says anyway?"

"Each director seems to have different 'boundaries' for how much freedom the actor has to experiment. Therefore, I would like to know, 'How much can I put in?'"

Two views

Representing a traditional and widely accepted school of thought is actress and author Uta Hagen in *Respect for Acting*:

> The director's concept must be followed and your job (the actor) is to make it live. It is your job to justify, make throb and make exist that which he asks of you, whether you agree or not.

And then conversely,

> In general, I like to be left alone … the director can then make what I'm doing clear or clearer. … The rehearsal process is the means by which the actor finds out what the scene is for oneself.
>
> —Kevin Kline, stage and film actor, *Directors in Rehearsal*

I have interviewed many professional actors and directors on the question of collaboration and what they feel is the job of each other's position in the company.

English actor/director Richard Clifford:

> For me, "The play's the thing!" All actors are servants to a play. We interpret what the playwright has written and develop a sense of inhabitation inside the roles. This is of prime importance, both as actor and director; we are interpreters.

Mutual trust

Veteran Broadway stage and film actor Stacy Keach:

> Mutual trust is the most important element, I feel, between the actor and director. Because it is a collaborative relationship, it behooves both parties to understand, respect, and appreciate the nature of their respective processes. When I am acting, I form an impression of myself as a musical instrument, and I regard the director as my conductor. As a director, I feel that my primary responsibility is to provide the actor with confidence and clarity. The late John Huston, one of my favorite directors (*Fat City*) said that a good director had but two directions: "A little less," or "a little more." Bad direction invariably stifles an actor's creative impulses, and invariably comes in the form of dictatorial or preconceived notions that ignore the actor's instincts. The transfer of positive energy becomes impossible, and the necessary mutual trust is helplessly eroded. Conversely, it is important for the actor to recognize and respect the director's obligation to present the audience with the total experience of the play, many aspects of which fall outside the parameters of the actor's character, such as set, costumes, lights, music, etc. As such, I have found that the most gratifying experiences occur

> when I adopt a posture of "what can I do, or what can my character do, to help serve the play and the production?" Generally speaking, I have discovered that this attitude produces positive results.

One on one

Actor Rick Foucheux:

> By the time we got into tech rehearsal for *Born Yesterday*, it had become obvious to me that there was a particular moment that wasn't "reading" for [the director] the way she had it in her head. I sensed this through her notes and by gauging her reactions to the bit in rehearsal; but I also sensed that she was searching for a better, clearer way to describe or explain to me what she was looking for. As we returned from a break I approached her and we both acknowledged that this was a sticking point we had simply not addressed fully until now. All that was required was a moment of quiet—again, one-on-one—trading of some ideas, and things became clearer for both of us. It served as a breakthrough on the one particular issue and helped pave the way for me to get closer to what she had in mind for the character in general.

The director is in charge of the production in all of its aspects, starting with casting and heading up the design team and final production. However, would you agree that the actor is in charge of their own characterization? You need to be confident in your authority as you bring your character's world to life.

Who's in charge?

You must recognize and be aware of the director's creative process, too, and approach rehearsal accordingly. You have to give yourself the freedom to try things, especially not knowing whether they will work. Your director has major input and hopefully many suggestions on how to bring your character to live in the same world as everybody else. What she or he sees can be crucial to your realizations.

However, what you do when you disagree with the director is a question that we struggle to answer in nearly every production. Disagreements can be about characterization, blocking, activities, a simple moment in the play, or worse: they can transform themselves into professional threats, abusive comments, and even harassment.

Of course, constant agreement can be sweet but not necessarily more productive.

I remember my graduate school professor, Jack Clay, saying in class that he had seen rehearsals that were veritable love fests but that the show didn't turn out well, whereas he had seen battles throughout rehearsal that turned into great productions.

"Following direction" is a curious phrase and, to my mind, denotes subordination of the actor. However, *agreeing* to try anything and everything a director suggests is more to the point. An actor *takes* direction, *accepts* direction, *wants*, *needs*, and *uses* direction.

It's essential for the actor to be inventive, to experiment, to problem solve, and to explore possibilities alongside and *in concert* with the director's vision for the production.

Being receptive and trying the director's ideas is equally essential in finding *your own* interpretation of the role. The director *needs* you to be independent to direct.

You can't drive a parked car, as the saying goes. The director does not need a servant or a robot that does whatever she or he believes is correct. The actor and director share equal roles in discovering and illuminating the story.

So, how *does* the actor truly collaborate with the person who does the hiring?

Both of you, being artists, need the temperament of thoroughbred horses that should give you an idea of how wild and unpredictable the rehearsal process can become.

From Zelda Fichandler:

> I think directing is an invitation to a conversation, rather than the handing out of nuggets of wisdom. It's sorting out divergent paths. Sometimes you try something that you want very much to try, and it doesn't seem to work right then, and you and the director can't reconcile your differences, so you have a little (maybe big?) struggle—as graciously as you can. You try something else; you may or may not go back to the first idea or even move on to a third attempt. Struggle is part of the hard work that achieving a successful production often requires. Theatre is a collaborative art; in the end, one hopes everyone is proud of the work and content with the way it was achieved.

Rush toward embarrassment

Regional actress Kate Eastwood Norris's approach:

> It's a wonderful thing to be able to work with a director who thinks exactly like you or where you can come to at least a compromise about your character: those are joyous and fulfilling experiences in an

actor's life. But the best review for a performance I ever got was from a Shakespeare scholar who told me, "You failed. But you failed in a great big ball of fire and I was mesmerized." This was in a show where I disagreed almost completely with the director and wasted a lot of time arguing over the table. But in the end I did my job and committed myself to playing the character he wanted. I actually won an award for this performance, which confuses me on so many levels to this day. I now use the following method in rehearsal all the time—get up and give a moment 100% to show the director if what he or she is asking of me makes sense, rather than talk about how I might disagree. It's also an efficient way to show your idea, which I failed to do with the director in question. We are not completely devastated when we come up with an idea that gets rejected while talking about it so why should we become so if it gets rejected while showing it? We are actors, not debaters. Rush toward embarrassment, it saves a lot of time and takes all its power away.

Director type

Among all of the other jobs, a director often has to determine how best to work with the different actors within the cast. He or she will discover that certain cast members need extra attention, some like to be left alone, others of us may be nervous and need reassuring. She or he becomes instant psychologist, teacher, coach, and doctor in helping us to discover our characters' actions and our own insecurities.

Just as it helps to know how your fellow actors work, it helps to understand how your director likes to work. Is she or he highly experienced; young; perhaps known as an "actor's director," which means that he or she may have once been an actor and is personally experienced with the actor's process.

The director has her or his job, and you have yours. Do not expect him or her to do yours or even show you how.

Responding

Director JoAnne Akalaitis is the founder of Mabou Mines and the former artistic director of the New York Shakespeare Festival. Winner of five Obie awards, she continues to direct in the major regional theatres of the United States and is professor of theatre at Bard College.

I trust actors more than ever, I think they know what they're doing more than I do. And if you give them some kind of freedom, but say, okay, you guys play, often, when people say, what do you think I should do, I say, well, I don't know. What do you think you should do? My job is not to teach them how to act, my job is to respond to their work, you know, if someone does a scene, all I can do is say, well, I think this worked, this didn't work, this worked great, this was perhaps not a good idea and you should go back to the drawing board.

Egoless

Actor John Lescault:

> The directors whom I admire the most are those who have the courage and the egoless-ness to say, when asked a question: "I don't know. Let's find out." I've noticed that that spirit creates the healthiest kind of environment in the rehearsal room, which may then lead to the all sorts of discoveries. The director who says "Yes, and. …" also helps to lead an actor to a potentially deeper understanding of the character or a moment. In contrast, the director who barks, "No!" to the first attempt the actor makes, can squelch and hinder the creative process, which is a very delicate entity.

Hindered, because suddenly the actor has to either accept or confront. *Delicate* because the director has made a definite decision, and you feel judged, limited, possibly devalued and have to decide whether to fight for your choice. I have found most directors to be positive individuals who are learning how to get the best work out of everyone individually and have prepared more than any of the actors have had the time or interest overall to do.

Actor/director Jerry Whiddon:

> But if a director is resistant or too autocratic, I know my job as an actor is to use that merely as a constraint, not an impediment, because the essence of creativity is working with the constraints; just use that as a constraint and make sure I don't choke myself off. It's just that a certain way to manifest the dialogue is not as fertile as it could be with another director.
>
> And I just have to find other ways of exploring, and there's always the point where you're still trying to find that in the third and fourth week in rehearsal; you're still frustrated by a director who's not willing to see another possibility. At the same time, it's my job as an actor to fit into what the show needs to be, for the sake of the other actors. Also, this director just might be right about this. I don't want to deny

> their vision of the show; it's their vision of the show that's got [to] be manifest. That's what it has to be, otherwise we're going to have a bit of a mess, where everybody's doing what they think the scene should be—that's the other end of the spectrum.

Make a choice

Ralph Cosham is a British actor who has made his career in the United States for more than thirty years. On Davey Marlin Jones: "There were no wrong choices in Davey's class (or in rehearsal). The only crime was not to make one."

Recently, I asked Jim Young whether he could look back and identify the most important aspect of rehearsal, and he said, "Come prepared and then be willing to cast aside your ideas in collaboration with the director and fellow actors."

Trust

Mark Lewis, actor, director, and currently a professor of acting at Wheaton College in Illinois:

> I remember a simple word that Vincent Murphy spoke once that has stuck with me for the many years since. He was directing *The Misanthrope* at the Alabama Shakespeare Festival, and I was playing Alceste. The role is a difficult one to establish a tone for. Irascible, misanthropic—comic? I was having a hard time finding the balance, in one scene in particular. After rehearsal I stopped Vinnie to ask him about it, hoping for a clear sense of direction.
>
> He looked at me, smiled slightly, and said, "Don't ask me; because if you do I'll tell you."
>
> What he communicated to me in that moment was so valuable. First of all, he did have an idea about the moment; this meant that he trusted himself—that he had a solid vision for the scene that I could rely on. Second, he thought it a better idea for me to continue to try to figure it out on my own. This meant that he trusted me.

Resilience and risk

Jerry Whiddon as director:

> As a director, the expectations actually start in auditions, or talking with an actor I'm considering for the role. Not just: is this the best person, do they enter the world of the play more easily, but also—and this is

key to my process as a director—can they bring a sense of resilience to the room? Can they bring a sense of adventure and a willingness to try, to go down un-traveled roads with this character and with the process? And subsequently, when I'm looking at an actor or talking with an actor or watching an actor audition, can I live with this person for four weeks? Can we, after the first coffee break of the second Tuesday, can we still have that sense of exploration together, and is this a person willing to bring their two cents to the table and actually risk something, show me something rather than tell me something?

An organic process

Joe Dowling, artistic director of the Guthrie Theatre in Minneapolis who has done extensive directing in Ireland, including founding the Gaiety School of Acting in Dublin and serving as artistic director of the Abbey, encourages the actor to be in control:

> I think it is different with every person and different with every show, isn't it? Because sometimes the director arrives with a very clear and defined vision of how the play should be and he or she is going to want to see that vision realized through the work of the actors. What I try to do most of the time is sort of wipe the slate clean and say, we start at day one and everyone starts at the same level, and we find the play in the course of rehearsal and by and large that works. But collaboration is the exact word, it's the right word, if it becomes a kind of, you know, "director directs and an actor responds," then it's a mechanical process, it's not a creative organic process. Whereas if—as you remember with *Caesar*—if it is an organic process, then the actor comes through the process feeling much more of a sense of ownership of the role, and a sense of ownership of the production. So the stakes are much higher for the actor than they would be if they're simply parodying what a director wants them to do. So I've long been of the view that while film may be a director's medium, that theatre ought to be an actor's medium, and it is a medium where the actor is in control, because night after night, he or she has to go out on stage and recreate the performance. So it has to come from inside, it has to be organic and imposing it from on top by the director, merely—I've seen plenty of productions fail on the basis of that, because it doesn't feel natural or real.

Bring something to the table

Steven Satta, associate professor of theatre at Towson University said it succinctly:

> The actor must bring something to the table from the beginning. The director shapes that "something" and guides it to a level of integration with the other "somethings" from the other actors. The best scenario is that the actor discovers the moments of the play and the director helps to highlight and make them manifest in the production. Certainly the director must have a vision from the beginning, but that vision simply establishes parameters for the actors to work within. If the parameters are too narrow, the actors become merely puppets. If the parameters are too broad, the actors will lose focus, and the energy will dissipate.

Understanding the author's work

Christopher Martin founded CSC Repertory (The Classic Stage Company) in New York City and has been a professional actor, director, writer, and musician for more than forty years:

> Both [director and actor] are working for the author AND ultimately for the audience. I tend to spend a good deal of time at the table for the first week or more of rehearsal, so that ALL the actors understand every moment of the author's work and how their contributions fit into the grand scheme of the whole. Perhaps it is my long connection to music. If the symphony orchestra doesn't become familiar with the musical sweep of the whole, their contributions may well work against the whole. Actors tend to focus solely on their own parts, their own scenes, their own lines. Think of a football player who chooses not to watch the game in progress from the bench, but goes back to the locker room until he is called upon to enter the game. If he doesn't know the status of things on the field at the moment he's called upon, he will not be able to effectively contribute to the game.

Ready to rehearse

Doug Wager:

> I like to collaborate with disciplined actors who proactively prepare and do their homework and bring clear, imaginative, provocative and actionable information into the rehearsal—and who prepare to

be affected by what the OTHER ACTOR is doing—to be ready to rehearse—not do their homework in rehearsal.

No monopoly on good ideas

Joe Dowling continues:

> Again it depends entirely on the relationship that's been established between the director and the actor. If it's one where the young actor feels that they have a point in the room then disagreement is not treason, you know, it's not an act of tyranny. The director is not necessarily going to be tyrannical about it … but if on the other hand there isn't that atmosphere in the room, the actor feels intimidated by the director's strictures, then the hard core reality is they've got to swallow their pride and do what the director asks, otherwise it would be unfair to say to an actor you can always stand up for yourself in these circumstances. I think it would depend entirely on what the relationship is from the beginning. Of course if it's collaborative and if people are working closely together, I never mind if an actor disagrees, they can argue their point and then usually it's for a very good reason that an actor will say, you know I don't really think that's what I want to do here, and then they've got to justify what they do want to do, and make it work … and if they do make it work, then my attitude is, there's no monopoly on good ideas.

Coaching a star athlete

Stephen Fried, professional director and instructor at the New School in New York:

> There are a lot of different metaphors I've heard used to describe the relationship between an actor and director, but I think my ideal version of this relationship most resembles that between a star athlete and his coach. The athlete brings to this relationship a specific set of skills and extraordinary talents that the coach recognizes and understands even though he doesn't possess them. The coach understands the athlete's work well enough to know exactly what that particular athlete needs to be put through (even if the athlete himself doesn't know this) so that, come game time, the athlete will play the best game he's capable of. The coach is able to watch the athlete's performance and give feedback on its strengths and weaknesses, and the athlete recognizes that the coach has the ability to make the athlete perform at a higher level than

he would perform at without the coach. But both coach and athlete recognize that, once the game has actually started, it's the athlete who's out there playing—at that moment, the coach no longer has any control of the game at all, and the game belongs entirely to the athlete. And the coach recognizes that what the spectators have come to see are the athletes, and not the coach.

Talking to directors

I have occasionally heard actors say to one another that a particular director doesn't know *how to talk to actors*. This can obviously mean something different for everyone who feels it but, in general, I suppose it has to do with the way a director gives notes, suggests blocking or character adjustments, and an overall judgment of the actors' progress.

Directors can be a negative force in your work or immeasurably positive. How they talk to you is always relevant and influences your experience but, more important, regardless of how directors talk to you, how do *you* talk with directors?

Approach:

I think "*with respect*" sums it up:

- for their *position* as guide, coach, supervisor, architect, maestro, and personal mentor on your characterization and as someone who chose you for the role and is trying to solve many of the problems a production faces;
- for their *time,* with regard for all of the people and concerns that look to them for decisions over long hours day after day; and
- for their *person*, with concerns of their own, a family or loved ones that may be far away and personal aspirations that include making this show a success.

Taking direction

- Enthusiastically and agreeably, as something you will try in order to find out.
- Without hesitation, not determining in your own mind whether it is or isn't something that will work.
- Suggesting changes, after trying something that you have been directed to do that you would like to build on or change. Show the director your change the next time you encounter the scene, perhaps warning her or him that you want to show them your new ideas.

- During note session—again, with acceptance. If the note confuses you or disagrees with what you're wanting to do, ask for a moment to be discussed in private, depending on the openness of the director to receive immediate feedback, and time concerns.

Maintain your sense of humor

A costume director at the Oregon Shakespeare Festival remarked during a particularly pressured week, "Relax a little, this isn't cancer research."

It pays to remember that it's a play. You're not at war, and nobody is going to get killed.

This is one more piece of your puzzle. Yes, it could be extremely important in your experience at university or in your professional career, but maintaining a sense of humor about the ups and downs of your career process will only serve to lighten the load and help you get through difficult times with élan.

Troubleshooting: disagreements about character or scene

Public: When it's a small matter and occurs in the moment of working on a scene or a conversation that the director brings up, being honest and expressing concern with reasons will go a long way toward collaboration.

Private: When it's a larger matter having to do with character and/or characteristics, blocking, or actions that you feel are inconsistent with the character in the script as you see it, find a time one-to-one when you can honestly express your reservations without taking up the limited amount of group rehearsal.

Personal grievances

Depending on exactly what this is, whether a joke at your expense, a tirade aimed at you, an unfair comment, or a feeling that you're being directed totally against what you have expressed is an important choice, again, it's a matter of timing, perspective, and respect, and the chosen location in expressing the grievance is important.

I suggest that the stage manager always be present, as witness and protection if it's an especially personal grievance. However, whether in public or private, I would encourage what is known as the classic psychological response to what feels like an attack or put down:

"When you say that, it makes me feel like …"

That's opposed to the judgmental and counter attack response, which often sounds like "You always …;" or "You never …;" "You can't talk to me like that …" resulting in "You don't know how to talk to actors," or more often behind their back with "They don't know how to talk to actors."

Rather try a straightforward approach: "When you tell me that I'm an emotional pygmy, it shuts me down and makes me feel totally taken for granted as a human being." I also like Catholic University's Head of Directing Eleanor Holdridge's humorous advice to young actors: "You're allowed one diva fit for every five hundred lines in your role!"

I know directors to be a modern and essential collaborator in our evolution of theatre. I was born into theatre thanks to a director's care and nurturing. The most important things I have learned about theatre have been in collaboration with a director as we gave flesh to a playwright's story. However, as in all movements, there are extreme examples where power corrupts and, for every supportive and commanding creative presence, there are directors out there who are misusing their control to teach actors when they should be learning from actors. There are directors out there who are anxious about time constraints, pressured by their producers, and impatient with the actor's process. There are dictators and emotionally abusive people who take advantage of an actor's great need to be in a play. Of course, the other side of that coin is that there are as many temperamental and narcissistic performers who make life extremely difficult for fellow actors and directors alike. Finding your most authentic way to respond to either bully can take time, trial, and error but, most assuredly, it's an important quality to begin developing and to be ready to employ.

In John Barton's *Playing Shakespeare*, Ian McKellen and John Barton briefly discuss the role of actor/director collaboration.

> McKellen: Shakespeare's plays, like all plays, of course, have to be organized and it's as well to put one person in charge. In the past in Britain, I think that person was the star actor, or maybe the playwright himself. David Garrick, of course, he wrote plays that he was in, and indeed amended Shakespeare's plays for his own purposes; and Henry Irving was very firmly in charge of his own company, and Herbert Beerbohm Tree and so on. But in the twentieth century, this new kind of person arose, I think probably out of the ranks of the stage management. People who perhaps had been actors, but had an eye over the general scheme of things, and now they are the men who are running the Royal Shakespeare Company and the National Theatre and all the repertory companies up and down the country. And it's true abroad as well, that directors are the people who decide which plays are going to be done and how they are going to be cast. They are the people who organize, who influence, who make the decisions.

> I am not against that system as long as the actor finds that he is not in a cage, but is perhaps released from the cage of his own personality by the director who can turn the key for him. But there are some directors who limit the process and don't give the actor enough freedom. I don't think you [John Barton] are one of them, but I think that Shakespeare or other plays can go wrong if a director takes too much power on himself. …
>
> Barton: Though directors have great power and great responsibility, I am most aware of how we are in a sense powerless and unimportant once a production goes into performance. I always feel when we've opened that the production doesn't belong to me any more; it's yours, it belongs to the actors.
>
> McKellen: However, I do remember on the last performance of a play, you came round to the dressing room and I'd finished the part forever, and you gave me some notes on that evening's performance.
>
> I do wish there was more room within our scheme of things for different sorts of discipline to come to the fore. I would like to see companies run by communes of actors, let us say, experimenting without a director.

The revolution that I'm interested in seeing is the one where more of us take control of our process, come into rehearsal more prepared, speak honestly with authenticity during rehearsal, demand a freedom to explore, and insist on ways to collaborate as much as possible while we find characterization under difficult *or* ideal situations.

9 Actors and designers

A common purpose

> Designers must remember that actors are constantly making themselves vulnerable and anything the designer can do to create a safe environment is essential. The obverse side of being vulnerable exists for the designer as well. I have described my most vulnerable moment as when the actors first walk on the set, taking in their world, reacting to it both positively and sometimes negatively.
>
> —James Kronzer, designer

Your questions

What questions do you have for these artists? Take the time to know them by name.

Presumably, you have been preparing. You've read the play exhaustively, you have a firm understanding of the story and your role in telling it. You've examined its history of productions, articles and/or books written about the play itself, and come up with personal questions that remain unanswered. Now, like a first date: which ones make sense in the context of the first week?

All of the designers and dramaturgs will be very interested to hear your thoughts.

You have the opportunity to get to know them personally. I would suggest becoming interested in what attracted the costumer to this project. What did they do last, and how did they find working in that genre? What *is* their favorite genre or what got them interested in costuming, set designing, dramaturgy, or stage management in the first place? How would you feel if a costumer approached you on the first day and was aware of the last play you did? What if the set designer came up to you and asked you how you liked working in Houston, because they had taken the trouble to look up your résumé and saw that you worked with someone they knew? Of course, chances are they'll ask you about your designer and, if you can't remember their name, well, *that's embarrassing*.

If the stage manager knows that you grew up in Indiana and wants to know how you got from Indianapolis to New York University, where you graduated five years ago, you're off to a good start.

Take the trouble to find out about the people designing your clothes, building your world, and managing your affairs for the next few months.

Designers

Costume and set

I have always admired the work of these artists, and only as a result of their expertise, experience, and collaborative skills have I slowly ventured forth into meaningful conversations and an increased awareness of what they do and how they do it.

They have always seemed more a part of the director's world than mine until they themselves broke through my ignorance with an interest in my own process or ideas about the play. Unfortunately, in the past, it always seemed to take a crisis to bring us together, such as a disagreement about a costume or a set that I felt was unsafe. Is the lighting too bright? It's in my eyes. When should a conversation between us take place, and what does the actor say? How is it any of my business what the designers do? So I asked them.

James Kronzer has more than 300 productions to his credit, ranging from Broadway and national tours to regional and TV work. He has received eight Helen Hayes Awards and two Barrymore Awards for excellence in set design. He resides in Washington, D.C.:

> Unfortunately there is all too often distance between the designer and the actor. The designer has first shot at the director during the design process and often the actor feels like a lot has been figured out without their input even before rehearsal begins. This culminates in the tech process where the actor is onstage staring out into a black abyss that is littered with glowing Apple computers and the occasional disembodied request to adjust one's position.
>
> I'm often encouraged by my interactions with actors. I think each party needs to go out of their way to understand the process of the other. I put a lot of thought into how an actor moves around the stage. Where furniture is, why a door faces the way it does (doors opening into a space are funnier: see Jerry Seinfeld's apartment door), how high a step is, etc. Sharing this information is essential and the designer needs to find the opportunity to do so. It's not always obvious as to when this can happen given donor presentations, first rehearsal chaos and the like.

During tech, I make a point of going onstage and checking in with the actors, even if nothing is being said other than a discussion of the weather. There needs to be a constant building of the relationships in the room. If an actor is having a problem with a prop or some business, I make myself available.

If I am working with an actor whose character has had something to do with the space they are in, I encourage their thoughts on what might be on the walls, dressing, and other choices. I think this makes the actor feel like it is more their space and there is some ownership. This also goes into backstage areas. Going back and problem solving, being a physical presence with a solution.

At the end of the day, everyone in the room is there for a common purpose and the more interaction there can be between collaborators and artists, the more vibrant the story will be. This in turn will read to an audience experiencing the play.

I interviewed John Conklin, costume and set designer on Broadway, American regional theatre, the Metropolitan Opera in New York, and many opera companies in Europe. He is also an adjunct professor teaching in the department of design for stage and film for New York University's Tisch School of the Arts:

Gary: What would you say to a young actor—who wants to know how to talk with designers?

John: We talk a lot about this at NYU where I teach—about the need for a free, open relationship and atmosphere that encourages that the actor and the designers to talk: the actor to discuss what is happening in rehearsal, where is his character going; the costume designer, for instance, to show that the design as it sits there on the paper (or as a muslin mock-up or partially-completed costume) is like the actor's rehearsal "performance," a work in progress. This is the time that the actor can and should enter into the discussion, and where the designer should be careful to listen to the actor (and vice versa). This emerging vision is not just the ideas or concepts that have grown out of the director's and designers' collaboration that the actors are forced willy-nilly into, but a truly developing and organic product that now includes the actor and the ideas of the rehearsal.

Gary: Sometimes we feel like our designers and directors are our teachers. We're often in awe at the designer presentation, which makes us feel distant.

John: Too true. To stick with the costume design, that is why a costume fitting occurring after the actor has had time to be in rehearsal is often crucial. The idea that the design is manifest in the costume sketch or the set model as a kind of inviolate artistic object that the actor has to conform to, is not useful—certainly not useful for the actors and really not useful to the designers either. I mean the set and costumes are, what I would call, a proposal, a way to begin. After perhaps endless discussions and perhaps false starts, you (the designers and director) have to eventually end with something specific and, practically, something has to be sent (usually with tight deadlines attached) to the scenic or costume shops. So it's a way to begin a discussion, a process, not the creation of a frozen artistic vision—it's a vision that should develop, mutate, grow restlessly and relentlessly until it ultimately manifests itself in the final product.

At the first rehearsal obviously, the director comes with an intimate contact with the design process—the actors have to all intents and purposes been excluded and the director-design team may appear to have worked out all the answers, but that changes. The actors' work in rehearsal often creatively modifies or happily completely overturns the director's (and even their own) ideas about what's going on and this often in turn can shift the designer's approach into new and highly creative and unexpected paths. But time frameworks, the pressure for instance of getting the scenery and costumes to the shops and supervising accurate construction, painting, fittings, or the constant, totally understandable but often insatiable demands from the prop builders (tell us exactly what you want now or we'll never have time to find it or built it correctly for you); these often mitigate against ideas of organic growth, which usually wants to go at its own speed. I think there's an attitude that has to be broken down in designers, and in actors—a certain misplaced awe of designers and their craft. What a good costume designer will look forward to is to be able to simply talk with the actor who has been in rehearsal for perhaps two weeks—to modify the costume because the actor has learned and developed and evolved a specific character. You (the designer) might want to say, I've put you in these big sleeves because I am after all the designer and that's the way I see it—because that's one way I express my vision of the character for this specific person. The actor could say, well you know, that's not the way I'm playing it. And then the designer should say, alright, well let's talk about the sleeves. Tell me more about what you're playing, and I'll modify my idea of the sleeves to what you're doing (or the actor might see where the designer was headed and be stimulated or challenged to a new outlook). Then in the fitting room the sleeves might be refit, if that's what seems to be indicated … OK, enough with the sleeves—please excuse the extended and somewhat overworked example here!—but you get the idea, I hope.

What's important is the freedom of the actor to talk, and the freedom of the designer to not be rigid and to encourage discussion. The actors don't necessarily need to know about the techniques of costume or set design, but what they do know about is character and a certain sense of what clothes that character would have, and the environment she might inhabit. Here goes another (possibly silly) example: an actor will say I don't like green, I look terrible in green and you have given me a green dress. If the actor can be eloquent about why—not that she doesn't like green personally but that this character that she's developing wouldn't wear green for the following reasons—then the designer might say then let's go in another direction … (if the material hasn't been bought already or the costume begun—here is where those difficult practical details intrude).

Gary: You're asking actors for a certain amount of specificity—and as soon as they can get there, the better—and in a two- or three-week rehearsal process, there's not much time, which encourages casting sooner and once you are cast, work starts. You've got two, three, four weeks, maybe two months, to read the play—to begin imagining yourself in this play and doing your work, so that when you meet with your designer you have a conversation as opposed to simply questions about their vision.

John: And you, the actor must have an ability to express that vision, that insight into character, without just saying, I don't like big sleeves. I won't wear green. That's not useful. But if you explain why you feel that way, and if the designer, on the other hand, can also explain and articulate his thinking to the actor, useful and revelatory progress can be made. I've often been in a situation where an actor's been uncomfortable and we'll really talk it over and by the end the actor goes, well, you know (sorry...last time), the big sleeves seem right now somehow, and maybe I will now use them as part of my character. So that it can be a two-way street, but both sides need to be articulate and open.

Gary: Playwrights speak about that, before you try to fix me, just try it. Try to say it as written and then let's discuss how it doesn't work, but try it.

John: Both actors on the one side and designers on the other side become too arbitrary because they're nervous about each other. One thing I often tell my student designers is: Look, you don't have to go out on stage. You may think the actor is being difficult, you may think the actor is being unreasonable, you may think the actor is being illogical, and they may, in some objective sense, be all those things. But they have to go out in front of an audience and it is your duty to make them comfortable (practically and psychologically) in their clothes and in their world. If you don't, if you have uncomfortable actors wearing ostensibly gorgeous costumes in front of a beautiful set, you will probably have in the end an unconvincing and unrewarding production. The sets and costumes and lighting and props are only as beautiful or meaningful or appealing as the focus and intensity of the actors who are performing in or around them. You can't have one without the other. And I think designers sometimes tend to think you can.

This is very important for designers, because I think sometimes, we designers get off onto our own world of visuals, craft and technique. We mistrust or even discount performance. Actors can be difficult, they can be demanding. But they are operating within their own interior performance logic, which we cannot really understand because we don't actually have or need that experience to create. We must be sympathetic—truly, sincerely understanding to what the actor is doing. And it's always much more rewarding when the journey includes everyone. It just seems that actors and designers are separated too much. It's complicated. Do designers not get paid enough to be able to devote an appropriate amount of time to the ongoing development/rehearsal stage of the production? Are they untrained or unfamiliar with the intricacy of the daily rehearsal process so that it often seems boring or a waste of time? Can they speak or understand the actor's "language?" Sure it takes extra effort and commitment, but the payoff is so great, it's certainly worth it. The actor's at the center, so why wouldn't you want to constantly be connecting with the center of anything? I always wait and hope for a production, at some point when it all begins to come together, to start to tell you what IT wants to do. And this often happens through the presence and the voice of the actor.

Lighting designers have always seemed like rock-and-roll cowboys to me. They're mavericks who climb rope, wrestle with equipment, wrench tight fresnels, and adjust hanging gobos. They work magic from behind space age computers. They have always felt totally out of my world and the least likely designer to have any interest in my own creative process. Not true.

Actor James Whalen worked many years on the production side of things but has now shifted into leading roles on stage:

I was playing *Dracula* at Actors Theatre of Louisville in 2010. The show was an annual smash for the theatre for 15 years and was recently revamped with new designs, a new script some five years prior. In one of the final scenes Dracula has a terrific speech where he lays out his bone-chilling vision of domination in the name of darkness, from atop a lab table in the center of the room surrounded by his pursuers. He is interrupted by the breaking dawn and has to furiously escape the room or face destruction.

The show is done in the round, and the "backdrop" for lighting purposes, in that configuration, becomes the stage floor. I had a hard time understanding how the day was breaking. My line just before my exit was, "Ah! But my friends, the lightening sky tells me I must take my leave of you. Until we meet again!" Then I jumped from the table and frightened everyone and "disappeared."

Tony Penna had been lighting the show for many years. It is beautifully lit and he really captures that gothic sense with lots of gobos of cathedral windows and great color choices. So I went to Tony and asked him to explain the cue. He said the dawn breaks slowly—as the line of dialogue suggests. I told him I thought Dracula was trying to mask the threat by saying "lightening sky," and that the light could maybe burst onto the scene just before the "Ah!," becoming yet another character in the room trying to corral and destroy the vampire. He liked the idea and changed the cue.

I thought the change was powerful, and if it didn't change anything for the audience it certainly changed a great deal for me.

Living in the light

Jennifer Tipton has designed lighting for major dance companies, operas and regional theatres across America and the world. She has twice won Broadway's Tony Award as Best Lighting Designer: in 1977 for a revival of *The Cherry Orchard* and in 1989 for *Jerome Robbins' Broadway.*

She has been an adjunct professor of design at the Yale University School of Drama, and lighting design advisor at theYale Repertory Theater since 1984. I asked her what she thought an actor should know about her process.

Once the play is onstage the production path of an actor and a lighting designer rarely cross in physical space but I, as lighting designer, live with every step that an actor takes. My aim is to create a "light landscape" for the actor to inhabit. I am constantly looking to find the areas that an actor needs, that are not at first apparent, so that I may fill them with light.

I always assumed that the actors felt secure and comfortable in the rehearsal room and insecure when they first came to the stage. I learned to my surprise from an actor that I was wrong. The actor felt totally vulnerable in the "bare studio" and immediately at home in the space and the light of the play. This knowledge has made me aware of the responsibility of that first moment for actors to be on the stage in the light. At that point the lighting is just begun but the "place" and the space must be clear.

There have been occasions (all too rare) in my life when I have been able to interact with the actor. I always ask them to come into the house and look at someone else in the light. They so often have the wrong impression of the aim. Being in the light and looking at the light from outside are two infinitely different feelings. When looking from the outside it often becomes immediately obvious that the object, most often, is to light the actor, not to make a "realistic" scene as the actor so often believes.

The actor who is aware of him/herself in the light is all too rare. An actor has many things to think about. I recommend that they make "living in the light" a part of their process in such a way that they never have to think about it. If it becomes second nature then they have all of their conscious time available to spend learning things specific to the play.

Making actors beautiful is my joy in life. (If their role calls for them to be ugly they must do it themselves.) The "role" of the lighting designer is to wrap the actors in the light of the play and make them totally comfortable on the stage. What a glorious responsibility.

10 Actor and dramaturg, stage manager, coaches and crew

A big tent

> In the play [August Wilson's *Ma Rainey's Black Bottom*], there is the young, talented—yet wounded—character, Levee, and at one point in the play Levee tells the story of how his father was burned alive and lynched. The actor playing Levee asked me to find material to help him understand the tragedy and trauma endured by his character. It was a powerful and potent exploration, yielding actual newspaper accounts, unsettling lynching descriptions and statistics, as well as a number of horrific and graphic photos. While my emotionally-charged research proved to be incredibly helpful to the actor, it also proved to be very useful to me—on more than one occasion, the history of Levee's family came up on post-show discussions, with particular reference to the historic realities of racial violence. Having done the research—work born out of dialogue with an actor—my role as a dramaturg, and the actor's role as Levee, were far richer for the experience.
>
> —Faedra Chatard Carpenter, freelance dramaturg

Dramaturgy

Freelance dramaturg and educator Faedra Chatard Carpenter (literary management at Arena Stage, Crossroads Theatre, among others; assistant professor, theatre, University of Maryland):

> There are essentially two types of dramaturgy work in which actors and dramaturgs have a chance to interact and work together for the benefit of the production: Production Dramaturgy for a "finished" play (a play that is no longer in development) and New Play Dramaturgy (a play that is currently being written or devised with a future public presentation or production in mind).

Production dramaturgy

When working on an already established play, Production Dramaturgs and actors usually don't meet until the production's first "meet-n-greet" and/or table work session. Ideally, this is the time in which the Production Dramaturg is offered the opportunity to frame who they are and what they can offer the rest of the creative team—within a very concise time frame (usually no longer than five minutes!).

While I want to be sure to let the actors know that I have a wealth of information and insight to share during that first table work session, I also want very much to know what their thoughts, questions, and impulses are in relation to the script and the production's articulation of the play's theatrical world.

So, my advice to young actors is to think of themselves as active dialogue partners with their dramaturgs—they need to feel a responsibility to help advance discussion by sharing insights as well as raising valuable issues and questions that can then be further researched and explored. A dramaturg's work with the actors may end after the show opens, but usually the dramaturg's job continues throughout the show's run in the form of pre/post-show or panel discussions, or similar audience engagement activities.

New play dramaturgy

In terms of New Play Dramaturgy, the aforementioned dynamics still apply, yet there is also an added need for actor feedback and response. While actors should always be respectful and sensitive in raising questions or offering talking points when in the presence of a playwright, a work-in-progress is undeniably strengthened when the playwright (and dramaturg) gets input from the actors. An actor's job as part of the ensemble is not to simply "be," but also to "do"—to be an active participant in the process at hand.

Parameters

While I hope I speak for most dramaturgs who welcome and encourage actors to be active questioners and thinkers when it comes to the play script, I would be remiss if I didn't also advise young actors to remember that there are also parameters and boundaries to the "collaborative spirit" of theatre. Respect and sensitivity, regardless of the nature of an exchange, is first and paramount. That goes in terms of how we speak to each other ("Do unto others …") as well as fully recognizing the hierarchy at hand. As a dramaturg, it is my job to champion the vision of the playwright (if I'm working on a new play) or the director (if I'm working on the remount of an established play). This means that as a dramaturg, I need to honor the story that the playwright or director is trying to tell—not the story I think they should be telling.

I say this because there have been many times when actors have approached me to get my vision for a particular piece or even directing advice for their performance (especially when they find themselves at odds with how the director is guiding them). While I find that incredibly flattering—I appreciate that they respect my opinion—in the end, it's not my opinion that matters. For me to express judgments that contradict or detract from the director's choices, only aggravates tensions and serves no one—least of all the production.

Mediator

Actors should know that behind the scenes I am tactfully sharing my notes, offering suggestions, and voicing opinions, but I'm doing so through the appropriate methods and channels and I would advise them to do the same. It is well within a dramaturg's job description to mediate concerns between actors, directors, and playwrights and to help both sides become aware of alternative interpretations or presentations (again, that's about engaging in a dialogue!), but it is never the dramaturg's role to pass along her own subjective opinion without the director's approval (so please, don't ask!).

Purpose

Freelance dramaturg and organizational change consultant Mervin P. Antonio (literary management at Arena Stage, Public Theater, Actors Theatre of Louisville, among others):

> The dramaturg is there to help you embody your character. Directors will often have a specific idea of what he/she wants the character "to be" and a good dramaturg will support that vision. And in many instances, you will see the dramaturg constantly refer to the text as a main source/fount for knowledge. This is especially true when working on a Shakespeare or any play rich with language.
>
> Good dramaturgs will meet the actor where they are, and dramaturgs love questions, so come prepared with your questions (anything from the concrete, like "how do you pronounce this word?" … or "what was life like in England during the Plague?" to the more philosophical/existential). For the latter, we won't give you a direct answer, but will help you navigate it for yourself.

Cuts

> Sometimes a dramaturg will suggest cuts to a director or playwright. Don't take cuts in your lines personally. Know that we're all there working to create the best possible play/production. If a cut really doesn't work for you, let the dramaturg and director in the room know why and maybe there is a mutual work-around. Again, dramaturgs are there to help you embody your role effectively, so let us know what you need and we'll do our best to get the information you need. If the information and research they pulled for you doesn't work for you, let them know. Many dramaturgs come from rich academic backgrounds, so some of the information you may get may be very hard "to act" so engage them in a conversation until you get the information you need.

Keeper of the story

Freelance dramaturg Martine Green (the Court Theatre, the Oregon Shakespeare Festival, and the Classical Theatre Company):

> A dramaturg is the "keeper of the story." The most common ways that manifest themselves in a rehearsal/theatrical process are: 1) providing historical information that aids the members of the artistic team and the actors in telling the story, 2) sitting in rehearsals and identifying when choices being made in rehearsal either help or hinder the telling of the story, 3) facilitating or assisting with textual questions and with cuts of a script, 4) helping playwrights in the development of their play, 5) aiding the audience with their understanding of the play by writing program notes and/or facilitating talkback discussions, and 6) working with education and marketing departments to develop material distributed in reference to the show.

To supplement

> The information that a dramaturg provides should not replace an actor's individual research—it should supplement it. The information we provide helps create a background for the world of the play but not necessarily for each individual character.

Patrick Tuite, head of the MA program at The Catholic University of America sums it up by saying,

> I recommend that actors introduce themselves to a dramaturg. Ask them questions! They love questions, and a good dramaturg will offer more

information than you care to use … a talented dramaturg will provide a variety of choices without advocating for one approach to the work.

Stage managers

> The SM is an enabler … what we do is enable people to work in a very emotional world.
>
> —Martha Knight, Arena Stage/Kennedy Center stage manager

Top ten

C. Renée Alexander (extensive New York and regional stage management credits):

> The secret to working with stage management is simple:
>
> 1 Be on time and call if you are running late. However if you constantly run late this is not just the actor's problem, this becomes the production's problem.
> 2 Dress appropriately for rehearsal.
> 3 Deodorants and oral hygiene will help you make long lasting friendships.
> 4 Ask ahead of time for what you need to help you; preferably not five minutes before rehearsal starts.
> 5 Acknowledge that stage management is neither the maid nor the mind reader for the production.
> 6 Silence is golden. (Your opinion is not always wanted or needed.)
> 7 Don't feel the need to compete with other actors who constantly tell stories of other productions.
> 8 Ask for line when you need help. Don't snap your fingers at the person on book.
> 9 Stage Management sets up a coffee station as treat; it is not a necessity. Take initiative, make a fresh pot of coffee or add more water for tea if necessary.
> 10 Stage Management are people who love what they do. Open and honest communication will add to an enjoyable experience.

"We're not the enemy—"

Martha Knight, 25-year stage manager veteran at Arena Stage and The Kennedy Center in Washington, D.C:

> I find actually in rehearsal, actors don't need to depend on the SM so much that's a transfer of power in a way … the director is the one the

actor is most concerned with, part of the SM's job is to make the actor aware of the fact that the lines on the floors are really walls or steps or whatever, sort of be a go-between with the reality of the designer's point of view.

The vocal coach

I've often heard it said that the voice is the doorway to our emotional life.

Kristin Linklater entitled her book *Freeing the Natural Voice*, which is the actor's goal, after all.

Your natural voice is one that you need in performance, but it's very common for actors to adopt a false sound when they try to project, get emotional, or have created a habit of a performance sound that is either deeper or higher than their natural resonance. Sometimes this is produced for effect or possibly just a sign of effort and stress.

In a summer workshop with Kristin many years ago, I remember her pointing to her shoulders, throat, and lower face near the jaw, mouth, and sinus areas, calling it the Bermuda triangle of lost impulses.

For some reason, it seems that much of our emotional tension lands in our jaw and the very places where we need articulating freedom. Our voice is considered one of the actor's instruments, but all too few actors practice it on a daily basis, along with the rest of our body if we want to in good enough shape to meet the demands of our role, especially on the stage.

Luckily, our theatres are often hiring vocal coaches as a member of the artistic team in mounting a production.

Working with a vocal coach

Erica Tobolski is an associate professor at the University of South Carolina and has coached for film, educational, and professional theatres, including Utah Shakespeare Festival and The Lost Colony:

> The Vocal Coach is an integral member of the production team, working primarily with the actors to assist them with all aspects of the characters' vocal life. In simple terms, the Vocal Coach helps the actor to be heard and understood and to fulfill the given circumstances of the play. Working collaboratively with the director, designers and technical staff, the Vocal Coach assists in creating an aural experience for the audience in order to amplify the meaning and intent of the production.
>
> A Vocal Coach may be involved in assisting the actor with the following:
>
> - A character's dialect or regional changes in speech.
> - Heightened text, such as that of Shakespeare, Moliere, or Shaw

- Specific vocal demands such as screaming, crying, or coughing.
- Tracking the vocal journey of a character within a play.
- Supporting the breath and sound for large theater spaces or speaking offstage.
- Being heard in intimate scenes.
- Vocal stamina for long runs or large roles.
- Freeing the body of undue tension in emotionally charged scenes.
- Working with a microphone in amplified productions.
- Enunciation in songs.
- Orchestrating overlapping speech in ensemble or crowd scenes

The Vocal Coach is not there to make choices for you or tell you how to play the role; that remains the actor's privilege. However, in an active collaboration with a Vocal Coach, the actor can maximize their chances of success. Here are steps to take:

Before the rehearsal begins:

- Find definitions of any unfamiliar words in the play.
- Locate pronunciations of words written in another language.
- Learn or familiarize yourself with the character's accent or regional dialect.
- Look for clues in what other characters say about your character.
- Continue to work on habits that interfere with free breathing, alignment or clarity of speech.

During the rehearsal process:

- Be on time for any voice sessions.
- Consider what may influence your character's voice: age, level of health, personality.
- Bring into a voice session questions or ideas you want to test.
- Take any notes from the Vocal Coach and try to avoid getting the same note twice.
- Ask if you can record your voice session.
- Stay hydrated by drinking plenty of water and alert the Vocal Coach if you experience vocal fatigue, hoarseness, raspiness, or pain.

Fight master

David Leong is a nationally recognized fight chorographer and chair of the drama department at Virginia Commonwealth University. He offers specific acting advice as you begin to learn your fight choreography.

Preparation

I think that one of the first things for an actor who has to do some sort of fight, is that they talk with the people putting it together, whether it be the director or the fight director. Sometimes there are two different processes that happen.

The fight director, after consultation with the director, comes in with the entire fight laid out. That's one way of working.

The other way of working is that the fight director shapes it with the actors. Whichever process is going to be utilized for rehearsal, I think the actor must get to know what the beat break-down is first. Really know how the fight is broken down, who is doing what to whom and why.

Don't get so excited about "fighting" that you forget that it's a scene. It's about, "I want something from you, and you're in my way."

Discuss with the director and the fight director, what's the beat breakdown, in other words, how do these moves help me get to achieve my goal in the scene, by doing this, by slashing here, by cutting there, by punching, it's not just a series of moves.

Rehearsing

Now, once that's been decided upon, you've got to spend a while on the technique. You can't play the concerto until you can play the scales.

Learn the choreography until it's down solid. Then, pay attention to the rhythms of the fight … the one and two, three, the slash, what are the whole notes, what are the half notes, where do the pauses go. The variations in the tempo will help tell the story. What happens to a lot of actors, for one reason or another they just learn the moves and say, "I want to do it," but they don't know that they have to pay attention to the rhythm.

The equivalent would be if, once they learned their lines, they said, fine, now that I've learned them I'll just say them, with no intention, all at the same pace and at the same tempo. Actors will often do that with a fight—once they get the moves done, they'll just perform it like that. The rhythms are based on the intention, so once they've learned the choreography, they have to break it down into knowing what's faster, what's slower, where are all the pauses, and all that sort of thing. That's the actual technique.

Now once that technique is done and you've learned it solid, go back and put it in the context of the scene. I want to do this to you because … and I either get it or I don't get it, and so the third part of that whole process is, I have to play the [fight] *scene*. I don't have to think about [the moves] anymore.

It has to be so solid so that you can play your intention for every single beat.

Crew

I was struck by something that film and stage actor Christopher Walken once said during an interview. He was asked about his acting process while doing a film, and he pointed around him to the crew as part of his process, support, and inspiration. I confess that in entering the theatre world as a professional actor in the early days, backstage seemed like a car repair shop to me. It was filled with mechanics and technicians who operated in a world totally divorced from mine. I was the new car and spent all of my time in the showroom. It has always been an uncertain marriage: theatre to theatre. However, while doing a play at the Huntington Theatre in Boston, I ventured into the shop one day as the set was being built. They were like pirates on a ship, and I wanted to be one of them. I asked them questions, and at first they treated me like a tourist, as if I was wearing a Hawaiian shirt, sipping a lemonade, curious about the natives. However, the more I watched them work, the more I admired their craftsmanship and passion about the production. We became friendly. Traveling through rehearsal after that felt different. I was a part of the whole, and it was different. It was better. Backstage looked more like sweat and long hours of artistry in the making. Since then, I leave rehearsal and purposefully visit the prop shops, scene shops, and costume shops more often than my scheduled fittings. I am part of a much bigger team and no longer the center of my universe.

I asked Elisabeth Wilson, with whom I worked backstage in a show entitled *Dark Paradise, the Legend of the Five Pointed Star* by Keith Glover at the Cincinnati Playhouse, to name any priorities that came to mind about the actor/technician relationship. She said simply and profoundly:

> My top three most important qualities for the actor/artist/technician relationship would have to be:
>
> 1 Communication
> 2 Trust
> 3 Respect.
>
> If an artist and technician can give these to each other, the working relationship should be a good one. If all parties can go into their project with job integrity then it shows in their work. After all, theatre is a team effort.

11 Shakespeare's mountain of words

Poetic language

> … And it's the soul, the spirit of real, concrete people going through hell—and sometimes moments of great ... achievement and joy.
>
> That is the pentameter you must focus on … and should you find that reality...all the iambics will fall into place.
>
> —Vanessa Redgrave*, Looking for Richard*

I have often heard that if you can play Shakespeare, you can play anything. He is the great teacher and the great leveler. Our western tradition of theater for the past 400 years has been influenced by this one author and his plays. Shakespeare has won the test of time, and the great roles such as Hamlet, King Lear, Lady Macbeth, Shylock, Portia, Beatrice, Romeo, Juliet and Richard III have been attempted by the most skilled actors in every generation since. There are certain roles that you can repeat over the course of decades and still be learning new things from the text.

Al Pacino recently starred on Broadway as Shylock in his third production of *The Merchant of Venice* and was asked why he wanted to do it again. "Actors in the past have done roles many times over the course of a lifetime. … "

This production was closely followed by another one in New York. F. Murray Abraham remounted his critically acclaimed Shylock for *Theatre for a New Audience*. I saw this production while writing this book. His portrayal of Shylock was vulnerable and vicious, poetic but human, grand but very nuanced. He spoke the verse naturally and forcefully. He never seemed to be reciting; he was revealing. You always had the feeling that this was *his* story rather than a famous role. It was one of the best portrayals I have ever seen.

How *does* an actor achieve such a oneness or seamlessness with a Shakespearean role?

Playing King Lear is often compared to climbing Everest or "getting on the mountain." However, any of Shakespeare's roles can be intimidating and incredibly rewarding once you start the climb.

There are seven established camps on the way to summit Everest. As playing Shakespeare can sometimes *feel* as if you're tackling something incredibly challenging and full of risk, I'll continue the metaphor and talk about Shakespeare rehearsal one camp at a time.

Base camp: your preparation

Peter O'Toole said that he keeps two books beside his bed, Shakespeare's sonnets and the King James version of the Bible. He confesses to being a "retired Christian" but loves the language of the King James version, and he is reported to know all of Shakespeare's 154 sonnets by heart.

Again, in the interview with Charlie Rose, he says:

> My generation was brought up on a simple principle—the theatre was, at its fundamental basic level, the human speech as an art form, both in dialogue, construction of plot, whatever, it's human speech formed into an art form. That is what I truly believe, that is one of the things that makes acting such a worthwhile thing to do.

I'm not sure whether you can actually communicate Shakespeare without loving language. And if you love it, you care enough to study it, to practice it, and to truly humanize it straight out of your emotional well-spring, your soul. For Shakespeare to live, it all starts with the words. Your base camp is loving and learning about language, your own and his. Shakespeare is considered one of the greatest poets in the English language.

Do you like poetry? How about epic poems such as *The Iliad*, *The Odyssey*, *The Rime of the Ancient Mariner*, *Enoch Arden*, *Evangeline*, *The Divine Comedy*, *King Arthur*, *Faust*, *The Song of Hiawatha*, or even narrative poems such as *The Canterbury Tales*, *The Charge of the Light Brigade*, *Gunga Din*?

Nursery rhymes? Cumulative tales such as *Green Eggs and Ham*, *This Is The House That Jack Built*, and Shel Silverstein's *Sarah Cynthia Silva Stout Wouldn't Take the Garbage Out?!* Do you like how strings of words are put together to affect meaning, emotion, and even action?

During my first season with The Shakespeare Theatre in Washington, D.C., I worked with a masterful classical actor in a production of *Love's Labor's Lost*.

Ted Van Griethuysen was a Don Armado for the ages. Since that production, we've shared the stage as Edgar and Gloucester in *King Lear;*

Hamlet and Polonius in *Hamlet;* Suffock and Gloucester *in Henry VI, Parts I, II, and III*; Antony and Caesar in *Julius Caesar*; and I played Pope Urban to his Galileo in Brecht's *Galileo.* Ted has lived in the robes of Lear, Prospero, Jacques, Falstaff, King Henry, Hamlet, Claudius, Romeo, and so many more over the course of a fifty-year career.

His approach to Shakespeare is as passionate in the doing as in the describing how. In our interview, he made it very clear that poetry is at the heart of expressing our existence and good Shakespearean acting as well:

> The human heart needs people to see the world in an honest fashion, so that we know somewhere the world makes sense, that there is a logic to the world that is likable. And poetry is one of the great means we have of liking existence, because it makes it bearable or coherent, or true, or funny, or friendly even.
>
> Generally speaking I think, actors are uncomfortable with poetry, actually, because the drama in poetry is different from drama in the theatre. Drama in poetry is essentially internal drama, while acting, by its very nature is external, visible.
>
> It is vitally important, therefore, that actors should know and study poetry. If you don't know what poetry is—if you don't know it in Wordsworth or Byron or Millay or Neruda, how can you know what poetry is in Shakespeare?
>
> There's that great misconception—and I don't like the phrase when it's used—that poetry is "heightened" language. It's not heightened language, it's simply more honest than customary. Poetry is probably the most important art form we have. It's the one that's mostly deeply connected directly to the human soul, through words. As much as the visual is important to the theatre—and I'm also a designer so I love visual things—Shakespeare is first of all an auditory experience.
>
> Going to a Shakespeare play, you should be able to close your eyes and know exactly what's happening all the time. John Barton importantly points out that the reason we are originally affected by Shakespeare—the reason the lawyer carries around Portia's "quality of mercy" speech—gets lost, usually, in directors' conceptions and production values, and character revelations.
>
> Shakespeare is what is said and how it's said. There isn't anything else. That's Shakespeare.

Camp 1: Speaking the language

Know what you're saying

Again, director Joe Dowling:

> … there are so many productions of Shakespeare where you feel that [the actor] definitely doesn't understand what h/she is saying, they know roughly what the dramaturg has told them, and the voice coach has told them, but they actually haven't felt it and realized it emotionally. It's simply being said … when you break it down—particularly with young actors—and … encourage them to think it through for themselves and find a way of delivering the text freshly each time, it just makes it so much more alive.

Language, it's all about the language, not something *in* your way: it *is* your way. As is often said of Shakespearean verse, the direction of how to do the text is in the text. It's in the punctuation, alliteration, antithesis and how it scans. Finding the operative or stress words can be the key to unlocking the sense and essence of a line and, often, your characterization.

In rehearsal, the approach, the techniques, and the sequence are all very similar to other plays, but the text demands special preparation and ability. Directors often say, "Does he or she have the chops to play that part?" referring to the ability to make clear the poetic and descriptive language in the play.

Early approaches to the script involve clarity, scanning, choosing operatives, and reading it aloud to get the mouth motors in gear.

You must become a talking machine, relying much less on subtext, physical blocking, and physical expression. Rely much more on communicating character, too, through your use of the words themselves. However, it's equally about what's happening; the givens and what you are doing. As Peter Brook said to Al Pacino during the film documentary *Looking For Richard:*

> The text is only a means of expressing what's behind the text. So, that if you get obsessed with the text … this is a great barrier to American actors who get obsessed with the British way of regarding a text.
>
> That isn't what matters. What matters is that you have to penetrate … into what, at every moment, it's about.

Talking Shakespeare

Some of the best Shakespearean performers in my experience have been those that did not sound as if they were reciting poetry or singing verse like elocutionists. They seemed to be talking, just talking to someone about something that mattered.

Ted Van Griethuysen addresses this observable manner of speaking:

> If the actors know what they're doing and understand what the line is, and they're saying it with emotion that arises from the line, audiences will stay with you, even though they may not wholly understand it. And anybody who expects to come to a Shakespeare play and have it be perfectly clear should have his face slapped. That's impertinent. It's not going to happen.
>
> We go to see these plays over and over again because every time you see one, you see it anew and see new things, different things. That's true for actors too. All the great parts in Shakespeare. You do them in order to find out how to do them. So, if you don't get a second chance, it's not fair. The first time through, you make all the mistakes, well, not all usually; there are always a few more that you can get to.
>
> When you speak the lines, you have to do two things: first, you must honor the fact that it's some of the greatest poetry in the English language. And, second, you must sound like a human being talking, and you must do both at the same time. You will spend a career learning how to do that. You start again every time you pick up one of the plays. It never changes. You keep finding out how to do it.

Television, film, and Broadway stage actor Sherman Howard spoke to my graduate acting class at The Catholic University of America of how he learned to speak "Shakespearean:"

> I've always felt that the fundamental challenge in acting Shakespeare is linguistic fluency.
>
> One summer in my mid-20s … I had heard that a Renaissance Fair was coming to town, and I got an idea that might earn me some pocket money and generate some fun in the process. I devised the character of a poet, whose tongue had been palsied by a witch's curse. The curse could only be lifted—temporarily—by the touch of silver to my palm. I set about memorizing twenty or so sonnets and costumed myself in tattered finery. When the fair arrived I was ready.
>
> I wandered into the crowd, searching for my "target audience"—romantic couples, preferably a man and woman holding hands. Grunting and stammering incoherently, in obvious distress, I would approach a couple and thrust into their hands a crumpled sheet of parchment, explaining my predicament in faux Elizabethan text. As they read through my plea they would quickly understand and, grinning, reach

for some pocket change. The instant their coins touched my palm, I would gasp for breath, shudder violently, and finally speak in perfectly aristocratic tones … "Thank you, kind sir! I have, but moments..." then, focusing upon the wife or girlfriend, I would recite a sonnet. The sonnet completed, I would bow deeply, and as I arose, gasp and shudder once again, reverting to the grunting, stammering creature, who first approached them. Clumsily bowing once more, I would make an awkward retreat into the crowd … and seek out another couple.

The first two or three times I performed this ritual, I delivered the sonnet in a manner consistent with the "Shakespearean style" I had learned in conservatory. I stepped back two or three paces, spread wide my arms, and spoke in a strong, boldly declarative voice—rather as if the woman I was speaking to was in fact, a small crowd. Within a couple of lines I could see that she wasn't really following the sonnet and seemed distracted at being the focal point of such a public display. By the middle of the sonnet, I could clearly see in her eyes that she had no idea what I was telling her and would probably prefer it if I would simply shut up and go away. I had lost my audience—an audience of one! From that moment forward, the slog through to the end of the sonnet was pure torture! As a young actor (or actor of any age), I could not have asked for a more brutally honest or more invaluable critique of my skills. After several similar failures, in sheer desperation, I began to alter my approach. I began experimenting, trying things differently, exploring—just as one does in rehearsal. Over the next several hours, through perhaps 30 or 40 encounters, my delivery of the sonnet transformed profoundly.

To begin with, rather than stepping back, I stepped closer. I would gaze into the woman's eyes in silence for several seconds, as if searching for inspiration … then, in the most intimate tones, carefully forming the words as if they had never been uttered before, I would speak the thoughts and phrases directly into her eyes. With simple honesty.

The response also transformed profoundly. These women were engaged; they followed every thought; they took the journey with me! I actually saw pupils dilate as the images landed and took shape in consciousness. Sometimes their eyes began to fill with tears. Many women looked as if they had been waiting all their lives to be spoken to in such a manner. By the end of the day I had acquired groupies—repeat customers—thrusting bills into my hands to hear sonnet after sonnet!

For ten hours a day, three days a week, for the next six weeks I spoke Shakespeare's sonnets. The following fall, when I returned to the theater where I was employed, our first play of the season was

> *Antony and Cleopatra*. The moment I began to speak my new lines—lines which I had never spoken before—I was stunned at how easy and effortless it was to shape the thoughts behind the words. It felt like I was speaking in my own tongue. Only then did I fully realize that it had never truly felt that way before.

Camp 2: Your physical instrument—your chops—get in shape

Physical preparation

Stillness. Bearing. Strength. Relaxation. Warm-up routine. Yoga.

Eleanor Holdridge, a professional director of productions all across the United States and a veteran of twenty-eight Shakespearean productions sent the following e-mail to her cast of *Cymbeline*, four months before rehearsals were to officially begin at the Catholic University of America:

> This production is going to be very active—there will be a large number of battles, many moments of hand to hand combat and lots of running across the space … You will be running, wielding your weapons and then speaking difficult text. That said, I suspect that some of you may not be in the physical shape required for this particular production. At the very least, you should be able to run a mile in ten minutes and have a conversation immediately afterwards, do 200 sit-ups and, from a plank

position, 20 push ups for the women, 40 for the men. Test yourself. If you can't do that, you are not in the shape to do any Shakespeare play let alone this production. So if you are not quite there yet, please start honing your physical instrument. Now is the time.

Vocal preparation

You must begin with a 24/7 consciousness. You will never be able to accomplish the demands of seventeenth-century text by waiting until official rehearsal hours to speak them. Over and over and over, in your room, waiting on the bus, in your car, in the shower, walking across campus. shopping in the mall, as you fall asleep, and as you wake. Anywhere and everywhere during your day, speak the words until they become part of you. You used to be able to spot an actor because they and the mentally deranged were the only ones talking to themselves. Now, of course, half the population appear to be talking to themselves with bluetooth.

Aloud and often, which means vocal warm-ups every day!

You may have been able to get away with your normal speaking voice in plays, but now, you have to develop super voice, better breathing, and a warm-up routine of centered sounds and articulation exercises. Your lazy tongue will need a workout as will your soft palate, lips, cheeks, and jaw.

The point is, while preparing for classical plays, this must become routine and the sooner the better. Would you expect to play a tough game of basketball or take a dance class without warming up?

Or what does it take to become really good at playing any sport or endeavor? You know that you have to do it constantly until you find yourself doing it in your sleep.

I learned to play basketball by carrying the ball with me everywhere I went. I dribbled up the road, over the railroad tracks, around pot holes, and onto the school playground. Hanging in the hall was my coat and, underneath it, a basketball. If I had been taller, this might have been a very different book.

Camp 3: Your givens; know the story and know exactly what you're saying

Prepare before rehearsals officially begin.

Eleanor began her notes to her cast of *Cymbeline* with the following recommendations:

> As you go on break and over the next months before rehearsal, I encourage you to read and re-read *Cymbeline* and let the images and

words of it enter your imagination. This is about the lead time you'd have in a professional situation, and it's good because you can start asking questions and let things stew within your imaginations over time, never knowing when a new insight may strike. Here are a few of the many questions you could start asking yourself about your character:

- Who am I? What do I like? What do I dislike?
- Whom do I love? Whom do I loathe? What makes me happy?
- What do I show to the world? What do I hide from the world?
- What am I most ashamed of? Of what am I proud?
- What are/were my parents like? Have I ever been in love?
- Do I speak in metaphor or simile? Do I mostly speak in verse or prose?
- Do I speak the truth?
- Do I know myself?
- How do I change as I move throughout the play? What or who changes me?
- What do I want? And how do I go after it? Of course this is what we'll do in rehearsal, but you could start thinking about it anyway.

You should come to the first rehearsal with your role(s) scanned, operative words circled, a paraphrase of the text if that's helpful to you, and know the meaning of all the words in your text. Know what you say and why. But more importantly let the images of the plays inspire you. Your character is not some alien outside of yourself, but is created by how you react and are inspired by the words that you say.

Eleanor is very clear about the amount and specificity of preparation she expects from her cast. What her cast may not realize is how much time and personal devotion it takes to get ready for the first official rehearsal. I've recommended a daily personal schedule for this, but I want to elaborate from my own personal experiences.

Scanning

Of all the books and workshops and classes that I've read or taken on this subject, for me, it has all boiled down to three or four elements that I've found most important in my preparation for a Shakespearean role.

- **Intention:** Know exactly what I'm saying and why I'm saying it, under what circumstances. Then transpose into my own words and thoughts when necessary.

- **Emphasis:** Underlining the operative words, the ones that I want to *hit* that further the lines' meaning and my intention.
- **Antithesis:** Using the opposite phrases to highlight the character's intentions.

Character is how I say the words and the effect that the words have on me.

Witnessing

Watching and listening to existing recordings of the play is often considered verboten or even heresy by directors, teachers, and some actors, too. I guess that they are afraid that your (or their) personal impulses and interpretations will be sabotaged by the work of another actor. You might feel this way as well, and this could turn out to be the case, if you are the type of person who will not be able to get "their" performance out of your head. After all, whoever has seen Derek Jacobi's Hamlet or Olivia Hussey in Zefferelli's film of *Romeo and Juliet* will have a hard time separating themselves from what was done so well. Conversely, however, such performances are inspiring. I have seen young painters standing in front of the masterpieces in art museums all around the world, drawing them for themselves. You can never replicate what another actor has done, but they may give you an idea of a way to go, a way to approach, a way toward understanding and, most important of all, personal confidence. When haven't we seen a great performance and thought to ourselves, I can do that! Or maybe, if only I could do that. So, why not try seeing and listening to it and see if it helps you?

Watch the leading players at work. They did. They certainly watched inspiring actors play the great roles.

> I'm not ashamed to say that I stole from people. I've never been ashamed of that. If something is good then take it, borrow it, as you will. When young actors copy my characterizations, I am flattered; as I'm sure Irving would have been of the generation who impersonated him. It's not arrogance, it is understanding. As I have said, I admired Barrymore and used much of his Hamlet in mine. In the case of Henry V, I have to acknowledge some of Lewis Waller's performance. I was fascinated by his vocal acrobatics and I'm certain some of them lingered on within me—honed to my performance, of course, but still there.
>
> —Laurence Olivier, *On Acting*

Camp 4: Character

> The text is the character. It fills him out and gives him his life.
>
> —John Barton, from *Playing Shakespeare*

Good S.O.I.L.—Script, Observation, Imagination, Living

Born from the *Script*, *Observing* people, *Imagining* who they could be, and *Living* with them.

It's all about giving humanity to the verse and letting the verse give you its humanity.

Techniques

In the film *Hoosiers*, Gene Hackman is the coach of the Huskers and takes his small-town team all the way to the final state championship in Indianapolis. The Hinkle Fieldhouse is as big a basketball court as the small town kids have ever seen in their lives, seating 15,000 spectators, a far cry from their home court (which I'm guessing sat 300). The coach asks one of the players to measure the distance from the foul line to the backboard. "Exactly 15 feet," says the player. Then he asks the player to measure the height of the basket itself. "10 feet," says the player. The coach then remarks, "I think you'll find that the measurements in this stadium are exactly the same as our little gym in Hickory."

Shakespeare may seem like Mount Everest, but I think you'll find that your creative rehearsal process is based in the same techniques and characterization process as every other play.

> This language [Shakespeare] is the language of thoughts. To do this in the theater, you must speak loud. There are very few actors who can speak loud and still be truthful. That's the actor's problem. Every actor knows the quieter he is, the closer he can be to himself.
>
> —Peter Brook, *Looking for Richard*

Prompt book: Just as in every other play that you do, begin your prompt book the minute you begin reading the play.

Beats: Just as in every other play you do, measure the beats; when does the subject change; where do the thoughts shift?

Off book early: As in every other show, you want to get ahead of the words and not let them dictate the speed of your work. Sure, you can hold the book and wait for the blocking choices and character work to push you further, but the sooner the words are in your head, the deeper work begins.

In your own words: The one difference with Shakespeare is that you can translate the verse into your own words to fully understand the meaning when necessary.

Overnight review: Never take the day's work for granted. Only with repetition and "reminder through" rehearsals on your own will you retain and deepen.

Visualize yourself in the space: Take the time to actually watch the movie of yourself doing the role.

Private rehearsal: I performed the role of Berowne in *Love's Labor's Lost* at The Shakespeare Theatre at the Folger in Washington, D.C. and felt as if I needed extra practice in the rehearsal space on my own. I swear to this day that without those private rehearsals, going over lines, blocking, and character choices for hours alone, I would not have had the same amount of confidence in my work and been able to communicate this character's highly poetic verse with human qualities.

Sleep with it: Let a difficult moment wait until the next day. After a good night's sleep, return to it.

Characterization will reveal itself through clarity of the script and your untiring commitment into the death zone.

Camp 5: The death zone

You're high up on a mountain now, where your commitment counts the most. It is here that the words will become your own with repetition and living with them night and day, dying to yourself as the character emerges.

Live with it

Take your words with you, saying them aloud as often as possible: walking up the street, across the park, in the subway, at home alone, walking around your house, lying in your bed, taking a shower. Live with the text everywhere you go—always ready to try it on for size.

Hal Holbrook was preparing for a Shylock he was going to perform at The Shakespeare Theatre in Washington, D.C. A few of us were standing with Hal in a casual conversation around a home bar at Louis Taper's house in Los Angeles. We asked Hal how it was going, and he began reciting a section that he had just learned. This was a perfect example of having it on call everywhere you are and not being afraid to do it for anyone, anywhere. It's part of your preparation, taking it with you everywhere you go, ready and willing to speak the words.

In rehearsal, the run-throughs are happening more frequently now, and you are learning the arc of the character's journey. You don't have to play all aspects of Richard the Third or Juliet in every scene. Every scene allows you to present different shades of their person and deepening need of getting what they want.

Camp 6: Talking Shakespeare

Having spent the amount of time climbing, repeating, studying, experimenting, and falling in love with your part; it's becoming a part of you and much easier to communicate. The pressure is falling away as is the effort. You're stepping up to the next level almost as if there's a plateau high up on the mountain to simply walk and talk.

Charlie Parker was an American bandleader, saxophonist, and composer who famously said,

> You've got to learn your instrument. Then, you practice, practice, practice. And then, when you finally get up there on the bandstand, forget all that and just wail.

At Camp Six and in a Shakespeare performance, you're on the bandstand. You're in the moment and playing your intentions, trusting that all of your practice with the verse will be there.

Charlie Parker: "Don't play the saxophone. Let it play you."

To the summit

Performing Shakespeare well is like seeing the world for the first time.

Shakespeare expresses thought, character, and human emotion better and deeper and more provocatively than anyone. You stand in the center of it now, pretending and believing at the same time.

Michael Gerson described it magnificently in an article for the *New York Times* entitled, 'Ourselves in Shakespeare':

> But the amazing achievement of the plays, as critic Harold Bloom and others point out, is when characters such as Hamlet, King Lear or Macbeth transcend the words, they speak and come to life—transformed into what the poet Shelley called "forms more real than living man." Other playwrights use characters as mouthpieces for their own wit or philosophy. Shakespeare's greatest characters seem to possess the spark of their own identity. They have somehow escaped the cage of the author's intentions.

I would go even further.

The creative genius that Elizabeth Gilbert (*Eat*, *Pray*, *Love*) described during her teaching on *Ted Talks* is an unexplainable force that sometimes attends us in moments of our yielding awareness, commitment, and openness.

> Even I have had work or ideas come through me from a source that I honestly cannot identify. And what is that thing and how are we to relate to it in a way that will not make us lose our minds, but in fact might actually keep us sane.
>
> A glimpse of God.
>
> The most extraordinary aspects of our being came from us or on loan to us—from some unimaginable source for some exquisite portion of our life to be passed along. …
>
> Don't be afraid, don't be daunted … just do your job … continue to show up for your piece of it, whatever that might be … if the divine cock-eyed genius assigned to your case decides to let some sort of wonderment be glimpsed, for just one moment, through your efforts … then olé, but if not, do your dance anyhow and olé to you nonetheless for having the sheer human love and stubbornness to keep showing up.

You've done the work, you're playing with all you've got, getting out of the way and letting Shakespeare's genius shake hands with yours. It's a mountaintop experience.

> From Hamlet onwards, I allowed myself to surprise myself, and I did that by becoming more and more still.
>
> —Ben Kingsley, English actor

12 Rehearsing the musical

An American original

> They always have to tell me to take a break, I never seem to want to let go, even for a five minute break. I'm totally there during the whole rehearsal process. I listen; I'm involved with the other characters.
>
> —Chita Rivera, speaking to the author

Acting is acting that stems from truth and a desire to fulfill your objective. Musicals are different only because they present another set of skills that do not detract from the essence of characters' living lives, and the author's telling us a story that informs, inspires, and entertains.

The trick is being able to focus your self and your character in the midst—or rather in the center—of the dancing, singing, and the occasional script that can occasionally seem to be two-dimensional.

Your job and your process remain committed to preparing as an artist and finding a character who lives moment to moment and fulfills his or her intentions.

In other words, your tools are basically the same. You can approach the work s-e-r-i-o-u-sly, and you can approach your character's music and dancing with some of the same creative processing techniques that we have already been suggesting. It involves even more preparation and practice. Give yourself permission, power, and protection as you enter rehearsal. The self-confidence and rehearsal techniques all stem from the same source, though a different (maybe faster) process of staging the musical demands an additional set of skills.

I have never been a triple threat (actor, singer, dancer), but I have many close friends who have made a living on Broadway and touring productions around the world. Allow me to defer to their expertise for this unique process.

My best friend was Gregg Mitchell. It was through my friendship with Gregg that I met and became friends with many of Broadway's finest. One

of his closest colleagues was Chita Rivera, renowned actress, singer, and dancer for more than five decades. I spoke with her about rehearsing for the musical.

The script

Chita: I always like to get my script, first of all, I like to meet as many people as I can that are involved with the show, mostly the director, the choreographer and some of the other people, especially if I know them. And just have a drink or something, just stop and say hi to start to get into that warm wonderful space that we have, and that we're lucky enough to have; and then I get the script and I like to read it and learn all of it if I can. Because, it's much easier when you get in and there are changes, you're much more familiar with it.

It was very difficult with *Spider Woman*, because most of that part was "fragments" and it was complicated to bring all of those dots together to make it a "person," one whole character. So that was an interesting process. But I get the script, I try to learn as much of it as I can so I'm a bit more relaxed when I get into rehearsal, because I'm familiar.

Gary: What else do you find important?

Chita: Listening, being on time, focusing, being exactly where you're supposed to be. If you're in that rehearsal hall, you're there, no place else. I can't believe that people have phones that are on in rehearsal halls, it blows me away.

From the inside out

Chita: For instance, back to *Spider Woman*, I really found my character through watching Brent Carver (Molina) … you find so much, not just your scene, you've got to be in all the scenes in order to know what the entire play is about, which eventually comes around to what you're about. People always ask, "Did you know that the shows that you did were hits when you were rehearsing it?" Of course you don't know, because as far as I'm concerned, you're busy being the "innards" of the piece. We're busy being the heart and the gizzard and the liver and the kidneys. There's not a camera, with me there's not a camera that's outside of where I am. I'm not looking back, I'm looking from the inside out.

I know it sounds weird, but I'm sure you understand.

I come from a time when we did as we were told, and then we were allowed when we really got in it to have variations—I mean, Jerry Robbins would have seven variations of one combination, or one section, I should say—you have that kind of freedom if you are a bit more comfortable and are not quite so frightened. I mean the first day of rehearsals are always so scary, that first reading, you're listening, you're judging yourself, you're not relaxed. It takes getting through that first day, it's a wonderful, interesting, scary process, but trust is important.

Songs and steps

Chita: I make sure I'm in bed long enough to go over everything that happened that day. But I try not to pressure myself, which has been a problem, but I get close to the company because the company will save you. It's like a family. You get a lot of courage and a lot of strength from your fellow actors. I'm involved with the other actors; I get a lot from watching the other actors.

I'm a sponge.

Rehearsal sequence

Luis Perez is an actor, singer, dancer, director, choreographer, and fight director both on and off-Broadway, regionally and in film for more than 30 years, working with legendary directors, musical directors, choreographers, and actors.

He is currently head of musical theatre at The Theatre Conservatory at the Chicago College of Performing Arts at Roosevelt University. I asked him to describe the process of a musical rehearsal.

Musicals … are a huge collaboration of writer, composer, lyricist, director, choreographer, musical director, set, light, costume, and sound designers, orchestrator, stage managers, producer, and of course the actors. As such, it is imperative that the actor knows and respects the job of each. Everyone is coming together to create a new piece of theatre.

At the first rehearsal, there will be a meet and greet where everyone will introduce themselves and what they do. Bring a writing implement and note what each person does. Following the meet and greet the director will go through the show with the set model and explain scene to scene what will happen. The costume designer will then present the costume design. Again make notes of anything that will affect you. This is the world you are about to live in, and as such it is a large part of your given circumstances. Following the design presentation there will be an initial read through of the show. Lyrics are generally read aloud and smaller parts are sometimes assigned during this read through. Have that pencil handy. After the initial read there is usually a lunch break, then the work begins.

Always pack everything you possibly need for rehearsal. A recording device, pencil, and notebook are absolutely essential. If you are dancing in the production, appropriate dance clothes and whatever shoes (jazz, tap, ballet) will be required, as well as knee pads for men, should always be with you.

Music rehearsals are the next step. Often there will be Chorus music rehearsal while the director does table work with the leads. Have a recording device with you! Record your parts in order to rehearse at home. You will be expected to be off book the next day when the choreographer begins to stage that number. If you are a lead, write down or record everything the director says, often nerves can shut down your ears. All the same things apply to the acting of a musical as apply to working on a "straight" play. Identification of the character's needs, examination of given circumstances, listings of primary attachments, character's voice, physicality and private/public behavior all have a place in the musical.

Learning the music

Make sure that you learn the music correctly the first time. Nothing will frustrate a musical director more than having to give the same notes over and over. Oftentimes the score will need to be adjusted for harmonies—be sure to have a pencil at every rehearsal! The process of learning a song is as follows:

1 Learn the rhythms and intervals with no words. Make sure they are correct by either plunking them out on a keyboard or using your recording and working methodically through the song.
2 Write the words out as a monologue. Find where you naturally breathe when speaking this monologue and where your new thoughts occur. Mark your breaths on your music.
3 Add the words to the song and sing through it.
4 You are now ready to begin layering a character into the song.

It is the actor's responsibility to be "off book" as soon as possible for all the music in the show. Music by necessity precedes staging, and there is nothing more cumbersome than trying to learn choreography with a script in hand.

Choreography and review

Choreography or blocking rehearsal will begin as soon as a good portion of music has been taught. Again, I cannot stress enough the need for a pencil, pad, and recording device for all rehearsals. You will not remember everything unless you write it in your script.

For a dance rehearsal, arrive early and warm up. Warming up will give you longevity. Be sure to have a towel with you if you sweat profusely and do not wear cologne or perfume. It is asphyxiating trying to work with a partner who has doused themselves in perfume. When watching the choreographer demonstrating, pick up the steps and style as fast as you can. Choreographers are hardly ever given the time that they need to put a number on its feet and will be working as fast as possible.

One technique I have used in the past is to do mental rehearsals before going to bed and in the morning upon waking. Visualize yourself doing all the choreography and staging that has been taught that day. Think it through as thoroughly as possible. This helps you with not only learning, but also with the connective tissue of the song or dance. Use every free moment you have in the studio to rehearse in front of the mirror or with your partner. The sooner the movement becomes second nature, the sooner you can begin to layer a character on the staging. Review everything you know every day. Do not leave a number to get dusty in a corner of your mind. Always rehearse full out unless the choreographer asks you to mark. If you are working with a partner, make sure to check in with them prior to rehearsal to see how they are on that particular day.

Basic rules

Basic rules for rehearsal:

1. *Always be on time!* Studios are extremely expensive and it is rude to your fellow actors to be late.
2. Be prepared. Bring all you will need for that day and do your homework from the day before.
3. Always write down any notes given to you. If you do not understand a note, politely ask; *do not* say something like "Really?" or give a reason why that thing happened. Take the note, and say thank you. Even if you don't agree, there was a reason the note was given—meaning that your current choice was not working.
4. Respect everyone in the room. That second assistant today may become a great director tomorrow.
5. Never leave the rehearsal until being dismissed by the Production Stage Manager and finding out what your call is for the next day.
6. Do your homework. Review what was taught during that rehearsal day and read through what will be worked on the following day.
7. Have fun in the rehearsal room—the process is wonderful when everyone is focused on creating something new.

Many times a director of a musical is not necessarily an "Actor's Director;" be ready to bring ideas on character and blocking into the room with you. However, do not say "What is my motivation to move over there," if told to do so. A famous director answered an actor who said that, with "Your understudy will know the motivation." Find the motivation in your creativity.

Organic and coming from the actor

Rob Marshall, four-time Emmy Award winner, six-time Tony Award nominee, Oscar nominee, and director of the film musicals *Chicago* and *Nine:*

> Rehearsing for a musical is so much more layered and in some ways, more complicated than just rehearsing for a straight piece because it has to all work as if it's coming from the actor. I mean the most important thing for me as a director is that it mustn't look like I'm creating it … it should seem like I was never there. It has to look organic, like all of a sudden, that move is happening. It's happening on this lyric—it should seem completely like it's coming from that person or from that character.

Heightened moments of discovery

Donna Bullock, veteran Broadway and film actress and my personal friend for thirty-five years, has had many leading roles on Broadway, in Los Angeles, and touring the United States. I've seen her countless times but was especially happy to see her in *Me and My Girl* opposite Tim Curry, and in the Broadway production of *Ragtime* as Mother opposite Brian Stokes Mitchell. She has this to say:

> Typically, the first stage of rehearsal for a musical theatre piece begins with learning the music. If at all possible, you should know your music before rehearsals begin. It will help with your overall confidence and you can get down to the business of discovery, making choices, and getting the songs into your body. I always first explore the lyrics as spoken monologue—much like Shakespearean soliloquies—repeating them again and again and again. Songs in musicals are usually heightened moments of discovery, revealing secret aspects or secret longings of the character. Characters sing what they wouldn't or couldn't say. Songs seek height and depth! The more you repeat them, the more they will unfold.
>
> Recently a director had me first explore my songs in rehearsal "externally," giving me permission to allow my body to be overtly expressive—to go too far! Then, in contrast, I explored the song "internally"—a more private investigation. It was a new approach and very effective. I quickly learned much about the landscape of my songs.
>
> Always come to rehearsal fully warmed up—both vocally and physically. Be ready to sing; be ready to dance! Doing a musical is very much like being an athlete. You must be aware of your own instrument's unique requirements in order for you to be in top form. Don't compare yourself to other performers. You need what you need. Get plenty of rest and stay hydrated!
>
> In a musical there are at least two chiefs—the director and the music director; three, if there is a choreographer. You may find one more helpful than another. That's OK. It's just good to know which pair of eyes you can really trust.
>
> Musical acting is no different than acting in a straight play. The books are often spare to make room for the songs, but that just means deeper investigation, discovery, and fleshing out of your character! There is no excuse for two-dimensional characterizations!

There certainly can be a misperception of musicals as two-dimensional experiences for the audience and the actors. It can smack of vaudeville sometimes, and you think you're watching an escalated version of *The*

Entertainer. However, as my friends have demonstrated, it is a multi-layered and demanding art form. Your preparation and repetition work are none the less important than for that of a straight play.

Donna continues with regard to confronting a common problem:

> Fear: I want to say something about fear, because most actors deal with it at some point. Almost everyone has some anxiety about the first read-through. The number of actors I've known who are sure they will be fired after the first day is amazing! You don't get rid of fear by stuffing it down or pretending it isn't happening. You're bigger than it is! You need to bring it in, breathe it in, embody it and allow it to be part of the energy you're working with. That may sound crazy, but it's the only thing that has ever helped me—other than prayer!

Brad Watkins, accomplished DC-area director and producing director at Olney Theater Center, on musical rehearsal:

> Preparation: The preparation as actors in musicals may begin long before being cast in a show. Knowing your voice, your range, your singing style(s) is all something that can be explored with vocal tutelage and can bring confidence to pursuing musicals.
>
> You've been cast—now what?
>
> So, you got cast! Get your script and score materials as soon as you can. Soloists can prepare their assignments with a personal vocal coach prior to the inception of rehearsals. This work should not focus on interpretation but rather execution of the sounds and vocal production you will need to do the show. Your director, choreographer and musical director will work with you to discover what the show is about. During the rehearsal period, you will be taught your music by the musical director. Hopefully, this will precede any table reads or choreography work. It is smart to bring a recording device with you so you can capture your specific solo and choral assignments for your personal review outside the daily rehearsal process. Think of it as an aural script. You could not memorize your lines without your script nearby. This recording will support you in a similar fashion—both in singing and dancing. Hopefully, you will be afforded plenty of repetition in the choreography. The kinetic aspect of dance can be mastered in private but lacks that living dynamic of collaboration and context–just like running your lines by yourself. Set your bar high on mastering the elements defined by the creative team. Get off book musically as soon as you are comfortable in advance of any requests from the directors. Learn your dances. Employ

rehearsal time when you are not on call to work with others off on the side, in an alternative rehearsal space, in the hallway on this mastery. The elements of a musical are not unlike mastering an accent. The sooner you have assimilated the nuts and bolts of a dialect, you can begin to park that technique and focus on acting. It is the same in musicals. While you build the character and music/dance in tandem, you are not really liberated to explore the action of the story until you no longer have to think about these three-dimensional challenges. Because of the increased physical challenge of doing musicals, your ability to pace your personal life becomes more important than ever. Sleep, diet, plenty of water all help. And give up down-hill and water skiing during this job.

Practice positive and embrace the struggle

You've got to keep thinking positive and not get into the negative thing and then indulging in getting yourself in that spiral . . .[do] whatever it takes to be buoyant, smelling the roses and enjoying even the struggle, the tasting of the struggle, almost welcoming it, expecting it, "bring it on . . ." and the toughness of it, it's almost like that visceral thing of being in a sporting event, where you're in it and you're hurting and you're really experiencing it and it just makes you feel more alive rather than letting it smother you.

You've got to develop that sense to be honest and direct and make it attractive and positive, that's something to practice, it's a skill to practice.

—Gregg Mitchell,
Broadway actor and dancer

13 Film, television

Less is more

> Because I come from theater where it really is all about rehearsing and then living it, I like the rehearsal part of it. Rehearsal for me is the exact opposite of what I think a lot of film actors think it is. They think it's "squeezing the lemons." I truly believe it gives you great freedom.
>
> —Rob Marshall, director

My daughter, Julia, was a rising movie star at age seven, having worked two years with major actors in major projects. Her highlight was playing the lead in a film called *The Tie That Binds*, directed by Wesley Strick and starring Daryl Hannah and Keith Carradine. Not long after that, she saw me in a production of Shakespeare's *Twelfth Night* at Arena Stage in Washington, D.C. Afterward she said, "Daddy there are three things: television, film, and acting."

The stage is the actor's medium. Like an athlete on the field of play, it's all happening right now, and you're the one throwing, catching, waiting for, watching, dropping, and shooting the ball.

> The theatre is really the only place we've got left, isn't it? Film is a director's medium. The stage belongs to the actor.
>
> —James Whitmore, American stage, television, and film actor

As will be said many times, television and film are the director's medium where the camera captures and sees for the audience. *However*, you are still throwing, catching, waiting, watching, dropping, and shooting. Your work continues to consist of living your through line and preparing to play, *but* the muscles are different, and the preparation will not have as much collaboration or time.

Helen Carey is an accomplished stage actress who has also worked continuously in television and film:

> The biggest adjustment when moving from stage to film is the scale of acting. Take any speech from a play and deliver it to your mirror. Now make a frame slightly larger than your face and repeat the same speech staying within that frame. You'll feel immediately how intimate the delivery has to be to be "real." All the emotion has to be present as it is in a play, but you convey it all through your eyes, or through the tiniest shrug or smile or tear. It requires a minimalist delivery—not small—minimal.

In my own experience with film, episodic television shows, and daytime soap operas, I found the experiences to be freeing in the sense that it began and finished in one day. The official rehearsal consisted only of lines learned, blocking established, and then jump! This created the need for my own mini-rehearsal process the night before a day's filming or in my dressing room, trailer, or on the darkened set before shooting began. One example I can offer is from one of my scenes in the series "*Something Is Out There*." I played an FBI guy who has captured "a creature" of a man. The scene consisted of dialogue while fixing him lunch and timed just so that I could enter through "the creature's" door at the right moment. No rehearsal. "Here's your kitchen, there's your food, over there's the door, the camera will follow you from here to there, we shoot in about fifteen minutes." The way my character would do it was all up to me. Character!? FBI guy? I was cast the same week, so the only thing I had time to do was get a haircut and memorize the scene, period.

So, while the director and director of photography were setting up the shot, complete with a little room crammed with lighting equipment and crew, I got busy. I saw the tray, sandwich meat, and bags of bread lying out on the counter, so I began to privately go over my lines and mime the fixing of the sandwich. My scene partner was game, so we quietly went through the scene together with no time to be distracted by everybody else doing their own setup. We were the actors getting ready for the shot, and they were the crew getting ready for the shot—what's the difference?! Just do it. When time came to shoot, we were one-take ready, dialogue, sandwich (take out your frustration with this guy on the sandwich making!), cross the room, enter the room and bam, get wiped out by "the creature" with food flying everywhere as he grabbed my throat and lifted me up to the top of the doorway where he was hiding. Done, over, in the can.

The acting techniques still apply. Creating objectives still apply. Repeating the blocking or movement of a scene applies, whether in your mind or in the dressing room. Know your lines cold to be open to discovery and changes. Using techniques such as subtext, personalization, and hidden story applies. However, it is such a condensed experience and often more about the shot, the schedule, and the lighting or design elements that it deserves perspective from many other actors with whom I have worked and who have done more camera acting than myself. It's very easy to feel insignificant in the overall setting, so you have to give significance to yourself and what you know how to do.

Stage, film, and television legend Hal Holbrook offers great beginning advice:

> What I would say to young actors about preparing for work in television and film is: learn your lines way in advance. Learn them so well that you don't have to think about them anymore, you just think about what is going on in the other actor's eyes and in your mind. Knowing the lines cold and salted away has given me a freedom that I cannot get if I'm worrying about what the next word is going to be.

I spoke with director Rob Marshall, and he cited examples from his films *Chicago, Nine*, and *Pirates of the Caribbean: On Stranger Tides* to illustrate the differences between film rehearsal and that of the stage:

> Rob: One of the first things that just comes to mind is a very specific story. I was working on a scene with Richard Gere and Renée Zellweger, and it was the scene where Roxie fires Billy Flynn. Because it didn't involve any singing or dancing, I wanted to rehearse the morning of. Richard, Renée and I were in this prison set working, and I said okay, let's just walk through what this could be, and so we started to do it. I remember Renée wasn't giving it 100%. I could tell she was just kind of barely marking it. I said, "Renée, why don't we do it full out so we'll see where it will lead us to," and she said, "You know what, let's not squeeze the lemons."
>
> I'll never forget that phrase. And then we did the scene later on, a few hours later, and she was fantastic, but obviously she didn't want to give it all away. That was her process.
>
> And I guess the difference between theater and film, in many ways, is that you're trying to capture something, the spontaneity of a moment. And some actors, who don't come from a theater discipline, feel that it's actually more helpful to not have really worked through that until the moment it happens.

Nine

> Daniel Day-Lewis's process is interesting because he doesn't like to rehearse—although he is incredibly disciplined. He knows the material

inside and out. But he very much likes to be surprised and be thrown into a situation and see what happens. … So with different actors it changes, and I find that not everybody has the same process. A lot of wonderful film actors that come from theater, like Judi Dench, for example, love the rehearsal process, and they want to rehearse. But a lot of film actors find it more freeing not to. So ultimately, I don't think there's a right or wrong.

Incredibly familiar

I do feel that the most important thing is to be incredibly familiar with the material. You really have to know the material inside and out to be able to be thrown into a situation without rehearsal. I can always tell when an actor is "acting" because they can't remember the lines or they're taking a pause, pretending that it's a dramatic moment when it's not. I know in a second that it's because they don't know what's coming up.

Another example of someone who thrives on the process without much rehearsal is Johnny Depp. But he has an extraordinary memory and his facility, his language facility is unbelievable. … He's extremely prepared. He knows the work inside and out and so he can try anything and it's great.

Gary: Do you think that comes from private rehearsing or personal preparation?

Personal preparation

Rob: It's personal preparation. That's what he does. It's all personal preparation. He's shy. … To be honest, he's shy about it.

I've found that some of the actors I've worked with, like Daniel, like Johnny, people who don't really love to rehearse, will rehearse for me because they know I like it. Because I come from theater where it really is all about rehearsing and then living it, I like the rehearsal part of it. Rehearsal for me is the exact opposite of what I think a lot of film actors think it is—they think it's "squeezing the lemons." I truly believe it gives you great freedom. I think you can be there experiencing it without having to think, "Well, I'm crossing here and moving here." But it's very interesting, that's not the norm for most film actors. The norm is "let's discover in the moment," and I appreciate that. I appreciate that 100%.

Gary: It's unfortunate for me if I don't get four weeks of rehearsal. I need time for discovery.

Rob: Yes. It's interesting, because I really do feel the more you work on something, the better it becomes. I come from the school where I don't necessarily believe that the initial instincts are always the best for the scene. I appreciate that they give a great immediacy and a sense of discovery that happens in that moment, but I feel theater training is the strongest for any discipline for theater, film or television.

Gary: I heard Peter O'Toole recently on a repeat of *Charlie Rose*, and he said that you can talk about Brando and the method all you want, but he did *Streetcar* thousands of times before he shot the film and that's how you get a masterful performance.

Rob: I agree. I have to say I agree with that. But luckily the people that I just mentioned—Johnny, Renée and Daniel—they do so much preparation on their own.

Gary: What do actors do to find that multi-layered experience when all is said and done? How has it come from them?

The moment of truth

Rob: What happens is, honestly, when I rehearsed both the films *Chicago* and *Nine*, I rehearsed them like a Broadway show. There was no difference whatsoever, zero. We got in and we learned the material and we put it on its feet, bit by bit, and you start seeing what works and what doesn't.

Also, you can teach a number and then not shoot it for two months. So, I actually continued rehearsal. I remember the producers coming up to me and saying, why do we need the rehearsal rooms? I said, "Because they're going to continue to rehearse while we're shooting, as we're not going to see certain numbers for two months, and they'll forget them."

In *Chicago*, Renée was new to musicals and she was amazing because she worked meticulously and slowly. I was so proud of her, because I thought, "Well that's a real example of rehearsing so hard and knowing something so well that then you're free to actually live it in the moment of truth."

I would come in to work, because we were still creating and working all through filming, and there she would be at 9 in the morning on a Sunday. She'd have her little hat on and her sweats doing something over and over and over again. She's a real worker. I mean the actors that I've worked with that are great, are workers.

They work like no one's business. Daniel Day-Lewis—I've never seen anything like it in my life. He gives everything. People think his process is bizarre because he assumes the character, but actually it's not bizarre at all. It's a total dream for a director. It's not like he's dropping and putting back on the character. He's there. So when you're ready to go, he's there.

But it's all up to the individual—whatever works for you—I think that is the key. And as a director I am always adapting my own way of working to adjust to the actor's personal process. I'm fine with that.

A new performance every take

Michael Pressman, actor (*Frankie and Johnny Are Married*); film director (*To Gillian on Her 37th Birthday,* among others); Emmy Award-winning executive producer for television (*Picket Fences,* among others):

> The key to acting in film or television is knowing your character and your character's relationship to the story, and to show up on the set available and open to surprises. The discovery process is key. It can happen in rehearsal, and even more while you shoot. The fundamental difference for the actor in film, rather than on stage, is that rather than repeating a performance every night that is basically the same, the actor in film can try different emotional things in different takes.

Here's what works for many actors with whom I spoke about their own rehearsal practices and priorities when working on a film.

Perspective

Yvonne Erickson has been doing film and television for twenty-five years:

> You were hired because you showed them something special in the audition. Your unique way of acting this role. Or your great look. Or your wonderful presence. Let that be there. Don't over think it. They will let you know if they want something else or something in addition to what you brought to the audition.

An audience of one

Actor John Prosky:

> As far as preparing for Film/TV, the best advice I ever got about that was from Pop [actor Robert Prosky]. I was cast as a lead in a Movie of the Week … straight out of Rutgers University, so, in a panic, I called

Pop and he said, "Do everything that you would normally do to prepare for a stage role but when you finally act it, think of it as an audience of one and they are standing right next to you."

More specifically: Take all of your "actions," "objectives," character ideas, etc., all the things you've prepared for the role and just think them, don't "project" them. You don't need to project them; the audience is two feet to six inches away from you. When your proscenium is literally around your face, anything you do is magnified a gazillion times, so for God's sake, JUST THINK IT. To most actors that can feel like they're not doing anything but after they see themselves on film a couple times, they see that it's more than enough and, if they've done their work correctly, it's interesting and very alive.

Deepening over time

Actor Keith Hamilton Cobb, co-star in television's *Andromeda, Noah's Arc*, and Emmy nominee for *All My Children*:

> Rehearsal for actors in television and film, particularly television, is most often found to be an element directly proportional to budget. Actors in major motion pictures with large budgets will be rehearsed. They will dissect text with their director, and explore in rehearsal rooms finding the subtleties of relationships in no way significantly different from rehearsing a play. And all that work, because it was done, will be there on film for the editor to work with, and to do with as he and the director will.
>
> In lower budget television which includes the plot-driven mediums of Soap Opera and Syndicated Action Sci-Fi, "rehearsal" is, for the most part, a thing for director and camera-ops. For the actor, the rehearsal, usually happening on the day of performance, is about where to stand, because the camera will be expecting you there. Where will the actor be when she turns to see her long lost love arrive with flowers? Where will he need to arrive and stand when he turns from the computer bank and walks toward the ship's view port in order to evince the horror of seeing the alien ship coming to attack him?
>
> Ultimately, to this end, casting directors in television begin to look specifically for actors who can do this sort of thing with ease, who need little rehearsal, who can begin to play a character on the first day and continue to play him, summoning up whatever emotion is needed in the moment, out of context, and at times with very little justification.
>
> Ironically, one thing that helps is the serialized nature of Daytime TV, where one might play a particular character for years on end. Each

episode might then begin to serve as a deepening of the character's drives and imperatives. In this respect, in such mediums, we might say we are always rehearsing, as each on-camera day allows us to feel more fully that character that we can only further create and embody as time goes on.

On-set rapport

Rehearsal in the mediums where I have spent most of my on-camera time seems to me to be a process of diligent contemplation as to who your character is, and then showing up on time with your lines learned. If you are a good actor, alert, aware, spontaneous, this will do much, as well as will a good rapport and time spent with on-camera colleagues discussing those very things that you would discuss in preparation for any stage play. A good actor brings a great deal just being his/her beautiful, sensitive self. You do the work. But don't be surprised—or put off—if all anybody wants to do is take moving pictures of you.

Quick choices

Actor James Horan:

Preparation is critical, and theatrical training is best, in my opinion. Not that you need a lot of time to "develop a character," but you need to be able to quickly make choices about the character from reading sides, or the script if you're fortunate enough to have access to it—as you know, this isn't always the case.

I once heard actors described as "emotional athletes"—in the sense that athletes maintain a high degree of preparedness and conditioning, so that they may perform at their best when called upon to do so. So my advice to young actors would be to always exercise your emotional muscles, as well as your physical ones, to be able to tap into vast reserves, even when you're faced with a limited time to prepare for an audition, or a job in film or TV.

Camera ready

Actress Yvonne Erickson:

Know your lines

You usually only see the actors that are in the scenes with you or who are filming the same day.

Know your lines dead cold. This means you really must be a quick study. You may get script changes shortly before you shoot (day of). Sometimes the director will feed you a new line. Don't make a judgment about the text. Say it as written. Your job is the subtext. Do not improvise unless you are asked to do so.

If you flub your line … don't apologize, fumble around, get mad at yourself, etc. Don't assume they will cut anyway. They don't really want to. Take a breath and regroup. Stay in character, and start the line over and keep going. They will tell you to cut if they want that. The actor does not make that decision. Relax! They hired you because they think you can do the role and they trust you.

Wait for the camera

Your "rehearsal" will mostly consist of setting the camera moves. You may get to go through the lines with the action once or twice (with feeling at half mast). Save the emoting for the take or takes. The director will let you know if he/she will film the "rehearsals." In that case, go ahead and act the scene full out.

I once had the producer of a film I was acting in (Jody Foster) come to me after about the 3rd rehearsal (a big group scene may have more rehearsals) to tell me to hold back till the camera rolls. I was the mother of a teen who had died. We were at the funeral and I was sitting next to the casket. I was to react to the minister's eulogy. I had to hold the weeping until the 1st take. It took half a day to set the scene. This was a day player role.

On-set etiquette

Be on time. Actually … be a bit early for your call. You will have to find a production assistant (do this right away; look for a guy/gal in a headset with a walkie talkie) to tell you where you need to go. Hopefully you have your own room in a trailer. Relax there 'til someone comes to get you. There should be a call sheet (daily shot list) there waiting for you with a mini-version of the sides of the scenes you are shooting for you in your room. If nothing is there … ask a PA (production assistant) for a "mini" and a call sheet for the day. You need the mini to see if there are script cuts or new lines. The call sheet will give you a lot of info … like if you will be back the next day!

Be respectful

When you are taken to hair and makeup, be friendly, but respectful. These folks are working. Be observant. Be helpful. Don't be a chatty

> Cathy unless you run into your long lost high school buddy. But even then … remember there is a schedule and you are a small part of it. If you find yourself next to the "star" in the makeup chair, smile and say hello. Be nice. Be relaxed. But mostly be respectful. They may be preparing for something big that day. You will know if they want to chat … go ahead and answer questions. But pretend you are a bit shy even if you are not. Let them lead the conversation.

Be flexible

Actor Mark Pinter, with extensive daytime television credits and leading roles on regional stages across the United States, says:

> The actor must do the work before he comes to the set and the decisions that the theatre gave us time to consider, must have already been mulled over—thrown about—retained and/or discarded. But, always keep your heart, mind and soul open to the possibilities—because the actor will be confronted with distractions and last-minute changes on the film and television set. There is no audience—generally no one gives a shit what you're trying to do—the response must come from within—stillness, honest and simple and real—which can, sometimes, be extremely difficult for the actor who treads the boards for a living. Being real is a very scary prospect for some of us. Be flexible and open on the set—and it will translate to film and television. Do the work first—then throw it all away and be ready to play.

Centered and relaxed

Actor Jeff Allin has enjoyed a successful career on stage in New York and in film and television in Los Angeles:

> In terms of TV/film, our imagination is sometimes the only opportunity we have to spend time with the character. Often on a film or high profile TV project there will be time and budget to rehearse beyond a "table read." In the world of episodic TV though, the rehearsal process is mostly a luxury. Most of the time, a guest star will not see their scene partner until they are called to the set. It may be before the set is lit and it will feel like a real rehearsal, i.e., run it a few times, block it for camera, have a pretty good sense of what it all looks like. It might also be in costume on a lit set, with the whole crew there, not much information and a very public experience less protected. In daytime TV rehearsal time can be even harder to come by. All this is by way of saying, what works for understudies also works in TV/film:

1. It is imperative to create tools to center and relax ourselves in these situations.
2. We want to spend some time at home imagining ourselves as these characters, in these particular circumstances, and sort of compress the rehearsal process into our minds.

Knowing the lines before you get on set is a sign of professionalism and a must

> One other thing worth mentioning for TV/film work: flexibility and openness are great assets on a set. Once you're there, you're surrounded by collaborators with different ideas, and it is a collaborative process. Don't allow yourself to be locked in to what you imagined in your living room or bedroom. A living, breathing character has lots of options. Better to think of that as an asset than a problem.

Actor Sherman Howard:

The readiness is all

> Meaningful rehearsal in film and television is rare. Film and television directors who have actually acquired a working knowledge and functional vocabulary of the actor's craft are exceedingly rare. Meanwhile, the vast array of technical components and competing considerations converging on a film set—the choice of lens, exposure, camera angle, camera motion, lighting, set, wardrobe, sound, continuity, editing intentions, etc—all tend to consume a director's attention because they are ALL coming together at once ... for the first and only time … and at very great expense! Time is indeed lots and lots of money! This is the prevailing reality on a film or television production set.
>
> In such a turbulent environment, rehearsal often consists of little more than blocking. Therefore the actor must arrive ready to perform! Know your lines; know your character; know your inner life; know your intentions; know your back-story; know your emotional preparation—know everything! Until the director calls, "Action!" Then throw it all away! Stay loose, listen and respond, remember to breathe, be alive in the moment and don't expect much more from your director than, "Could you...uhhh...maybe have more fun with it?" (Translation: "I've no idea how … but please make it better.")

Dan Southern, a veteran stage, film, and television actor:

Let the camera do the work

I got a two-part guest spot on a TV series opposite Fred Dryer, again I believe, because I was tall enough to stand next to Fred, an ex all-Pro NFL defensive end. On this shoot, there was another bad guy I had to do a scene with in a warehouse. The thing about TV is that there is NO TIME for rehearsal of any type, beyond just blocking the scene for the camera. This is about the only thing that is set.

On this shoot, the words didn't even seem to matter. Fred, who was the executive producer on the show as well as the star, would change lines at will. "Nah, I don't like that line, I'm gonna say this" and I'd say, "Well, if you don't say that line then my line makes no sense." "Change it, then," he'd say, and I would. I remember being concerned that we were making no verbal sense after a while. But what I recalled as incoherent looked perfectly fine on network television. It was a big lesson for me to realize that the camera through reaction shots, cutaways and long shots along with dubbed music and post-production, could do a lot of your work in terms of scene intentions. It went a long way to allowing me to relax on camera; I realized that acting had to go through the camera to reach the audience, and where the camera was placed and how the scene was set up was somebody else's job—meaning it was beyond my control.

Hit your mark and say your lines

The camera is fickle. … If you aren't interested in her, she's very interested in you. The moment you begin to notice her, she makes you look like shit. It's tricky because of course you must be aware of her at all times. You don't want to blow the take by stepping out of frame. As a stage actor, one has to let go of the longing for more rehearsal, the comfort of having played the scene a dozen times, sifting through all the various different choices and coming up with those you are confident in are the best. The process is truncated in the extreme. Every time I came to the set attempting to compress 3–4 weeks of rehearsal into one take, I would find that the director would give me the same direction which, in essence, was "do less." I survived and lived to act another day on camera because I took pride in being able to do the basics well: hit your mark and say your lines. Hang on to your intentions and try not to notice that camera sticking in your ear that will bloody your nose if you turn too suddenly to the right. Trust that at such small remove the camera will do much of your job. Don't be too wedded to your choices. You may find that acid remark that you planned to deliver in a heat with rising inflection may be much better in a conversational tone with a simple lift of the gaze beneath a hooded brow. The canvas is smaller.

Improvisation

> Being comfortable with improvisation is very important in doing on-camera work. On the second feature film I did, my character had a name but I have no memory of it because we never used it. I showed up for the first day knowing all my lines and we never used any of those either. Everything we did was improvised and shot in one or two takes after a couple of run-throughs. I had an idea of who my character was in the script—a young sharp business guy working for a boss he greatly admired, who was slick and a bit rapacious. The improvisations were very helpful by the way in which the other actors related to my character. And, of course, much more of your acting on camera comes between the lines, without the lines, in counter point to, or against the lines.
>
> The opening scene in this second movie is a contract signing between my boss (Pierce Brosnan) and two guys across the table gloating over the presumed deal they've negotiated. My character is just standing there behind his boss who, at the conclusion of the scene, reveals to the buyers that, in fact, they have paid two times more than anybody else had offered for the property. He then stands and exits. My only business was to reach forward and pick up the signed contracts off the table. Well, I made the choice to let the professional demeanor slip just a bit and give the two guys a big "gotchya" grin as I grabbed the contracts. The director of the film loved it and gave me a full face close-up in the retakes. Cinematically, it's the defining moment of my character.

Study, explore, repeat, be independent in your thinking, taking ownership in an uninhibited way with a spiritual perspective on the entire experience. You may not be given the focus of the experience by everyone else, but you can give it to yourself whatever the medium.

Sky diving

Actress Helen Carey:

> Rehearsing for film and TV is sort of like saying you are going to "rehearse" sky diving from a plane.
>
> Sometimes you have the luxury of knowing the actor opposite you; more often, you meet for the first time on set. There is a camera rehearsal but that is for the crew's benefit—lighting, sound, camera angles and measured distance from the lens. Unlike stage work where the audience is at a comfortable distance, the crew can be inches from you.

> Preparing for all that requires great concentration, solidly knowing your lines and serving the needs of the director. In film, you are going to be spending long hours repeating the same thing and sounding as fresh as the first time you said it three hours earlier. You will be picking up or putting down props on exactly the same word each time so that all the shots match. You will do all this for the master shot, the medium and close up shots and for all the reverses when the camera is filming other characters and only the back of your head is visible.

As in every aspect of this business, you can take tips from those who have gone before you, but you'll find your own way just the same. Hal Holbrook defines the work on film and everywhere:

Who you are

> The other thing I would point out is that being at peace with who you are becomes very important after you've worked for a while. Just accepting who you are, that that is going to be okay, that you don't have to cover up anything or put on anything, just be the human being that you are. You'll come out O.K.
>
> If you have thought about your role a great deal in advance, you won't have to think about it in rehearsal. Just take your performance from what the other actor gives you.

Part III

On your own

> Nobody can help you, nobody. There is only one single means. Go inside yourself. Discover the motive that bids you … examine whether it sends roots down to the deepest places of your heart, confess to yourself whether you would have to die if it were denied you.
>
> —Rainer Maria Rilke, *Letters to a Young Poet*

Part III is about being on your own, becoming a problem solver, and creating your own rehearsal process by trial and error over a period of time. You're continually laying the foundation for how you approach your work and how you approach your life. Both approaches will be under extremely tested conditions when you enter the business of acting. You'll be practicing your rehearsal techniques during a production and every day of your life. The following chapters suggest rehearsal techniques to add to the ones you find on your own that will suit your independent and creative process of living and rehearsing.

14 Practice your own rehearsal process

A declaration of independence

> It seemed to me that a careful examination of the room and the lawn might possibly reveal some traces of this mysterious individual. You know my methods, Watson. There was not one of them, which I did not apply to the inquiry. And it ended by my discovering traces, but very different ones from those which I had expected.
>
> —Sherlock Holmes, "The Crooked Man," *The Memoirs of Sherlock Holmes* (1893)

You solve problems, observe mysteries, and ask questions *for a living* as an actor. The production of a play can easily fit many metaphors, but a puzzle is surely one of them. A play is in pieces, revealing the picture little by little over the course of time. It demands patience and a skill in answering questions, trying solutions, and discovering another piece that fits, but it's almost always a piece that made little sense until it's placed into another piece of the picture.

Nothing is impossible, and everything is what you make it. With a habit of preparation, a willingness to overcome adversity, and a daily devotion to achieving your goals, even luck will be on your side. You've got a better-than-even chance of having a career.

With humility, patience, and an interest in what makes life tick, you can become an artist at whatever you do.

Two actors who know each other meet up on the street, and one asks the other, "How's it going, getting any work?"

"Nah." the other one replies, "I can't get arrested, nothing's going on. You?"

"Well, I've had a lot of auditions and a few call backs but nothing for almost a year. You know, sometimes I wonder how you get out of this business."

I stared at Jarlath Conroy, who told me the joke, blankly, thinking, what's so funny about that? And then it dawned on me that out-of-work actors don't consider themselves out of the business, and we evidently keep deluding ourselves that whether we are working or not, we're still actors. He told me that we all have the same reaction: waiting for the punch line.

It's because we believe. It's because we are actors whether we are officially getting hired to do it or aren't; we are artists and keep forgetting that at some point, we have to make a living at it, too!

Painters are not any different in my opinion. I once lived in a place called the VanDyke Studios in Manhattan, thanks to painter George Wingate's letting me crash when I was between apartments. These studios were famous loft spaces that have been rented by painters for almost 100 years. It had great skylights that provided natural light for their daily painting but also was known as Fort Apache because of all the break-ins from the roof. I used to sleep with a hammer by my bed.

Nearly all of the painters on that floor had to do something else for monthly income, and their walls were covered with amazing art work and a progression of their styles as they matured. Most of them were focused on developing their style but also hoping that a gallery would show their work. However, gallery or no, none of them doubted their calling, their gift, and their constant attention to their daily responsibility to paint.

Rainer Rilke tells the writer to go inside him or herself to discover the motive that bids her or him to write. He also says that nobody can help you but, in the theatre, it is a team of players. Listening, reacting, building on what happens immediately in rehearsal and performance is the wave that we surf on. Even surfers, however, know that it's not all wave. Good surfing requires heart, passion, technique, and practice.

The life of an actor is a living experience, 24/7, but you need an *RP*, your own *rehearsal process*, for any job you get and even for the audition to get it.

Your **givens**

First things first. Before you begin to adopt a personal and creative rehearsal process, what are *your* givens?

Who *are you* as a working artist? What would the play analysis chart look like with you at its center? To repeat a phrase from the first chapter:

> You are bringing yourself to the process of rehearsal along with the riches of your life and stage experiences. You're bringing your imagination, your work-ethic, your questions, your fears, your inhibitions, interests and the way you look.
>
> But, how do you like to work, bottom line? Are you satisfied with the way you approach an audition and a rehearsal?

As there are archetypal personalities, there are similar attributes in an actor's persona and a need to become as authentic as possible. Where are you on the astrological acting chart? What are your natural tendencies?

Are you naturally inventive or do you prefer lots of direction? Do you need crisis to create, like the proverbial rock star who feels that he or she cannot write unless their life is always in a state of anarchy and physical deprivation? Do you start out fast and grind to a halt or, like the thoroughbred, Silky Sullivan, wait until the last eighth mile to close like a rocket?

How do you like to rehearse, and how might you like to change it? Will you apply some of the personal techniques suggested in the next chapter, or will you always need a director to guide you through them?

What is your natural temperament?

It was long into my career before I was introduced to the work of Keirsey and Bates, which amplified the famous Myers/Briggs psychometric questionnaire to help us determine our basic temperaments, from such temperaments and psychological types as extraverted versus introversion; intuitive versus sensing; thinking versus feeling; and perceptive versus judging. You can take the test yourself by buying the text (*Please Understand Me, Character and Temperament Types*). Understanding how you basically approach life circumstances can help you understand how you approach rehearsal and whether it is consistent with how you *want* to approach it.

The more realizations you have about yourself and how you approach life will only illuminate your approach to people, problems, and practice in rehearsal.

The rest of your givens can include what's the job at hand? What are the demands of the gig? Where is it taking place? When and why do you want it?

Does it fit into your schedule, your life and, most important, does it fit into your overall objective for your career? There are many detours, and I don't subscribe to the model of taking work anytime and anywhere it is offered. *You* must determine where *you're* going and the kind of work *you* want to do. Believe me: the business will follow your lead eventually. Please don't misunderstand: I also believe the maxim that work begets work, so your decisions are always important, and one gig can lead to another.

The audition

Your preparation includes rest and diet and an uncluttered mindset but also specific approaches that include more information than you might ordinarily suppose.

This is an interview for a job! It's not just an evaluation of yourself as an actor or a person, so do your homework on the theatre, the playwright, the director, and your role.

Audition homework?

- The theatre: Look up their current season, their history, their staff, actors, and directors; you might know someone.
- The playwright: Look up and read other plays, read the entire play that you are auditioning for (see story below).
- The director: Who is she or he, where else has he or she worked, has she or he written any books or articles? Be familiar.
- The role: Read the play and have questions, look up reviews from previous productions, know who has played it and how they were reviewed. Look up commentaries and become your own dramaturg for the short amount of time before the audition.

Dustin Hoffman was appearing as Willy Loman for a Broadway production of *Death of a Salesman* in 1984 and personally helped conduct the required Equity principal auditions at the Equity lounge in New York City. There was an obvious buzz, with such a famous film and stage star conducting the low-level auditions himself. An actor who was in the lounge at the time recounted to me how Hoffman himself came out of the room at one point and very seriously spoke to all of the actors waiting their turn and said that if they hadn't read the play, he didn't want them to come in!

I have suggested doing much more than reading the play before you even get cast. It is a lot of work, but this is an interview for a job, which could change your life and certainly advance your career. You're not only hoping for this job but wanting to make the best impression possible. You are there to make a fan and will do so by showing up knowledgeable about all aspects of the production.

Obviously, if you get the call the night before the audition, only a limited amount of research is possible. However, with the Internet, you can learn a great deal in a very short time. The advice is to be as well informed and as practiced in the role as possible in the amount of time you are given.

The entire premise here is approaching your audition and your eventual rehearsal process and performance seriously with commitment and transforming whoever you have become into the type of person who will succeed in your endeavor to become the best actor you can become. It's up to you and you alone.

Enter: your personal creative and collaborative rehearsal process

What works for you in rehearsal may be totally different from what works for another actor or even the director. And as you get older, your ways of working will evolve, but it's important to begin developing your own creative rehearsal process now and as something you can build on as you mature.

Director-proof

It's naïve to believe that all actor/director collaborations will be good ones. For whatever the reasons, you may disagree with your director's approach to the extent that you come to realize that a majority of the blocking choices, character discoveries, and repetitive scene work is up to you. The phrase *director-proof* has long been around, and I mean that the onus is on the actor to deliver a performance regardless of the people, pay, or circumstances. I was very interested to hear artistic director Ed Herendeen, from Contemporary American Theatre Festival, echo this in his description of actor training:

> I think another thing actors should be trained to do is to be director proof. If they're doing their job, I trust the actor, I try to hire actors who are going to amaze me and surprise me and teach me what the play is about.

It's also often said that a particular play is *actor-proof*, meaning that the story will be compelling even if the actors aren't very good. Along with this theme, if your director is at the beginning of her or his learning curve, opposed to what you're trying to do in the play, or very distracted and unprepared, it's your job to be able to reveal your character and tell the story of the play regardless. You can do it, one play at a time.

Actor independence

The figure overleaf shows a suggestion of methodologies and qualities that combine to achieve an actor's independence.

In-rehearsal philosophies

There are consistent themes that are evident in my director, playwright, and professional actor interviews.

- Use whatever it takes for you to find an *authentic* voice and spirit in your approach to the world alongside your approach to the work.
- Develop your *creative state* on a daily basis and live your life as an actor who observes, appreciates, and is incredibly curious about what makes life tick.

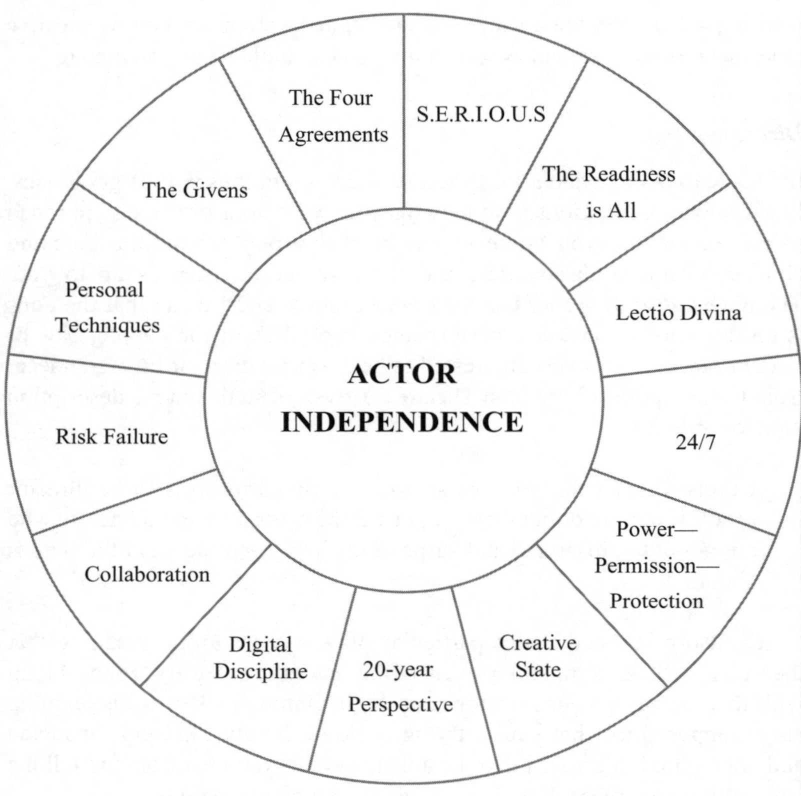

- *Preparation* appears to be the key in everyone's mind to doing well in rehearsal. Understanding the author's work.
- *Reading* the play many times before rehearsal and continuing research of the play and playwright throughout the process are the cornerstone to discovering your world in the play and give you strength with the director during rehearsal.
- *Commitment* is a quality that gets you into the room and brings you back.
- *Risking* and diving into rehearsal with your original choices appears to be a consistently winning strategy. "Make a mistake, loud!" and "Rush toward embarrassment."
- Collaborating in a positive and self-confident fashion with all of the artists involved with the production is an essential quality to doing your own work.

- Solo rehearsal and repetition of your daily discoveries are essential in retaining them.
- Warm up for rehearsal, transitioning from the outside in: dressing-room rituals, makeup patterns, pre-show character warm-up, time alone, or relaxing time in the green room, centering.
- Control of the digital media in your preparation is your challenge toward a disciplined rehearsal period.
- Trust your director. Mutual trust is the ideal, but work by example, and know that your director has the entire production to consider and will give you as much space as you are prepared to take.
- Sleep and nutrition. Taking care of your instrument is basic and essential.
- Be open to your fellow actors, your director, and your own instincts.
- Establish a one-to-one relationship with your director, finding private sessions of dialogue and problem solving.
- Be aware of basic rehearsal etiquette: being on time, call for line but stay in the scene, prepared for that day's work, personal hygiene.
- Maintain the givens: your given circumstances for wanting the job and becoming an actor, the given circumstances of your character in the play, analyzed and studied.
- Utilize techniques that work for you. There are a hundred techniques to do on your own and try in rehearsal. Don't wait for the director to tell you what to do or what to try, just do them.
- Maintain a twenty-year perspective on your learning and longevity.

> Somewhere in talking and rehearsing, there is a magical moment where actors catch a current; they're on the right road. If they really catch it, then whatever they do from then on is correct and it all comes out of them from that point on.
>
> —David Lynch, American filmmaker,
> film review: *Lost Highway* by Steve Biodrowski

15 Reading and researching the role

Rehearsal techniques

> It has been said that an actor must have the hide of a rhinoceros, the courage and audacity of a lion, and most importantly, the fragile vulnerability of an egg. It also has been said, and I'm not sure by whom, that the moment of not knowing is the moment that has the greatest potential for creativity. The professional and private lives of most actors are filled to the brim with moments of not knowing. Actors are survivors and will continue to strive because they have the need to celebrate, in performance, that sacred communion between actor and audience.
>
> —Actor Robert Prosky, 1930–2008

It's a profound responsibility when you accept a role in a production, and it deserves your patient study and undivided attention. In memoriam to the veteran Arena stage actor, Robert Prosky, Zelda Fichandler said this about his artistry:

> There was the gracious gift of time; for Bob, decades of time … time to build one experience upon the other and one different from the other, but in some basic way each one asking for the same imaginative use of self. There was permission to see a creative "failure" as something to be understood and learned from, to be incorporated into the work, rather than as a career-threatening event. There were occasions, many occasions, for Bob to ponder that the process of acting was ultimately mysterious but that you could grab hold of a way—a technique, both inner and outer—to open the door to it.

Opening the door

Using the lectio divina method as a structure, the following techniques are a beginning in learning how to effectively rehearse on your own.

Read, reflect, respond, and rest

Reading

Of all the advice I received from professional directors and playwrights with regard to an actor's preparation for rehearsal, reading and reflecting on the script were at the top of the list.

Private study

- Read the entire play without interruption!
- Read all or portions of the play every day.
- Take notes.
- Read other plays by the author.
- Read some novels and find some paintings that capture the period or place where your story lives.

When Zelda Fichandler moved on after forty-one years as artistic director of Arena Stage, she began another career as a master teacher of acting and chair at New York University's Tisch School of the Arts' Graduate Acting Program.

Coming into their final year, the students received a packet of materials concerning their work to come, which included their casting and season of plays. Also included was an open note to the students, written by Zelda, entitled *Preparing to Rehearse.* Zelda has generously given me permission to cite a major portion of this material and its basic principles.

Preparing to rehearse

> Maybe you'll have time over the summer to begin to think about the plays you'll be in, the roles you'll be playing and in general, what preparatory work you can do to begin before you go into rehearsal.
>
> How does one begin? You've got the script, you know what your role is, you have the enthusiasm and the curiosity. Now what? Here are my suggestions:
>
> Read the play a number of times—each time with a different point of concentration. The first time, read for a general impression of where and when the play is happening; what happens in the play—what's the story; who the people are and, in a general way, what happens to each of them from the beginning of the story to the end. You might ask yourself: where am I, and who are these people around me, and what do I want from them, and what do I think is the best way to get it? Get a general sketch of the play. Reading number one will blend with reading two.

Read a second time for a deeper understanding of the characters and, of course, especially your character. See if you can find in the text clues about their past—especially the past of your character—about his/her temperament, about his/her needs, wants, frustrations, about the relative ages of the characters, their relationship to each other, the web of connections among them. Your emotional understanding will arrive in bits and pieces; don't expect more, just collect evidence of the inner life of your character and what you do to get what you want. As impressions come to you, here and there, hold onto them in a loose, open way. Be curious about what you can pick up: if a moment grabs you as real, bless it and hold onto it. This is the area in which you can make a great contribution to the rehearsal process.

Read a third time to see if you can make sense of the whole: what the playwright meant us to know from it (even though he, himself, might not have been aware of it!); why he might have written it when he did; how he himself felt about the characters—does he care about them? Does he judge them? What might be the overall action of the play (which unites the actions of the individual characters under one theme)? What does the play make us think about, how does it change us? How do we feel when we've finished reading it? Try to understand and appreciate how this play is different from or similar to other plays of the playwright or other plays you've read or been in.

Read only when you can get all the way through the text without being interrupted. Always read with a sense of curiosity: you are opening a door, what's inside? Who's there?

Never go to a first rehearsal without some thoughts and feelings about the play, some questions, some tentative decisions about the characters, especially the one you are to embody. It's good to come to the first exploration with your mind open but not empty.

That's because you're a collaborator in the process of making flesh and blood from the words, and therefore, response-able and responsible to the process. I know I can't work with actors I have to push around like chess pieces, which is why I love working with an acting company, and I know other directors appreciate work-ready actors as well.

Do research that grows out of what you need to know to bring the play, and especially your character, to life. How do these people lead their daily lives in this particular country at this time? To begin, think about what things affect your own life. What are your own anxieties, how do you worship, how do you relate to the opposite (or same) sex, how were you educated? Who are your parents? What do you wear, eat, drink, read, and dance to? How do you get from place to place, what do you hope to be, achieve, in your life and what might stand in your

> way? What do you do in your leisure time, who governs your country and in what way are these forces to be relied upon or to be feared or challenged or even attacked? What changes are in the air for you? What makes you feel hopeful? Where do you see yourself in the next five years?
>
> Then ask the same questions on behalf of your character. Your character is, after all, but another version of you—some other arrangement of you.
>
> Use all available research tools that you can think of. Listen to music of the period, especially dance music. Study photographs and paintings. Buy postcards and prints of them from a museum and keep them around you.
>
> Go at it with curiosity and exhilaration as if you were unraveling a mystery. In point of fact, you are.
>
> At points in the rehearsals, researched information will just fall into the text and illuminate it. It will bring the character into you and help you to enter into the life of the character. The point of research is to make real for yourself the circumstances the characters live within. You take these for granted in your own life because you're actually living it now. You don't have to construct it—there it is!
>
> Come to the rehearsals with information. The more information, the more imagination.
>
> All of this preparation can make a collaborative unit of the actors, directors, designers and make each of you a real contributor to the process. Try it out.

You need to read the story without interruption so that you experience the entire story and get a sense of how your character fits into the scheme of things. Carry it with you; the more you spend time with it, the more the story *inside the story* will reveal itself to you. You are bonding with your work. Give it the time it deserves, rather than fitting it in between texts, tweets, classes, phone calls and whatever other distractions you deal with every day.

Start to read your part aloud as you go through it. It's the beginning of making the words your own and hearing your own voice in the story.

Playwright Lee Blessing:

> Read the stage directions. Actors are often taught, I understand, not to read them—to cross them out instead and base their performance solely on the clues they tease out from the dialogue.
>
> I've always regarded this practice as arrogant, wrong-headed and deeply insecure. Directors and actors need to read not only what a

playwright's "heard" (i.e., the dialogue) but also what he or she has "seen" (stage directions). They don't necessarily need to "do" the stage directions, but they do need to know what they are, because it puts them in the ballpark of the playwright's intention for the moment in question. The director/actor team may well find an entirely different way to get the quality or value intended in a moment, and I think that's completely justifiable.

But I consider it an unconscionable shortcut to black out stage directions without reading them. Unless actors and directors know what that playwright's intention really is (as stated in the stage direction), they'll just be guessing. Actually, they'll be writing something that's already been written (hence the arrogance I mentioned), but they'll be doing it in their own way, and quite possibly worse.

The best actors I've worked with have read the stage directions and do them—or, knowing the stage direction, may search to find something that works as well for the moment. But they are at least, by doing things this way, working from a base of knowledge and not ignorance. The best actors in my experience are also line perfect, right down to the punctuation—which, like the stage directions, is there for a reason.

Reflecting

Homework

It's a job and a journey; give yourself a map.

An outline of the play's information will give you a head start. It's not always about being spontaneous, reactive, and waiting until your fellow actors and your director begin to discover the play on its feet in the rehearsal room.

Actor Edward Norton spoke about co-star Robert DeNiro's approach to the movie *Stone* in a *Washington Post* interview by Jen Chaney:

> Because he's not very verbal, he's got this rep as kind of a savantish or all intuitive, and it's so not true, he's like the most clinical, right brain—he's like a librarian. I've never seen anybody who's more about the voice-recorder and the notepad. He's like this wonkish, detail guy for weeks and weeks and weeks. Then he just pushed it out through this membrane [during shooting].

Reflecting is homework. Using your imagination and imagining the story and your character: it's outlining the facts and ideas that occur to you.

Reflecting includes study/analysis of the play's given circumstances and the character.

Start your prompt book

Prompt books have been used by actors for centuries. I recall picking up the prompt book of Edwin Booth's *Hamlet* when I was working on a one-person show based on his life. Seeing the penciled notes along the margins was emotionally charged and helped me feel more connected to him and our profession's legacy.

The prompt book contains your script with room in the margins or on the back of each page for notes. These notes will be blocking notes, your thoughts about character, character activities, actions, substitution ideas, or even personal motivators alongside your lines in the script.

It's also the book where most everything lands during the course of your entire rehearsal process. It can be your diary of role evolution. It can be the place where all of the dramaturg's research notes get stashed. It'll be where you'll keep your director's notes that are given you during previews.

It is the bucket that my friend Cain Devore refers to, because it's where everything ends up and where you turn for review.

In addition to this larger book, it's good to have a smaller second copy of the script from which you memorize and carry with you during blocking rehearsals. You can then transfer any spontaneous notes that you've taken while rehearsing and that will give you another session of review.

You should try to take your prompt book with you all the time (or a smaller version) in case an idea strikes you or you see something during your day that could contribute to your work on the character.

Story fact sheet

Marjorie Hayes (University of North Texas) created a very thorough Play/Character outline (researched from *Influence Your Behavior* by Clurman, Fran, Hodge, and Barton and a character analysis outline adapted from Robert Barton's *Acting, On Stage and Off)*.

With her permission, I have included it here (along with occasional comments of my own, in italics).

I. PLAY ANALYSIS

A. SYNOPSIS OF THE PLAY: Describe what happens in three sentences.

B. STYLE:

1 Type of play (drama, melodrama, satire, farce, tragedy)
2 General aesthetic style of theatre (e.g., realism, romanticism, vaudeville, absurdism, Brechtian, magical realism).

C. CULTURAL CONTEXT

1 Date the play was written
2 Date play is set
3 Cultural, socio-political, historical, and/or philosophical influences in the text.

II. SCENE-BY-SCENE ANALYSIS

A. GIVEN CIRCUMSTANCES

What relevant facts and circumstances influence your behavior?
(*Who, What, When, Where, Why, and How questions*)

B. BEATS

1. The scene breaks down into the following beats:
(Generally, when the subject of the conversation changes, it's a new beat—mark it, because almost always you will make a physical and/or vocal intention change at the same time).

The givens of the play/scene by scene

Who is your character (or who do they think they are) in the scene? There are also status actions. We tend to behave differently in different situations, depending on who is in the room or watching us. Our parents bring out a different aspect of ourselves than do our friends, bosses, or people we're trying to impress, and on and on. So who is your character in each scene?

What is your character doing? What do you want? Where are you, and how do you react to their surroundings? When is it during the day and how does that affect your mood, dress, energy, on and on?

To find character, simply play the circumstances truthfully, and the character shows up!

Right now, wherever you are, reading this book—you have myriad information that I would want to know to play you effectively, including time of day, how you dress at this time of day, depending on where you are, and what you're wanting from reading this book. What else is going on with you? Worried about a relationship? Money? Grades? Getting cast? Are the concerns temporary or looming, such as graduation or unemployment?

Your actions, both physically and emotionally and the way you deliver lines, all stem from your personal subtext. Your character has them too, and that's why you're reflecting on this—coming up with a more complete world to support your actions and reactions.

Stanislavski

The Russian actor Vasili Toporkov recounts a conversation with Stanislavski about character in his book, *Stanislavski in Rehearsal*. In Kataev's play, *The Embezzlers*, Torporkov was playing the cashier, Vanechka, and had worked out many line readings for the scene they were working on.

> Stanislavski directed, "Excuse me, but you're using a certain 'tone' which you have already worked out .... " I didn't know what he was talking about. Stanislavski explained that the most valuable thing in acting is to be able to find a living person in every part, to find oneself. He continued, "You're playing a character type and not a living human being."
>
> "Tell me, what's in your office?"
>
> "I don't understand ... '
>
> "You're a cashier, so what's in your office?"
>
> "Money ... '
>
> "Yes, money. And then what? Give me more details. You say money. Fine, how much? What money? What kind? Where do you keep it? What kind of desk do you have, what kind of chair, how many lamps are there? Well, tell me how you run things."
>
> I said nothing for a long time ... and I wasn't sure why I should know all this.
>
> "You see, you don't know what's most essential about your character, his daily work. What he lives for, what his concerns are ... here we have the cashier, Vanechka, a mild modest young man. His

office is his home. It is his holy of holies. It is the best thing in his life. Everything about it reveals the nature of his concerns: the cleanliness of the place, the order in which all the things he needs for his daily work are arranged, from the large steel safe to his nice red and blue pencil, which he considers his best friend. … "

Characterization premise

I believe that characterization stems from simply pursuing your through line, fulfilling tasks, objectives, and actions that are prompted in the script and in the eyes of the person standing opposite you in the scene. Characteristics can be found in yourself, other people, and the world at large. This is good ground, good soil.

S-O-I-L

1 **Script**. The author has created these characters. You add the flesh and blood, fulfilling concrete tasks, following impulses and through actions, choosing activities, and employing honest reactions based on whatever the other actors are doing, instinct, and practice.
2 **Observation** of other people and yourself, too. You were cast because the director believes you can act the role and that you already have qualities that fit the role. Use yourself to start the characterization process. Other people: like a writer, you embody from people you know or research … characteris*tics* and behavior you've observed and will use in rehearsal.
3 **Imagination**. Characterization starts with the script, using yourself and your observation of others, and then grows from your limitless imagination to connect to your emotion. Your imagination shows you who you believe them to be, in looks and behavior. Try things.
4 **Living with them**. Take your characters into your day. Privately, behave as your character outside of rehearsal. It will enliven your ideas and discoveries. Then, publicly, assuming your character is contemporary, take him or her to the mall and buy something as your character, ask directions, cause a scene—but don't get arrested.

Remember, *you* were cast; you *are* the *character-like* human being the director was looking for. Start with yourself, your imagination, and your observation of people.

I was watching an interview about the movie *Unstoppable* with Denzel Washington on the Fox movie channel, and he had this to say about the process.

You don't have to know what's going to happen, you have to be free enough to allow that—you absorb, I'm in the people watching business.

You watch behavior and you take chunks of this and pieces of that, the script informs you of certain things, the other actor informs you of certain things, the director has things on his or her mind ....

What is it about the process I like? The process ... the opportunity to play.

Character biography

Creating a biography from the information in the text can be essential for you if it helps you to create your character's history. It's there for you to *think about* when you're on stage, just as *you* think many things during an everyday scene of your own. It's what gives you nuance and change of expression, funny ways of saying things as if you were thinking about something else. So, think about something else having to do with the story or something in your own life that somehow supports the story.

Your character needs a world of thoughts and memories that come from her or his world in the play. Here's a continuation of Marjorie Hayes' play analysis.

III. CHARACTER ANALYSIS

A CHARACTER'S PAST

Note whether your answer comes from the text with quotation marks or whether you are making an inference without quotation marks.

1 I come from:
2 My childhood was:
3 My family conditions were:
4 Experiences that made a profound and lasting impression on me were:
5 The most important given circumstances in my life are:
6 The five most powerful members of my private audience would be:
7 Crucial events that occurred prior to this scene were:
8 Conditioning forces on my scene entrance are:

B CHARACTER'S PRESENT

1 My physical description and condition is:
2 I describe myself as (quotes from the entire play):
3 Other characters describe me as (quotes from the entire play):
4 The playwright in the stage directions describes me as:
5 I describe others as:
6 How do I group other people?
7 In public situations, I tend to:

8 My physical life differs from that of the actor playing me in the following ways:
9 My vocal life differs from that of the actor playing me in the following ways:
10 My usual style of clothing and type of accessories include:
11 My most distinguishing characteristics are my:
12 My temperament could be described as:
13 My favorite things are:
14 I am most interested in:
15 I am not interested in:

C CHARACTER'S FUTURE

(*Your character's thoughts, not unlike your own, are sometimes occupied with bigger hopes and dreams than just the ones being discussed or the situation at hand.*

"What does this have to do with where I'm going?"
It can help to give your character depth, purpose, and a sense of being occupied with aspirations and feelings about his or her future—which will change your approach to the scene and objectives.)

1 How do you envision your best possible future?
2 How do you envision your worst possible future?
3 How do you envision your wildest dream come true?
4 My super-objective in the entire play is to:
5 My primary objective in this scene is to: (Restate this at the top of your script.)
6 My other significant objectives, in order of importance, are:
7 I face the following major obstacle/s:
8 Specific tactics I employ during the scene include (actions you might employ to get what you want):

D CHARACTER ABSTRACTS

1 Images and symbols that I, the character, relate to:
2 Images and symbols that the actor relates to:

E ENDOWMENT: HOW THE ACTOR (YOU) RELATED TO THE TEXT

1 Other characters: Who are they for the actor in real life? (populate your imagination—thinking about people you know as the characters in the play).
2 Events in the play that the actor relates to:
3 Place: Where is this for the actor?
4 Set pieces or props: Is there any personal significance for the actor?

The hidden story

There is a life to be discovered and enacted underneath the text, though it stems from the text. You're thinking about it, looking over your shoulder, and silently playing it alongside the actual words. It's a sense of being preoccupied. It could be physical, like having sore feet or a back ache, headache, tired, or having to go to the bathroom. It can be organic, such as I'm saying such and such but thinking of this and that, which might have something to do with another character, a later scene, or a personal character trait that you are trying to hide. However, don't indicate it or show us, unless it's a physical obstacle, in which case, keep it subtle. Simply think it and feel it, and the audience will see it.

Subtext

However, unlike the hidden story, subtext has to do with exactly what's underneath what you're saying, why you're saying it, and what you hope to achieve by saying it. If you were to speak it aloud (a good exercise), it might be something very different from the line. It's what you're thinking. In other words, the line may be, "Would you like another drink?" However, your subtext is really, "Would you like to spend the night?"

16 On your feet and in your sleep

More rehearsal techniques

Actions three and four

> It's a cathedral of acting. You're there to be specific and the details are what the art is about, which is what some people have said, it's in the details—if you're gonna be a tomato, you can't just say tomato. Are you a beefsteak tomato, a little green one, what kind of a tomato are you? Is it young, is it hard?
>
> What can a tomato do and what can it not? This is what we're taught. I mean I swear by it to this day … and actors understand it. Now you go out into the world and get a job, and they say, okay tomato, you move over there and you say, No … I don't have legs; and then that's where the imagination starts, maybe I can roll. …
>
> —Dustin Hoffman, *Inside the Actors Studio*

I was once auditioning for a commercial to sell grass fertilizer. I hadn't done many commercial auditions because, at the time, I considered myself a classical actor, and so I felt slightly humiliated at the possibility of being seen in a green grass suit. However, as I sat outside the casting office with the script in my hand, I began thinking about how to play a blade of grass that envied the lawn next door. It was fuller, greener, and healthier than me.

I thought about the givens.

I must be grass that's brown, dry, and thirsty. I am probably angry at my homeowner for letting me deteriorate and sort of embarrassed by being shorter, discolored, and even itchy!

I suddenly had a character and was able to justify my audition as a pretty cool acting lesson in how to play an angry, jealous, thirsty, itchy, and pissed-off blade of grass! As Mr. Hoffman says, it's what we do, whether for a commercial or a scene in Hamlet. It's in the details, and these are the weeks you really begin finding them.

Responding

Active work

The following techniques are categorized by the physical, the mental, and the emotional or spiritual aspects of our work.

Physical

Prior to working on the play, as in *Lectio*, it is important to engage in a *transitional* activity that takes one from the normal state of mind to a more creative state.

This could be a change of clothing, getting to the rehearsal space early so that you have time to warm up, do some breathing exercises or stretches, a little time looking over the scene you'll be working on.

Warm-up

Practicing the art of getting ready to work, your body will recognize this as a normal experience in getting ready to create. If you practice this at the beginning of rehearsals and throughout, it will calm you for your performance phase during previews and opening and the run.

Use yourself

With all of the notes that you've taken on the character's past, present, attributes, and ways that you're alike or different, you still need to start walking and talking the words of the script as yourself but in the situation (given circumstances) of the character.

As mentioned in reflecting, remember, *you* were the one cast. You are the person most character-like that the director was looking for, or at the very least the one who the director trusts can play it.

Take the pressure off trying to be somebody else. Begin playing the given circumstances with commitment and honesty, and the character will begin to emerge. All of the reflecting you have done on their past, present, and attributes will contribute to your choices little by little as you pursue your through-action in rehearsal, one moment at a time.

> The script sits in front of you—I come along, I pick it up, the words come into my eyes, my mind and my body … it flows around and then the part becomes a part of me.
>
> —Peter O'Toole, Charlie Rose interview

Film actor James Cagney put it less romantically: "Plant your feet, look into their eyes and mean it."

Rehearsing the scene

As students when you are (or were) assigned a scene, you are generally faced with the dilemma of creating your own rehearsal process in preparation for presenting it to the class. I advise my own students to read the play, begin their prompt book of ideas and questions, read the scene every morning and every night, and work with their scene partner at least three times a week and:

1. Read and discuss the play, then discuss the scene: what's happening, who are you, what do you want? Read and discuss other scenes between your characters.
2. Arrange the setting where the scene takes place.
3. Begin to move around the set, script in hand, repeating the scene simply while you focus on talking to each other.
4. Go over the scene completely in your own words with the basic sense of the scene.
5. Get off-book.
6. Repeat your scene off-book for security and continue to try different moves or simplify your blocking. Follow your instincts. Everything is okay: there isn't a right way. Add activities and props if they're consistent with what your character might be doing.
7. Introduce a few techniques to the scene (explained more fully later in this chapter). You've already done it in your own words; now try a (Meisner) repetition exercise. Say your line, then your partner repeats it as a question; say your line again in answer and so on, four or five times until he or she says his or her actual line and then you ask it as a question, and so on.
8. Subtext through: Say your line and then, before your partner says her or his actual line, he or she says what he or she is really thinking in response to your line; you hear it but react only once his or her actual line is said; to which you respond with what you're really thinking before you say your actual line in response, and so on.
   Often, the thinking out loud will change your reading of the actual line in such a way that it forces you out of a generalized "line reading."
9. Extremes: Try running the scene, and surprise yourself and your partner with different approaches: quieter, angrier, indifferent, or confused. You're still playing intentions and following your objective, but there are many ways to ask for things, and you're still experimenting.
10. Time change: If it's a three-minute scene, take ten minutes to do it, see what happens and how you fill the space. Then take two minutes to do it; see what happens if you charge through it.

11 Improvise the scene: Say your chosen *theme lines* often, out of context, along with your actual lines to keep the driven reasons for the scene cooking. Just throw them in there whenever you feel like it.
12 Repeat the actual scene five times in a particular rehearsal, without much discussion between; just see what happens, not trying to do it the same way, and just stay open to what you want to do over the course of five run-throughs.
13 Dress it, using all the props and the costume pieces you've chosen; ask a friend or two to watch.
14 Present it in class.

Five one-hour rehearsal sessions

In Alice Spivak's *How to Rehearse When There Is No Rehearsal, Acting and the Media* (2007), she introduces a five-hour rehearsal sequence for a five-minute scene used in her Technique One class at HB Studios in New York. The following is a brief and condensed version of her impressive sequence (pp. 54–59):

1 1st rehearsal hour: Discuss the play and talk about the story. Label it according to where it comes in the story: this is the scene where he or she does what? Read aloud to one another, looking up as much as possible with no obligation to act but rather imparting the information of the lines to one another. Do this first reading as many times as you wish, becoming more and more familiar with the text and one another. It's simple communication. Begin to discuss the circumstances of the time (past, present, and future), prior relationship, your objectives, and activities.
2 2nd session: Set up the physical place and bring in the props as you begin to move around the space, finding your blocking, not worried about picking up cues but keeping in touch with the other actor(s). End the session with another first reading as in the first hour.
3 3rd session: Divide the scene into three equal parts (a minute-and-a-half to two minutes), rehearsing each part for relationship, inner objectives, and activities until comfortable enough to move on. Script is still in hand, but probably lines are starting to stick. The scoring of the script (beats) can be noted more specifically in this rehearsal.
4 4th session: Use the same procedure as the third session—three parts, one at a time, only now put the script down and refer to it only as needed. Blocking begins to form spontaneously but not set; activities may change, and you may start and stop, but always be occupied with the ever-deepening primary objective.

5 5th session: A dress rehearsal, going over the scene as many times as possible.

Script in hand connection

More and more professionals are beginning to enter rehearsals nearly off-book or close to being fully memorized. However, most actors still prefer to learn the script more organically, after working with the other actors and while they associate early blocking motions with their lines.

Regardless of when and how you learn your lines, as you're learning them, remember to look up from the page as often as possible and connect with your scene partner(s). It's assumed that you can read the scene, but what you're discovering is how to communicate what you want and need. Once again, this is rehearsal and not the performance, so generally there's no need to worry about pace and pauses. Take them, size up the situation, and look into your partner's eyes after and during your line. And when it's not your line, look up from the script and listen by looking at your partner. You're searching for the truth in the scene, and you just can't do it with your head buried in the script, but while you have it in your hand, make it secondary to what you're looking to do.

Character warm-up

Prepare your body and voice for the particular needs of your character. Do they automatically have *your* body or have you found reasons to look and sound differently than you. New rhythms of movement and speech will take practice outside of official rehearsal and possibly special warm-ups in preparation for rehearsal. Before a performance, maybe you like to run through the first scene or two in a found space before the show. You may have discovered an improvisation during rehearsal that gives you the right trigger to begin feeling and thinking in your character's mood and story line. The actual words of your character can go a long way to prepare you for entering his or her thoughts.

Character object exercise

In *Respect for Acting*, Uta Hagen introduces a simple two-minute object exercise that asks the actor to perform two minutes of a daily task in the studio, realistically. It should answer all of the given circumstances simply by rehearsing the two minutes up to two hours so that every move, thought, action, and activity in completing the task is practiced to the point of being able to repeat it honestly and believably in public. The actor should actually experience the two minutes on stage.

It's also a good characterization exercise that you can do on your own.

Choose an activity that your character might engage in during her or his day and practice it over and over until you feel that you've mastered a particular activity or minute in her or his day. This could be getting ready for bed, filling a pipe, sitting down to supper, shining shoes, reading a book, or writing a letter. As that character, just do it. It might even work its way into the play in some way.

Spontaneous reactions

There will also be times when you can't help yourself but react spontaneously to what the other actor does in rehearsal. Sometimes it's inappropriate to your character but, more times than not, it's a great moment to keep. Use it to further the action of the scene.

When I was rehearsing the role of Mercutio from *Romeo and Juliet* at the Folger Theater in Washington, D.C., Ed Gero as Tybalt entered the scene and said something in a way that struck me as funny, and so I laughed during the rehearsal, at which point Ed laughed too, and the laughter kept growing until everyone on stage was laughing. This came during the confrontation between Mercutio and Tybalt, which at first would have seemed inappropriate, as we're mortal enemies in a high-pressured and nervous situation. However, it totally worked, especially in antithesis to the insults and sword fight that was about to take place. What began as a rehearsal reaction stemmed from something honest, and so it fed the antagonistic relationship in an unexpected but truthful way.

In your own words

This technique is often used in rehearsing Shakespeare but works equally well in contemporary plays or even movie scripts. It is simply a translation of the text into your own words to get initially close to owning them in the way that you would say them.

Very recently, one of my students was practicing Tom's final monologue from Tennessee Williams's *The Glass Menagerie*. He was having trouble with the first line: "I didn't go to the moon, I went much further, for time is the longest distance between two places."

> "I hate this first line," he said. "It throws me right out of the play every time, it's so stupid."
>
> "Well, how would you say it? Try saying it in your own words, what do you mean by that line? How would you put it?"

He stood behind the three chairs we had placed in the middle of the room to serve as a fire escape ... he stared at the floor for a long time, thinking (also a good thing for Tom to do in that final moment of reflection and regret).

Finally, he looked up and said sort of haltingly as if he was saying it for the first time with a lot of history, hesitation and regret, "I didn't go anywhere; I just went to a lot of cities and stared at the same spot." More silence and looking at the floor.

"Well, that was very believable, now, think of it that way, and try the original line again in much the same way you said your own line."

He said the original line, keeping his thought process, the stare at the floor, sense of regret and hesitations. He owned it this time through. It's just a simple adjustment technique that can help get at your sense of the meaning and *talking* with the words instead of reciting them.

Costume your character

Start putting together your costume trunk for rehearsal. Actors through the centuries have been responsible to have their own costumes for roles that they often played. Today, the actor needs a costume collection as well, for rehearsal. Specifically, you won't be getting your costuming until late in the process, although you might be provided shoes. So consider what kind of clothes your character might be wearing and find some approximations to wear during rehearsal. The costume rendering they show you at the beginning of rehearsal will give you the idea. Borrow and buy whatever clothes you need to approximate the costume you'll be wearing in the show. It will take you a step further into characterization.

In general, it's a good idea to begin collecting all manner of clothing that could fit many genres of theatre. Thrift stores and vintage clothing stores are perfect places to shop for interesting clothing that could get you through a rehearsal period for plays that are set from 1850 until now. For earlier periods, keep an eye out for season-ending theatre sales. They often try to thin out their stock of props and costumes, and you should be there trying things on for your costume trunk.

Sotto voce

When actors are stepping on stage with their scene or character for the first time, I will often ask you to "*take it off the stage.*" In other words, this is a small space, he's standing right in front of you, it's very early in rehearsal, just talk to him. No need to reach the back of a 600-seat auditorium today. And really, no need to do it until later in the process. I find that young actors and pros alike have a built-in habit of projecting their lines early on, and it sounds (and usually is) "fakey," like recitations instead of conversations.

Repetition exercises (known as the Meisner technique)

This is one example of a technique for finding immediacy in your reasons for saying a line and reasons for responding to a line that can rattle the lines away from any obvious delivery habits. Some directors may incorporate repetition exercises in rehearsal but, generally, you will probably have to find a time when you and your scene partner can do it on your own. It is just this kind of commitment to working on your own that will make the difference in your performance. I have interpreted the technique in the following manner:

Say your line with intention and meaning. Your partner repeats your line as a question. Say your line again as an answer to that question. Your partner repeats your same line as a question again and you repeat the sequence four or five times until your partner says his or her next line, and you repeat that line back and forth in the same manner four or five times until you speak your next line and so on.

The key here is to really be present, attentive, speaking the line with its intention and asking the question as if saying, "Is this what you said, really? Am I really *getting* what you said?"

Really?
Really.
Really?
Really!

Such as:

Actor A: Do you want a cup of coffee?
Actor B: Do I want a cup of coffee?
A: Do you want a cup of *coffee?*
B: Do I want a cup of *coffee*?
A: Do *you want a cup of coffee!*
B: *Do I want a cup of coffee??!!*
A: DO—YOU—WANT—A—CUP of COFFEE!?
B: Do I want a cup of COFFEE??!!
A: Do you want a cup of coffee?
[Move onto the next line]
B: Yeah, I'll have a cup.

A: Yeah? You'll have a cup?
B: Yeah. I'll have a *cup*.
A: Yeah? You'll have a cup?!
B: Yeah—I'll—have—a cup!
A: Yeah? You'll—have—a cup??!!
B: Yeah, I'll have a cup.
A: Yeah? You'll have a cup?

Continue. The point being that you connect, speak, ask, reply, ask again, reply again and again and again with intention and response to what you've just received.

Psychological gestures (known as the Michael Chekhov technique)

Physical manifestation: Michael Chekhov has taught that the way into a character is not through analytical understanding but physical. Define the essence of your character, and then find a gesture or movement that defines that essence. Find a physical representation that is strong and exemplary of their most primal nature. This will give you a way into unconsciously understanding and portraying their essence even at first acquaintance. From his book, *To The Actor*:

> Ask yourself what the main desire of the character might be, and when you get an answer, even if it is only a hint, start to build your psychological gesture step by step, using at first your hand and arm only. You might thrust them forward aggressively, clenching your fist, if the desire reminds you of grasping or catching (greed, avarice); or you might stretch them out slowly and carefully, with reserve and caution, if the character wishes to grope or search in a thoughtful and diffident manner; or you might direct both your hands and arms upward, lightly and easily, with palms open, in case your intuition prompts that the character wants to receive, to implore, to beseech with awe … now you continue developing the psychological gesture, correcting and improving it, adding to it all the qualities you find in the character, slowly leading it to the stage of perfection.

Physically finding a symbolic manifestation is a terrific exploration, and you can try it without anyone's approval or suggestions. You'll be working from instinct and experimentation. It's another piece of the puzzle to forming your character.

The actors around you

> My breakthrough was: I realized I could always learn from the actors around me. If I could do that, there would be no end to what can be learned in rehearsal. And I learned that in the last hours of the rehearsal process, so I also discovered that great things can be discovered all the way up to the last minute of rehearsal. Never think you are done rehearsing.
>
> —Andy Prosky, actor

To reinforce this simple technique of watching what everyone else is doing, I repeat the words of the great Chita Rivera as she worked on *Kiss of the Spider Woman*, for which she won a Tony:

> For instance, back to *Spider Woman*, I really found my character through watching Brent Carver! (Molina). So, you find so much, you've just got to be, not in just your scene, you've got to be in all the scenes in order to know what the entire play is about, which eventually comes around to what you're about.

Expand the text

Whether you are alone or in the rehearsal room, you can get at what you're really saying by expanding and expounding as you go through, literally making up words that further amplify your intentions. This is rehearsal. Introduce your need for this improvisation to your scene partner and the director, and then add whatever lines you need to say exactly what you mean with your lines.

Extend the scene

As you're going over your scene for review, something else may occur to you. You'll feel like leaving the words in the scene and continuing the thought with more words, extended words and thoughts … let it happen. Soon, you'll find yourself in an extended scene that begins to further flesh out your character's ideas and way of thinking. It will further inform the words in the script with the fact that they could go on if you let them.

It's not unlike the follow through of a great golf swing … the ball has been struck already, but you follow through with the momentum of the swing … the momentum of the line. It's as if the film director does not say "cut" once the scene is through. The actor's job is to keep going.

Riffing (short repeated phrase) the character theme

When directing a scene, I occasionally ask an actor what is the essence or central theme of her or his scene. Put it in a phrase. Not unlike the psychological gesture, it's a one-phrase summation of your character's intention. Say it aloud.

It should be simple and direct, such as: "I want to change!" or "Why don't you believe me?!" "I can't trust you" or "I love you so much." Whatever the scene, find the essence of what you mean and, occasionally, throw that in along with your other lines; it can be an line from the scene itself.

Examples could include the Isabella/Claudio scene in Shakespeare's *Measure for Measure*. Claudio could repeat to his sister, "*Let me live*," interspersed throughout the scene. It will amplify his desperation. Afterward, take the theme line out of the scene, of course, but play what you found when you used it.

Independent activities

If I ever meet actor Dustin Hoffman, there is one question I want to ask him.

> During your Academy Award winning performance in *Kramer vs. Kramer*, who put the cookie on the counter that you grabbed as you were exiting the kitchen after that scene with your son?

I am convinced that a props person did not put it there and that he had to have asked or even brought cookies into the scene himself. It was just that little bit of business that communicated "home," demonstrating with an activity that he really lived in that apartment. It fit the character and the moment. You have to think outside the box, outside the confines of the written scene, and create the world that your character lives in.

Ron Leibman made an impression on me with character activities in his portrayal of Herb in Neil Simon's *I Ought to be in Pictures* on Broadway. The scene takes place on a Sunday morning, and Herb enters to find his estranged daughter waiting for him in the kitchen. As the scene begins, it's not in the script, but he is carrying a copy of what appears to be *The New York Times* and, automatically, one by one, throws unwanted sections into the trash can while beginning the scene with his daughter.

There are hundreds of independent activities you can find that will further amplify character qualities or characteristics. Actor Casey Biggs introduced me to the idea of independent activities when he told me he was playing a lawyer opposite actress Delta Burke. He decided he wanted to be distracted and busy during the scene. So, as the type of guy with never enough time, he asked for a hot dog that he could eat during their conversation on the street, as he readied himself for the case. So, here was his upscale well-dressed lawyer, about to engineer a big defense, casually eating his hot dog, wiping his mouth, brushing off crumbs, and speaking between bites, adding characteristic dimension to the relationship, character, and mind-set.

Dan Southern chose an independent activity for one of his films:

> Pick a bit of business that keeps you in the scene and focuses you there, hit your mark and say the lines. I had decided my character was really stunted with the emotional make-up of a 10 year old. There was a scene where two guys walk into my living room to find me watching TV. I brought a bag of M&Ms to the set and played the scene sorting the candies out by color, and throwing all the brown ones as if they were hand grenades or little bombs at the TV, making the sound effects of the bombs exploding, etc. Again, one take. This was also very frustrating as, inevitably, a better choice would occur to you after the one take and you'd suggest it but the answer was always the same, "It's in the can, baby. Next."

These are almost always actor-generated, though attention needs to be paid to whether they add to the scene or distract. Smoking a cigarette and looking for your matches is one thing … leaving it smoldering in an ash tray is a scene stealer. When you are thorough about the givens of a scene and answer the questions about what your character might otherwise be doing, *if the scene wasn't there*, you begin to see what independent activities they might be doing.

Interrupting

Once when I was auditioning for an understudy role for a Broadway production of *A Long Day's Journey Into Night*, the director, Jonathan Miller, showed me what he had done with the script. He said that actors are always yellowing their scripts on their own lines so that they don't begin speaking until it's their turn. Instead he had them begin speaking their own lines three or four lines before their scene partner had finished speaking. He insisted that it was more realistic.

When I saw the show, it was very interesting to see actors beginning their next speech before the other actor was finished. It gave the scene urgency and immediacy, even though you couldn't always follow the exchange. Playwright Eugene O'Neill may have hated this version but, as a rehearsal technique, it heightens the listening and intentions.

This technique is used very sparingly and only in rehearsal or concert with the playwright for performance purposes. If the playwright wanted overlapping, he or she would have written it that way.

Occasionally it happens by accident, when you don't exactly know your cue, but as an experiment, warn your fellow actor and director that you intend to shake up the lines and let your responses happen more immediately and as soon as the thought for them enters your head, before your cue. With overlapping, once you drop it, you'll find yourself wanting to speak, attempting to speak, waiting to speak, which is giving you active thought and responses without the boring waiting routine that is often the case when an actor is too dutiful of beginning her or his line *only* after the partner is finished.

Physical choice

This is something physical that cues you into the character and the through line of the character's objective. In Chapter 18, "Actor's block," several professionals describe how choosing a particular physical ailment or costume helped them to discover their character or scene. Actually depending on the given circumstances to inform you of your character's situation and your own biographical sketch of the person, you will undoubtedly discover many physical attributes that change the way your character approaches his or her story. Try things on for size in rehearsal.

Just do it

"Just do it." I'm a closeted fan of the Nike school of acting, coined by actor/playwright and friend, Barry Mulholland. I believe that simply doing what the character does and saying what the character says with *empathy*, *commitment*, *and imagination* will transport the actor into his or her skin.

Remember my grad student who was studying the role of Laura in Tennessee Williams's *The Glass Menagerie*? She read about production history, the life of the author, and the world of St. Louis during the time of the play. However, when it came time to step into Laura's shoes in the rehearsal room, she froze. "Now what do I do," she said. "I have all this information, but I don't know who she is or how to play her! I don't know what to do."

So, how would you know who she is? Simply do what she says and do what she does in the play. Do that with intention and empathy. *That's her*.

Again, ask yourself: What would somebody need to know to play me? If I were the character and you were going to play me, would knowing that I was born in Indiana bring you closer to reacting like me? Do you need to know what was happening in Indiana the year I was born? I certainly didn't know what was happening even though it could have affected the way my father treated me, if he was out of work and pressured. That's back story, however. What I say and how I react over and over (in the script) will begin giving you the important clues to my temperament, mind-set, and objectives.

Rehearse me first and foremost from what I say and do in the script. Try *just doing it* and trust that the audience will see it. This is the approach that will get you into the water.

Private time on set

Whether on a darkened half-built room on a television set or the stage, lit only by the house lights during a break or after hours, I have found that a private rehearsal in the actual space to be very valuable. Obviously, you're going through your lines without anyone giving you cues or prompting your reactions, but the very act of walking through your words and actions benefits not only from the repetition but by doing so in the actual space. It creates a mental familiarity from which to be more at home when you engage later, and ignites your imagination at the same time.

You should find that after walking through your lines, blocking, actions, and activities many times alone, new thoughts and impulses begin to prompt you and even deepen your understanding of the scene. Again, it's purely an imaginative exercise, as you need the flesh and blood of your mates to prompt your reactions, but it's good ground work.

Your imagination has filled in the world around you and, therefore, it is not a false run through but a supported practice on the set.

I was playing a priest in a daytime soap opera in Los Angeles and was to baptize Sonny's newborn son. We rehearsed in the rehearsal room that morning, surrounded only by tables and chairs as the director choreographed the movements and camera angles. We were probably four hours from the taping and so after makeup and costuming, I walked up onto the darkened church set, complete with pews, platform altar, and simulated stained glass windows and walked through the scene, holding the imaginary baby while pouring imaginary water onto his little forehead from the imaginary chalice. By the time the church was filled with extras, the regulars from the show, the crew, and cameras, I had been through the scene on the set four or five times and was completely at home in the space, as if they were now entering *my* rehearsal room.

Hand recorder

In this case, like DeNiro and many actors, a hand recorder records your ideas as they come to you and can be transferred later.

Home space

I like to arrange my home or hotel space in a configuration similar to that of the set, so that while at home, I can walk through my remember-throughs in the same manner as our blocking rehearsal.

Since childhood, I have always been nervous about standing and speaking in front of a large group of people. When I played Tom in Tennessee Williams's *The Glass Menagerie*, I had to face the audience in direct address several times during the show. So, even though I would be *in character*, it still brought back intimidating memories from childhood memorization contests that would scare me for weeks on end.

Tom was written to stand on top of the fire escape staring out at the 600 people below and deliver several long monologues about the state of the world and his own life. At the apartment that the theatre had provided, there was a raised bedroom loft space overlooking the rest of the apartment. In my mind's eye, I filled the place with the audience, stood on top of that bedroom balcony, and found the essence of those speeches night after night after night, soon erasing childhood fears because I knew these lines like my mother's face.

While rehearsing Arthur Miller's *The Price* in Washington, D.C., I arranged the basement space of our home to resemble the tiny attic space where the play takes place. It was in our basement where I became most familiar with the blocking of the play. There just isn't enough time during the official rehearsal to imprint the moves and familiarize your brain with why you move, where you go, and the hundred little hesitations and thoughts that get you there.

Overnight review

A given: Always run through the day's work again at night before the next day to further set your discoveries in your mind and body memory. If you rehearse at night, walk through your previous night's work first thing the next morning.

Move through review

There are times when all you need is a brief repetition walk through of the blocking. Like a choreographed dance, walk out the moves of the day's blocking … without lines or characterization, simply review the moves. Add lines after you've scored the blocking correctly.

Extremes

Try your scene as you feel it could/should be played and then pump it up in the same direction × 10 or × 100! My mentor James Young was awfully fond of saying, "It needs a thousand per cent more!" Today, we almost always hear a director repeating the phrase "the stakes need to be higher." So, as Gregg Mitchell would say, "Go for it, full tilt!"

The director can always bring you back to a more normal rendering; in the meantime, pump it up. Then the next time through, take it in the opposite direction for fun: just do it, just try it, just play your character shy if the time before you played him or her outrageous.

Then, interestingly enough, you may find aspects of each extreme that you can use in the characterization. I would say that the most common direction I have heard over the years from directors to actors in general is to play the scene with higher stakes … to take the scene more toward the extreme, assuring the actor that they will bring her or him back to something more subtle if necessary.

Repeating scenes—keeping green

I feel that the best directors have always wanted to repeat the work on a scene before moving on to the next one. I resisted this as a young actor because it was hard. I would work through a scene the first time and usually feel relieved when we moved on to the next one. However, in spite of myself, whenever we immediately repeated what we had just finished, the scene always deepened, and we would find even better moments.

Joe Dowling was directing a production of *Julius Caesar* at The Shakespeare Theatre in Washington, D.C. I was playing Mark Antony and it was time to do the forum scene: "Friends, Romans, countrymen, lend me your ears. …" It is a very long scene involving a mob of angry citizens who have just given rousing allegiance to Brutus, one of Caesar's assassins. Now it's my turn to convince them that Brutus and the conspirators are in the wrong.

The first time through was tenuous, off-book, forgetting lines, melodramatic, and not knowing where and when to move where and when. "Let's do it again," said Joe, with only a few suggestions. So, off we went, finding our feet a bit with an idea or two popping through the memory-run of what we had just done. Joe had earlier dropped the bombshell in rehearsal that he didn't like anything done the same way twice, especially in rehearsal but also that the flexibility would also be encouraged in performance! So we were all scrambling to find pieces of blocking that we could hang our hat on and yet recreate the scene again and again. We did the forum scene a third time, getting a few notes afterward, and I thought, "Finally! A cup of coffee and a break." Finding your way through such a gigantic scene the first time can be stressful, and I was grateful to be finished with the first go at the impossible speech in what felt like an impossible scene.

"Want to do it again?" Joe said, smiling. This rehearsal must have had my name on it. We took a minute and then did it a fourth time! By now, I had made the mistakes already and there was no need to feel shy about trying things. We were encouraged to experiment, so there wasn't any pressure to perform, and the scene began to take on a life of its own.

Citizens were bolder to shout responses to my every line. At one point, I picked up the substitute cloak of Caesar's, which had been slit with holes representing his wounds, and it occurred to me to place it on one of the citizen's shoulders as I continued the speech. The room fell silent, and a moment was born. We later compared it to someone handing you the coat of John Kennedy after his assassination. This was the fourth time through, and we were still finding new moments and repeating what had been learned already. The cloak moment lasted the entire run of the show, and it was placed on a different actor every night.

There's always time for that cup of coffee, but it's rare when a director asks for a fourth go of the scene. For me, Joe was the epitome of a collaborative director and took all the time needed to secure a scene in the actor's heart and mind.

I became a believer in running a scene as often as a director will allow, and often ask if we can *do it again*, rather than being relieved that the first awkward work-through is over. However, if the director doesn't repeat it on the same day, find a space and do it yourself. You can do it alone, just for memory, but usually new ideas and acting breakthroughs have a way of sneaking into the repetition work anyway.

Al Pacino's interview in *Playboy*:

> After 70 performances of *Richard*, something started to happen. A scene that I thought I would never get or understand, I began to understand. I knew that there was a lot I had to learn. That's why I can't wait to get back on the stage. See, repetition is a big thing with me. That's technique, repeating. Someone once said, "Repetition keeps me green." I like that saying.

Practice your character in real-life situations

I worked with actor Ray Reinhardt in a production of Arthur Miller's *The Price* in Vienna, Austria; he told me the story of a difficult situation with his cable company and how he adopted a character that he was playing to affect a result in a real-life situation:

> I was on the phone trying to get through and they were giving me a hard time, so I used a Russian accent and it gave me the freedom and

permission to say ridiculous things. Like, "I vant speak supervisor, you telling me, please I'm holding, and I'm holding and nobody says answers za phone, and a voice says hang up and dial again—I do, I dial again and I get no satisfaction.

"So please, I vant now, right now, please, vat's your name, please, huh, give me supervisor, I'm tired of vaiting, thanks you very much …" it was very direct and very aggressive. It helped.

Practice them outside rehearsal

In *Words About My Father*, Edwin Booth wrote about the technique of his famous actor father, Junius Brutus Booth:

> Whatever the part he had to personate, he was from the time of its rehearsal until he slept at night imbued with its very essence. If Othello was billed for the evening he would, perhaps wear a crescent pin in his breast that day; or if Shylock was to be his part at eight, he was a Jew all day, and if in Baltimore at the time, he would pass hours with a learned Israelite, who lived nearby, discussing Hebrew in the vernacular and insisting that, although he was of Welsh descent, that his nation is of Hebrew origin, a belief for which there is some foundation.

Speed-through review

If you learn the lines in a slow manner, getting them right and perhaps delivering them with a specific rhythm, don't be surprised if they are stored in your brain at exactly that pace, especially during the early rehearsal period. So, to have them at your command whenever and however you need them, practice speed-through sessions of the scene and your monologues. Sealing them into your brain at a faster pace will have them rushing at you during the scene, for you to deliver them however the moment dictates or changes. Often late in rehearsal, directors will run what's known as an *Alitalian*, or speed-through of the show. These can be hilarious as you're running the play at breakneck speed, but they are best when done with great speed that also includes accurate blocking and intentions, obviously heightened by the speed; but keep the rhythms, too. You can run them on your own to further solidify lines and security.

Mental

Substituting

Actress Susan Greenhill played Laura in our production of *The Glass Menagerie* at Stage West in Massachusetts. Once, she was asked by the director what she was thinking about during a particular moment. Susan relayed to me later that she was imagining a roach in her lap! This gave Susan the sense of fright and anxiety at the moment she learned that the gentleman caller was coming to her house. Susan said that she assumed that the director was expecting her to respond with "Laura's thoughts" rather than her actor thoughts, which she was using to convey Laura's anxiety.

Thinking in character

Perhaps the most underestimated and under-rehearsed secret to believable acting is thinking. I don't mean thinking about the mechanics of the scene but about what's inside the scene, as the character would consider them … including subtext and the reactions that are not written.

I have occasionally stopped a scene in class and asked, "What are you thinking about? What *do you want* to make happen right now?" Whenever I've asked this, my students have assumed that I want them to tell me some pertinent fact about the play or the character's circumstance in that particular moment. However, the scene is not about the facts; it's about thought-driven actions. What prompts me to ask is usually behavior that appears to be driven by the blocking of a scene rather than the human needs of the person.

The rehearsal exists to explore the character's story and the ways you are finding how to do it. Obvious, I know, but actors often make the mistake of trying to do something perfect before ever experimenting with other possible inroads to the character.

What do *you* think about in rehearsal and in performance? Are you thinking about your next line or where to move? Are you wondering whether what you're doing is effective and whether the director or other actors will be impressed? Does the audience seem restless and you wonder whether you should speed up the scene? Are you pissed off at what your scene partner is doing and you can't believe he or she changed the blocking?! Are you congratulating yourself when a section of dialogue goes well?

Obviously, fleeting thoughts about lines, blocking, and reactions to unexpected changes are all a part of your craft. However, allowing yourself to focus your thoughts on what you want and how to get it is "the stuff" that begins creating character and maximizes your rehearsal.

One of the best descriptions of thinking in character was told to me by New York actress and CUA professor Marietta Hedges when referring to *The Warrior* by Jack Gilhooley. The play tells the story of Tammy, a veteran of the Iraq war, who is back home dealing with posttraumatic stress disorder.

> Because of the previous reads I was going into rehearsal with a lot of knowledge about the play and the character—far more than what

an actor normally has when starting rehearsal process. Despite this I was determined to approach the rehearsal just like any other—meaning I wanted to explore the character, experiment with choices and collaborate fully with the artistic team.

But early on I began to encounter some trouble. During read throughs and table work I felt relaxed and free. I looked forward to getting on my feet and the physical freedom I'd have as I was already somewhat off book. But as soon as I got on my feet I was in trouble. I felt nervous, tense and self-conscious. As one who struggles with physical tension and a considerable amount of stage fright, I was not too concerned as I recognized this as a familiar part of my process. I always go through something like this early on, usually because I am just getting to know my fellow actors and directors. But in this instance, I had already worked with and performed with this team. We were all very comfortable with each other and it was the strength of my performance that had been the determining factor in the theater's decision to produce the show. So what was going on? I felt like I was going through the motions of acting but I was not present in the role. I was observing myself from the outside and was having trouble motivating what I was doing. I was just reciting lines rather than speaking for a reason.

The director stopped the rehearsal and gave me a note that is so basic that we actors often overlook it or just plain forget to do it. He told me to think in character. It was a light bulb moment for two reasons: first because I felt that I had been given back the key to my spontaneity and creativity; and secondly because I teach acting and this is one of the fundamentals that I consistently stress. How could I, who tell students every day "think in character," have forgotten to do this myself during rehearsal?

As soon as we went back to the beginning of the play I could feel the difference. I was focused, I was more relaxed and when I spoke, there was a reason and a need to communicate. Thinking in character continued to help me all through rehearsal and into performance. It anchored me in my character and was effective in combating performance anxiety as I could think my character's thought rather than thinking about the audience or my performance.

The more I thought in character, the better able I was to "raise the stakes" and invest in my character's circumstances. I also found that my character's thought became habitual for me; I thought the same thoughts at the same places night after night. I could re-live Tammy's circumstances through thinking her thoughts. It's what I tell my students—don't repeat work but find it again—live it again in the moment.

Back story

Actor Sherman Howard:

> Several years ago, as my wife, Donna Bullock, and I were preparing to play Beatrice and Benedick, we discovered several oblique passages in text that suggested to us the likelihood that Beatrice and Benedick had been previously attached in a romantic relationship which had ended badly. This possibility piqued our imaginations. … What could have previously occurred between the two of them to have incited such bitter, vitriolic antipathy as is reflected in their first encounter in the play?
>
> Donna and I gleefully set about constructing a romantically torturous, on-again, off-again saga of passionate expectations, dashed hopes, miscommunication, and mutual disappointments that extended all the way back to their adolescence. The culminating blow to their failed romance had been a letter which Benedick had written to Beatrice on the eve of a battle in which he was certain that he would die. In a mortal epiphany of self-revelation, he wrote his final farewell and swore to her his eternal love, devotion, and infinite regret that his impending demise would rob them of a life together. However, the next day, when he survived the battle, he simply went on his merry way, enjoying the carefree life of a mercenary. Meanwhile, poor Beatrice had spent six months weeping over his final letter, mourning his tragic death … before she discovered that he was still roaming the world, drinking and whoring like an aging juvenile! The entire story was wonderfully vivid in each of our imaginations, cast with people we knew and envisioned in exquisite detail.

Populate your imagination

Another experience Sherman Howard related, many years ago, was about rehearsing Hamlet in Louisville, KY. He discovered that if he took the advice of a well-known acting instructor of his in Los Angeles, he could perform the role with much more immediacy and passion. Larry Moss instructed his students to *populate their imagination* with real people that they knew in the guise of the characters around them. Once Sherman used someone specific such as Claudius, Gertrude, Horatio, and Laertes, he said that he began to "feel and have history with them" instead of pretending those passions toward the actors playing the parts.

Subtext

When you're rehearsing a scene, it can help to begin an entire sub-scene of character thoughts and responses to what is going on around you. Instead of trying to remember what line is next or where you move, think of the sub-scene in your head and say to yourself those things that inevitably stem from what you want to happen in the scene anyway.

Sometimes, your character is actually saying what she or he wants in the text, but often, he or she will only think it and perhaps act on it, while saying something totally different.

So, which is it?

It can help to do this aloud in a rehearsal—with permission from the director—or by yourself when you're going over lines, say what's underneath the scene aloud as an extension of what you've just said or in response to what he or she has said before you say your next line. As suggested in the last chapter, unlike the hidden story, subtext has to do with exactly what's underneath what you're saying, why you're saying it, and what you hope to achieve by saying it.

Inner monologue

There is also the inner monologue going on constantly in your character's mind, just as there is one in yours, right now. What are you worried about existentially? What are you happy about? You might express an excitement about what you're having for dinner when what you're really excited about is something else that's happening in your life. You just got the job you interviewed for, and now everything is expressed with exuberance.

If I asked you to speak your inner monologue, you might launch into aspects of your life that are at the front of your brain and what you're happy about or worried about or even distracted by, such as the color of the Kleenex box across the room. Perhaps you're thinking about the immediate tasks that you have to take care of today, so you launch into a tirade about how everything is a mess in your apartment. Your script could be about the weather, but when I ask you for your inner monologue, your feelings about the state of your apartment come out, which is what's coloring your comments (text) and attitude about the weather.

Similarly, your character's inner monologue is about whatever *you invent,* which is from either the text or your imagination. Composing an inner monologue will give depth and a multi-layered reality.

It can be based in reality or, as I was told of Marlon Brando when asked what he was thinking during a particular moment while filming a scene, he said that he was translating the line into French!

The other day in class, I asked a young woman to add numbers in multiples of six during her speech. It gave her entire monologue a sense of immediacy as if she was saying it for the first time and had to think of what she was going to say next.

Visualizing

Jacques D'Amboise, best known in his youth as a star dancer in George Balanchine's New York City Ballet and later known as a choreographer and founder of the National Dance Institute, wrote an essay for *Daedalus* called "The Mind in Dance," quoted with permission here, from MIT Press (vol. 153.3. Summer 2006, pp 76–77).

> Early in the morning or on my days off, I sit in the empty auditorium, gazing at the stage. I am envisioning a variation from my repertoire, imagining, in detail, first how I will look in costume, then how I will enter the stage and from which wing. As if watching a movie, I then dance the variation in my mind the very best that I can, or even better—the leaps a foot higher, the space covered double what I have done in the past. I picture the expression on my face, the use of my arms and hands, and the speed at which I move. …
>
> At first, I run this imaginary film to rhythmic counting alone (without music, melody, theme, harmony, etc.)—creating a blueprint of mathematical time. For example, I launch into a leap on the first count (or beat), float through the second and third counts, and land noiselessly on the fourth. Next, I rerun these movements, adding, in my head, the melody of the music in place of the counts. Each of these processes I repeat multiple times.
>
> Now I am ready to make the imagined concrete. Up on the stage, I rehearse what I have envisioned—step by step, count by count, without music, over and over again. Sometimes I spend as much as two hours on a dance sequence that is perhaps one-and-a-half minutes long. During these repetitions, I count the beats out loud as I dance, even rehearsing how I will breathe. I also practice the dance movements in three different tempos: slow motion, ideal, and accelerated (in case the orchestra conductor has an adrenaline rush during the performance). I am now prepared to handle any tempo that may emanate from the orchestra pit.

360

When you're first on your feet in the rehearsal room, there is a lot of standing around while you begin to determine where you move and why. It's essential that you don't begin to adopt the physical rhythms of this early physical and mental stammering.

You'll develop a "your turn-my turn" syndrome or a "you speak, then I'll speak;" you move and now, if it's my line, I will possibly move as well. You act, then I'll act, as opposed to seeing yourself and your character constantly in motion, both in thought and physicality.

Active thought is very apparent when watching actors who are constantly ready to do something or say something. You know that they're thinking something, because they have a sense of being *occupied.* Practice this in rehearsal. What are you doing? What do you want? How are you going to get it? It's constant, it's 360.

Listening

In David Hlavsa's very insightful book about the four-week rehearsal process, *An Actor Rehearses,* he speaks about listening in a way that I want to repeat here, as one of the techniques you have to give priority (p. 50):

> I've come to realize that the listening my teachers were talking about is not a function of earnestly hearing everything the other guy has to say, to the point where you could repeat it back verbatim if there were a quiz. It's about trying to figure out what's going on with that other person … and especially about what they are trying to do to us, do for us, do with us, do in spite of us. For actors, the skill of "listening" is the ability to tune into a whole range of verbal and nonverbal signals.
>
> For all your work on building an inner life for your character, the best possible way to get to know him is to pay attention to, react to, jam with, what the other actor is giving you. When you speak your character's words, how does the other guy respond?

There is an *effect* that your words have on your scene partner that creates a response. The audience needs to see that you take in their reaction, which often prompts your next line, after all.

What's your secret?

Every day and in every conversation, you have a secret. It could be a new relationship that you haven't told anyone about. It could be a bad grade that you have received and don't want anyone to know. You might have gotten so drunk the night before that you're trying to hide its effects, or you might have decided in your heart to break up with your boyfriend and haven't told him. You might be gay and haven't told anyone; you might want to become an actor and haven't told anyone. You might be about to give up acting and haven't told anyone. Our secrets are ad infinitum. Your character has them as well—and it's up to you to find them or decide what they could be and then hold on to them. They're yours to know and hide or reveal only in your averting glances.

The interesting thing is that the audience can tell you are holding something back … more than the script might indicate. It will add to your character's mystique and a depth in your performance if you construe a story of your character, often hinted at in the text if you look long enough.

Memorizing

Whether you begin to memorize immediately or simply super-familiarize yourself with them by reading your lines every day, you'll be much farther ahead of the game once you start the official rehearsal.

Various approaches

1. As you rehearse: you are familiar with the script as you begin to block, seeding thoughts and actions into your work as you become even more familiar and repeat in rehearsal so often that you lay aside the script, having memorized the lines *organically by doing* during the course of rehearsal, usually two to three weeks.
2. Simple repetition: one line at a time, until you have it without referring to the script.
3. Tape recorder: listening to them over and over or leaving blank spaces for your lines by asking your cast mate to record the scene with you so that you have his or her voice doing his or her lines instead of your own.
4. Writing the words out over and over until you begin to learn them.
5. Rote learning or grocery list: one page at a time, rote, repeating them by learning the first line; add second line; repeat first and second; add third; repeat first, second, and third; add a fourth, and so on, especially effective for monologues.
6. In your words: learning the thoughts, in your own words, and then replacing them with the actual lines. However, if you know the thoughts and the intentions of the scene, you'll be able to say something to keep the scene going.

Drill them. Repeat what you've learned aloud as often as possible. However, be careful not to monotone your words as a simple remember-through. If you do this often enough, it can possibly color the way you say them during the scene. Give your lines intent, even when practicing.

Reflecting: What are you saying and why? When I am learning my lines, I usually won't open my eyes in the morning without going over a section that I've recently memorized. I keep the script next to my bed to refer to it for parts that I don't remember. Never struggle to remember a line! Ever had the experience of forgetting a line in the exact same place every time? My theory is that you've memorized a blank spot by repeatedly struggling to remember it. Simply look it up if it doesn't come, which should fill in the blank spot.

Off-book early

This approach was once considered verboten and is still often frowned upon by purists who believe that lines should be remembered alongside the actions and learned after the thoughts that prompt them are discovered. Many actors I've spoken with are now learning their lines early to get the book out of their hand sooner. Without the script, you are able to follow your physical and emotional impulses without stopping to look for your next line.

I remember that the first time a director demanded that his cast arrive at first rehearsal off-book, there was a near mutiny among the shipmates. Most everybody felt it would threaten their creative process. However, with only three weeks to rehearse John O'Keefe's *Wild Oats* at The New Jersey Shakespeare Festival, director Christopher Martin wanted the cast without scripts in their hand. I was playing the lead, Jack Rover, while performing Orsino in *Twelfth Night* during that summer's repertory. So, early in the morning with a review late at night, I drilled the lines scene by scene until I had them down.

As the first rehearsal arrived, we began blocking immediately. Chris would sit on the stage with the actors to hear the scene first, giving us a chance to speak the lines aloud in front of one another and then to get up on our feet and find the movement of each scene.

Everybody loved it! Nobody expressed difficulty changing their interpretations from their home kitchen to the stage, and within one week we had the play on its feet and were beginning run-throughs off-book and able to focus on the characters through-actions rather than learning our words. All of the stops and starts inherent during the early work without scripts was eliminated.

In an interview, I heard Rob Reiner say that actor Jack Nicholson arrived on the film set of *A Few Good Men* totally off-book. When I did *King Lear* with actor Hal Holbrook at The Great Lakes Shakespeare Festival in Cleveland, OH, Hal had spent the last six months learning his lines.

Actor/director Jerry Whiddon agrees:

> And I think it's an old wives' tale that you learn them in a certain way and it's hard to break that pattern that you've learned, I never found that as an actor to be true. If I familiarize myself as much as possible

> with the script, I walk in and I'm much more on the ball of my feet emotionally, intellectually and physically to be able to respond to what a director asks me to do. I just find it much more fun; to make these words very much an active part of my being. If the director and I want to go in a different direction, it's so much easier than having to refer to the script so assiduously.

Memorizing calendar

I've always found it helpful to mark my script with specific days to have sections memorized. It's a goal that motivates daily work on the words.

Directing other actors

Never. However, Stephen Spinella (Tony Award for *Angels in America*) turned to me during rehearsal of *The Crucifer of Blood* at the Berkshire Theater Festival one day and simply said, "*May I suggest something?*" I was playing Inspector Lestrade to his Sherlock Holmes, and he thought of a funny bit that I might employ during a scene. I thought it a classy way to introduce an idea to another actor without imposing.

If you've established a rapport with your company and possibly suggested to another actor to make suggestions, many minds can be better than one. However, it's tricky territory when you see a moment that can or perhaps should be played differently by other actors. Give them their process as you want them to give you yours.

Positive feedback: where do you see my character?

Sometimes all you need is a positive recognition of when your director sees your character. I like to ask, "Let me know when you see him. …" be it a line, a reaction, an action, or a movement. From that, I can build a more complete version.

Emotional or spiritual

The power of positive thinking

You will find your character or your character will find you. You just have to simply have faith that there is not another option.

Synchronicities

Actress Kathryn Kelley explains how sometimes the world conspires to help you with your work when your antenna are high enough:

When you commit whole-heartedly to becoming an actor, you line yourself up to be used in the service of revealing humanity to itself. Expect to experience synchronicities, especially early in rehearsal, or during the time when you become deeply attracted to a role being cast. Coincidental encounters—with people, books, objects, films, weather, music, stray bits of conversation, dreams—anything observable can become soul-charged and piercingly meaningful to the role you're seeking, or the role which is seeking you.

A few examples—within a few days of being cast as Sheila in *A Day in the Death of Joe Egg,* I overheard a young mother talking to a friend in a thrift shop about her severely handicapped daughter, very similar to Joe in Peter Nichols' play. I knew I needed to get to know her, so I approached her and she let me into her life. We felt we were guided to one another.

Another time, during the first week of rehearsals for *Playing for Time,* the actresses who would have their heads shaved to play Auschwitz prisoner/musicians went to a little shop to purchase wigs, which would be removed after the early deportation scenes. "Why are all you young women looking for wigs?" asked an elderly woman in the shop. When we told her we'd be playing in Arthur Miller's holocaust drama, the blood drained from her face and she drew us close to her. "My four sisters died at that camp, but I survived." We were shattered and inspired by that encounter. Theatre reminds us that we are "more than we know."

Heat and light

Actor Paul Morella told me that:

> One of [the] dynamics I found very useful and enlightening was the concept of "heat and light"—something a director shared with me a number of years ago—or emotion and clarity. It's the idea that many actors want to ride the emotion in a scene or moment, without trusting the clarity of the expression to carry the emotion. To really make every point land, every intention count, every motivation clear at all times—and then let the emotion or "heat" take care of itself. It's very easy to have an argument with another character and get swept up in the emotional dynamics at the expense of what that argument is about, and what the characters truly want from one another. I found it very valuable to focus more on making the points—really landing them—than it was to color or inform them with emotion. The "light" carries the "heat"; the "clarity" carries the "emotion."

Body cries

Actress Kathryn Kelley suggests "If a scene is falling flat because the stakes seem too low, try 'body cries' to aggravate a character's need: Help me! Love me! Take care of me! See me! Respect me!

"Simply scream the need from inside you, silently. Let every cell of your body participate in this silent scream!"

Meditation, prayer, and centering

As the pressures of a short rehearsal period surround you, it's important to stay as centered, focused, and positive as possible. Alongside your rehearsal schedule, find a way to strengthen your personal resolve and keep the rehearsal in perspective to the rest of your life, be it religious devotions, daily yoga exercise, meditation, tai chi, or reading materials that take you into a relaxed and uplifting mode.

You'll return to the daily focus of your show with a renewed energy.

Resting

Sleep on it

Whenever I'm stumped, whether I'm acting, directing, or engaged in a tough memorization sequence, I resort to what I thought was a great personal secret. I take a nap! Strangely and consistently, whether it's a nap or overnight sleep, the lines start to come, and the ideas often start to gel. I always assumed that the unconscious mind continued to work once the seed was planted, and it turns out that I was right.

My wife, Christie Brown, recently earned a second degree in psychology; she directed me to formal studies that confirmed it: sleep improves memory and learning:

- "Naps help move new info from short-term memory storage in the hippocampus to long-term storage in the cortex," said U. C. Berkeley's Matthew Walker at the annual meeting of the American Association for the Advancement of Science in San Diego.
- In *Sleep, Learning, and Memory,* Dr. Robert Stickgold discusses how sleep plays a role in memory, both before and after a new learning situation. "Research suggests that sleep helps learning and memory in two distinct ways. First, a sleep-deprived person cannot focus attention optimally and therefore cannot learn efficiently. Second, sleep itself has a role in the consolidation of memory, which is essential for learning new information."

- In *Psychology Today*, "Sleep Boosts Memory. Another benefit of a good night's rest: better recall" by Colin Allen [October 1, 2003]. "Apparently, in the process of cleaning up our scattered thoughts, sleep also finds the ones that were about to slip through the cracks."

It may be obvious, but sometimes actors fail to associate the amount of sleep they're getting with the creativity needed in rehearsal and the ability to not only learn words but live in them.

Director JoAnne Akalaitis:

> I think if you can't solve a problem in the moment, then you say, let's drop this, let's go onto something else and we'll think about it tomorrow. That's become more important to me.

Let it go

Although a 24/7 consciousness will continue your creative state—consciously letting it go will make room for new thoughts, too. You've got to forget about it on occasion to give it space and breathing room to return. There is a certain amount of healthy indifference that will make room for continued creative impulse that is not strangled by too much effort.

While privately rehearsing a long speech on stage in my leading role of the twins Hugo/Frederic in Anouilh's *Ring Round the Moon* at my graduate school, Southern Methodist University professor John Stefano happened to be walking backstage and heard me practicing. He walked up to me, put his hand on my shoulder, and said the words to me that I have carried with me in every role since: "Don't work so hard."

There's good hard and bad hard in everything. I knew exactly what he meant, for my work was without ease and full of effort. I was pushing out of fear and not trusting the material.

Let it be

It is what it is, it is where it is. One step at a time. One day at a time.

- Relaxing events: Go to a ball game, a museum, a movie, or a new restaurant. There is much to be said for healthy alternatives during an arduous rehearsal process.
- Exercising: Work out daily. An hour on stage can feel like four hours at the office. Your body is depending on you to release the tension through daily exercise.

- Indulge not during rehearsal: Go easy on anything that will throw you off physically. You can spend half your time recovering instead of rehearsing; remember, you're in training.

Staying healthy

Repeating an admonition from playwright Eric Ehn: "Watch your sleep and nutrition, exercise patience, and expect that the answer will be more in your body than in your head, and more in your hearing than through any other sense."

Specific summary

Based on what you know about yourself: do a character sketch! What kind of rehearsal process would this person most likely engage in?

Here's a summary of options I've suggested: can you describe them?

Good ground
Approaches

- Creative process
- Digital discipline
- Permission, power, and protection
- *Lectio*: Four actions
- The four agreements

Get S.E.R.I.O.U.S.
24/7 Consciousness
Collaboration emphasis with all the artists

Techniques:
Physical

- Private study
- Reading, reading, reading
- Prompt book
- Play analysis sheet
- Givens of the play/scene by scene
- Characterization S-O-I-L—from script, observation, imagination, live with them
- Character bio
- Character analysis sheet
- The hidden story
- Physical warm-up
- Use of self

- Rehearsing the scene
- Five one-hour sessions
- Script in hand
- Character warm-up
- Character object exercise
- Spontaneous reactions
- In your own words
- Costume your character
- Sotto voce
- Repetition exercise
- Psychological gesture
- The actors around you
- Expand the text
- Extend the scene
- Riffing the character theme
- Independent activities
- Interrupting
- Physical choice
- Just do it
- Private time on set
- Hand recorder
- Home space
- Overnight review
- Move through review
- Extremes
- Repeating scenes
- Real-life situations
- Practice outside of rehearsal
- Speed through review

Mental

- Substitution
- Thinking in character
- Back story
- Populate your imagination
- Subtext
- Inner monologue
- Visualizing
- 360
- Listening
- A secret
- Memorizing techniques

- Making suggestions
- Positive feedback

Emotional and spiritual

- Positive thinking
- Synchronicities
- Heat and light
- Body cries
- Meditation
- Sleep on it
- Let it go
- Let it be
- Stay healthy

17 Understudying

The readiness is all

> I was understudying Alan Alda in Neil Simon's *Jake's Women* on Broadway and as I watched from the back of the house, I kept having to turn around and watch over my shoulder so I could remember which way he was actually walking on the stage!
>
> —Munson Hicks, New York actor

Understudying is tricky territory, and most all actors at one point or another are asked to stand by for a role that has been created by another actor. Learning the lines and the blocking, watching the performances, and reproducing the character during afternoon understudy rehearsals demand a unique set of muscles that can be practiced. Preparing to *go on* at a minute's notice is a high wire feat that can take even more rehearsal than originating the role.

Gregg Mitchell, Broadway dancer and actor, told me that " … your best dancer should be your swing," those ready to step into any role at a moment's notice. So, it should be considered a compliment when asked to stand by and carry the show in case of crisis. There is a lot of money resting on your ability to keep the show going and sometimes improve it by bringing a new level of immediacy and danger to the rest of the cast.

Conrad Feininger knows this better than anyone. He is an accomplished actor who started his career in Washington, D.C. by understudying major roles for major players:

> I think the purpose of understudying is to create as seamless a transition as possible between the actor playing the role and yourself so that the production itself isn't impacted by the absence. There isn't really creative freedom … if you think it's ridiculous for the character to have that hissy fit down right, well, get over it. Your process has put

you in a position where you are trying to achieve the other person's performance, not your own.

The laws of understudying

Conrad's Ten Commandments:

1. Start early and watch early—read often—for understanding—the more you hear it, the easier it will be—so that when you play it, the rhythm of the role is familiar.
2. Make a calendar—deadline of days to get pages done with ruthless, ruthless review.
3. Don't be a toady (a brown noser):You've got a job to do, that's all. There is no need to suck up to the stage manager or the actor(s) you are covering. Everyone knows you are there and working to be ready.
4. Keep the ball in the air: In other words, when you go on, if you can't think of the line, say something, but keep yourself active, physical and in the play because the minute you deflate and feel bad about what's going on, you're already so dead and there's no point in continuing.
5. The Stage Manager is your best friend. He or she has all the notes on the blocking and will be the one who coaches you through the blocking, line notes and calls you when you need to go on. He or she is also the one supporting you when you do go on.
6. Don't get greedy. When you have to go on, ride the wave but don't get greedy; the performance may go incredibly well, much to your surprise. No need to watch yourself or revel in the glory of having saved the day, scene by scene, because catastrophe is right around the corner. Stay focused and thank your lucky stars with every realized scene without thinking too much about it. You have another scene to do!
7. Suspend your disbelief higher than anyone else. You have to be more in the given circumstances of the play than anyone acting or watching. This is your job, this is what you know how to do, so just do it.
8. There is safety in repetition: It takes rigid, rigid work. Hit the script heavy in the morning, once in the afternoon and at night. There is no amount of preparation that will have seemed too much when you have to go on. So, over-extend yourself in the weeks prior to the event. You have to be ready and there is no substitute for a daily and religious work-out.
9. Keep going. Make a mistake? Move on—don't ever look in the rear view mirror, it's not there anymore. Undoubtedly there will be a line or two, a blocking moment or an action that you may fail to complete in the heat of the action. Forget about it and move on … the less

you dwell on the mistake, the less the other actors, the audience and especially you will give it any weight.

10 Achieve their performance, not yours.

My interview continued with Conrad as he explained understudying traps and tips.

Understudying traps

> Trying to be perfect: You don't want to be too good as an understudy starting out in your career … (which is not meant to be discouraging), but you can develop a value as an understudy that could exceed your value at that point in your career and it's hard for directors to think of you in another way.

Tracy Letts, actor and author of *August: Osage County,* agrees. In a *Washington Post* article, he reports being asked on a second occasion to understudy for the Steppenwolf theatre company. "I said no. I turned 'em down. It was at a time when I really needed the job, too. But I thought, they're gonna think I'm the understudy if I keep doing this. And I don't wanna be the understudy."

Conrad continued:

> Covering multiple parts: You treat them individually; when you're looking at one, don't look at the other. Attend every rehearsal.
>
> Don't rank by size: Say you're covering Lysander in *A Midsummer Night's Dream*, plus a soldier in the Athenian court and Sugar bun, the little fairy. If the fairy is supposed to bring Bottom the horn that gets Bottom his big joke and you weren't paying attention to that because you were learning Lysander's lines—then … "things are bad."

Tips to remember

- During previews, never take your ears off it, and if you can, your eyes—watch from the wings.
- Never let them see you sweat—but if you're sweating, you meant to!
- Self-preservation requires competence.
- Everyone has an agenda, such as the ambitious young director who wants to pump out a good rehearsal—so you shouldn't let other people's agenda be yours. Take the time you need to understand exactly what you have to do.

Information

Understudy rehearsals generally don't begin until preview week. There is a good chance that you're already in the production and have known you would be covering a particular role since the beginning. So, you've been able to live with the actor's process and discoveries all along the way. You have had your own work to accomplish in your role, (which could be sizable in certain companies, even though you're standing by for someone else) which creates a domino effect once somebody misses. Nevertheless, understudy assignments are a union requirement, and the theatre generally tries to protect its production by assigning those who are most capable to cover.

Now is the winter of our discontent

Actor Jeff Allin, on understudying:

> *Meditation*
> … I was actually hired to play Ratcliff and cover Richard for a few performances during the nine-week run.
>
> First off, I knew it would be imperative throughout this process, learning and performing one of the larger roles in Shakespeare with little or no rehearsal, to maintain a sense of equanimity and calm. There would be so many variables over which I had no control; I had to be able to manage the one variable I could control, myself. I wanted to be intentional about my time, my energy, my thinking. I mean, quite literally, my thoughts and attitudes in the midst of it all. So what did that look like? For me, it meant noting when my thinking was unproductive, anxious, fearful, doubting, negative (fill in the blanks, we've all been there), and halting that train of thinking by shifting my attention to a more useful activity i.e., picking up my script and studying lines, breathing, stretching, sitting in on a scene, anything to break the negative pattern and move into a healthier, more productive mode … Tai chi, yoga, certain methods of prayer, breathing techniques, affirmations, all of these allow us to interrupt patterns and redirect our attention. I'm not suggesting that we must eradicate negative thoughts, I am suggesting that it doesn't serve to get lost and trapped in a stew of negativity.
>
> *Imagination*
> From the time I took this job on, well before rehearsal and the learning of lines, I began to imagine myself as Richard. Of course, as actors that's what we do, isn't it? We imagine, we pretend. Now, in this case, I wasn't going to have the benefit of a five-week rehearsal process,

> experimenting, discovering, playing, but I could begin to condition my mind, my self, to the idea of me being the king of England. That's a very important part of the rehearsal process … convincing ourselves that we can say these words, wear this strange clothing, stand on that stage and inhabit, embody this being. So I did it in my mind.

Much to everyone's surprise, Jeff ended up going on eighteen or nineteen times in all, saved the theatre untold amounts of money, and provided the cast with security and consistency.

The lines are the thing

Sherman Howard understudied the well-known American stage, film, and television star John Lithgow on Broadway in *All My Sons*:

> In the theater, security is in repetition, which is why we rehearse eight hours a day, six days a week, for four to six weeks before facing an audience. As an understudy—even under the best of circumstances—you will receive a very small fraction of the preparation you need.
>
> Learn your lines early and say them often. Should you find yourself in a worst-case scenario—thrown on stage in an emergency, with little warning—you will be swamped with adrenaline and your concentration will be under constant assault. Therefore, it is imperative that you know that you know that you know your lines! No matter what! To maintain a rock-solid sense of confidence, I find it necessary to thoroughly go through my part twice a day.

Now I am alone

Author

I was standing on the Arena Stage in final rehearsals for *The Way of the World* when I wondered aloud what I would be doing next. Without hesitation and totally out of the blue, actress Rosemary Knower said, "You'll be doing Hamlet." That very same week, Daniel Fish, assistant director to Michael Kahn at The Shakespeare Theatre in Washington, D.C. asked me if I thought I could learn Hamlet in eight weeks. They wanted me to alternate the role with Tom Hulce (Academy award nominee for playing Mozart in *Amadeus*). I leapt at it. Rosemary was clairvoyant. And the next morning, I wondered how in the world I would learn the role and play it without rehearsal?

I was guaranteed six performances, designed to give Tom an occasional break from the grueling eight shows a week.

Before my opening night, Daniel would walk me through the blocking of every scene and try to include a member of the cast whenever possible, but I would have only one complete run-through. I was told that I could play *my own* Hamlet, but I needed to keep the blocking and basic intentions of every scene that Tom had developed in the role. Ironically, understudy rehearsals were going to officially begin after I had already gone on!

I began to read all of the research materials about the play that was given to the cast by the dramaturg. I needed to begin discovering the role of Hamlet for myself after all, but this was obviously going to be a memorization marathon, unlike any rehearsal process I had experienced.

Memorizing calendar

I have always had a three-day learning pattern whenever I had to memorize by rote:

- Day 1: Read it over and over, breaking the ice.
- Day 2: Capture it until able to repeat it without the script.
- Day 3: Secure it with review, and repeat the words anywhere and everywhere.

I set myself up a calendar with target dates to learn the entire role. The following is the basic pattern I used:

- Break the ice at night (read it over and over, occasionally looking away).
- Learn the same section in the morning (often by rote in the bathtub where I was unable to get distracted. Stay with a scene or monologue until able to repeat it without referring to the page).
- Work the same section on my feet in the afternoon (imagine walking through the scene).
- Secure it at night (repeat the day's work in my head with eyes closed and then break the ice on something new before turning off the light.
- Repeat the pattern the next day with a new section.

Every third day was a review of all three days in the same pattern:

- Review all three days at night.
- Review and capture all three days again in the morning of the fourth day.
- Walk them that afternoon.
- Secure all three days again that night.

Starting the three-day pattern again on the fifth day, one day at a time until the seventh day, I would review those three days' work and also review the entire week's work as well.

This pattern continued one week at a time until I reached the end of the third week, in which case I would review all three weeks in the same pattern: review the three weeks at night, review and capture them again the next morning, walk them in the afternoon, and secure all three weeks that night.

Constant review

Constant review before moving ahead too far was the key to actually getting them in my body, psyche, and confidence. There would be no room for a weak link in the process. Harder phrases were not put off until later but kept in sequence until they were learned and reviewed again and again.

I did not have the luxury of associating the words with the blocking or the security of learning them while looking into the other actor's eyes as a reaction. Those eyes would be completely new to me when it came time to perform them, so the words *HAD TO BE* second nature, rushing into my mind for me to choose how and when to say them.

About six weeks in, or two complete cycles of my memorizing pattern, I had them: three weeks for Act I and three weeks for Act 2, as I remember.

The first few run-throughs of the scenes with the actual cast were rough. I was nervous and, as these rehearsals were earlier, I was still learning the scenes and they were fragile.

But was I doing *my* Hamlet? In all of the memorization, where was the guy?

Parachuting in

I was desperate for a director. Daniel Fish was very encouraging as he walked me over the tightrope of learning Tom's blocking while I was beginning to experiment with my own interpretation. However, his time was limited, and they were all opening the actual production, while my rehearsal was happening in the bathtub or reviewing words while walking around Capitol Hill in Washington, D.C. I called Christopher Martin, founder of CSC Repertory in New York, and asked if he could come to DC and whip me into shape. He had done the show four times and knew every scene, soliloquy, and syllable. With only two days to step through the show, he pulled no punches.

Chris hammered the "givens" of the role into every scene and soliloquy, challenging me with questions. I realized that in my zeal to learn the words,

I hadn't taken enough time with the *who, what, where, when, why, and hows* in the text. "Who is Horatio? What do you want your Mother to do? Where are you coming from into this scene? When do you realize you're being watched by Claudius and Polonius? Why don't you *just* kill Claudius?"

Simply calling me Hamlet and saying *you* instead of *him* began to stimulate my sense of ownership and oneness with the guy. The thousands of words that I now had in my head began to intersect with intentions and personal substitutions.

The run-through came with the entire cast on Friday afternoon, before I was going on that Sunday. The first time through with lights, sound, and costumes on the set felt surreal. However, I quickly turned it into a chance to rehearse and not only find *whether* I could do it but *how* I would do it! As I steadily worked on the *how*, the *whether* faded away. It was up to me to start and stop as I needed. "Can we please do that again?" Tom couldn't have been more generous, allowing me to follow him backstage during a particular performance so that I would be familiar with where the props were set and exactly what the world looked and sounded like before making an entrance. He wasn't competitive in the least and appreciated what it meant for me to do it, while giving himself a vocal rest at the same time.

The week of the performance, I thought I might have a panic attack of some kind, as it alternately felt like impending doom or a great triumph. No matter how many times I could run it in my head, during walks or even private run-throughs with someone on-book, the question remained in my head: could I do it on stage in front of an audience?

Friends had asked whether they could come the first night. I thought, "But who knows what will happen?" Jack Stehlin said, "Well, that's the night to see it! Who knows what will happen?!" I had to agree … high wire, indeed. Will I fall off? That's what makes good theater, right?

Standing backstage, dressed in black and about to go on as Hamlet, I thought, "This is the actor's nightmare." I was not at all certain whether I'd be able to get through it. I had heard of actors turning toward the audience, apologizing, and then walking offstage because they couldn't remember their lines. However, instead of dwelling on that kind of fear, I decided to look at it like a dream come true.

Nevertheless, when I began speaking to Gertrude, the reality hit me, and I began to get dizzy. I actually thought I might faint during the line, "Seems, madam? I know not seems … " The house is full, what if I make a mistake? Can I really get through this entire play? Steady, one scene at a time, Sloan, one scene at a time. I remembered Ben Kingsley's lecture-demonstration in Ashland, OR describing his own first night as Hamlet. He said that when he came to the speech, "Oh that this too too solid flesh would melt … " it was the way that he actually felt. So did I. Hamlet's words become our own.

When Horatio arrived and I threw my arms around him and said, "Horatio or I do forget myself!" a little miracle happened. I was home. I relaxed. This was my stage, my company of players with whom I had performed Berowne, Mercutio, and Edgar. There was no help in judging how the scene was going, I was in it, not watching it. I started having more fun going from scene to scene than I could have imagined. The words led me and sustained me. They became my best friends in the world.

I would perform it five more times during a month of shows, so I guarded my knowledge of the script every day by running the entire play somewhere, usually on the stage.

I recently saw an interview with actress Katharine Hepburn who was recalling her advice to self during the filming of *The Lion in Winter*. "Just say the words, Kate, just say the words."

I learned Hamlet's lines but, for some reason, I kept looking for *him*. Yet, there he was all the time, in his words; waiting for me to *do* them. When I stepped onto the stage, dressed in black, *my* Hamlet was already there, "a little more than kin and less than kind."

18 Actor's block

How professionals break through

> Everybody is very eager, you know, to act! Rather than saying, when somebody throws the ball at me, I'll throw it back. And before that, I'm just kind of looking to find out where the ball is.
>
> —Nikos Psacharopoulos, co-founder of the Williamstown Theater Festival

Practice makes perfect

My first breakthrough occurred in college, but it made a lasting impression on my professional habits. My scene work in college was lazy, and I always put it off until the last minute. My work was often received by my mentor slamming his clipboard down onto his lap in disapproval. I was much more committed to the swim team than I was to drama, and I was usually unprepared because I waited until the night before class to memorize my lines. One time, however, accompanied by a beautiful blonde scene partner, I decided to see what might happen if I actually rehearsed, a lot. I went over the scene with her countless times, finding any available space. It began to feel like I knew it backward and forward and, when it came time to perform it for class, I don't remember thinking about the audience, my teacher, or what my next line was supposed to be. I had it down cold and, for the first time, was able to throw myself completely into it. When we finished, my teacher, Jim Young, slammed his clipboard down onto his lap as so many times before as he said,

"You are so frustrating. You can be so good sometimes!"

His reaction was probably one of those little moments that began a thirty-year career. It seems like a distant dream now, but I can still remember thinking, you mean, all it takes is practice?

Or was it the blonde?

In this chapter, I invited professional actors to speak directly about situations during rehearsal that baffled them and how they overcame their particular problem. Though I don't introduce each of them individually with their credits and awards, all of the following stories come from colleagues whom I esteem highly.

Physical afflictions

> I was having trouble as The Cook in *Mother Courage* at The Shakespeare Theatre Company. The director had begged me to come play the part, and once I agreed, he trusted, apparently, that his own opinion that I was "perfect" for the part would prove to be correct! He was, therefore, unhappy to discover that I myself was not quite so sanguine. There ensued hard feelings—on both sides. Until one day, in utter exasperation, he snarled, "Okay! Look! If you need a clue from me—your feet hurt! Okay? Now leave me alone!" Oddly, those painful feet—that suggestion—was all I needed. Suddenly, the whole man—his feet, his hygiene, his self-regard, even his sense of humor, were apparent to me.
>
> —David Sabin, actor

> I was playing Dr. Chumley, the beleaguered director of the mental hospital, in a production of *Harvey*. During the early stages of rehearsal I couldn't seem to get a handle on the character that would make him in any way interesting—until I decided that he had hemorrhoids, painful hemorrhoids! That made all the difference to his mood and actions.
>
> —Ralph Cosham, actor

A world on hold

> I am an easily bored and distracted person. I crave stimulus and excitement. I have discovered that when I am rehearsing a play, I need a huge amount of discipline to channel all that scattered energy into a working force, and that when I set up my life as best I can to achieve that, I am at my most powerful. What this means is that the rest of the world will just have to go on hold for a while. Friends, that new book I want to read, cleaning the house, laundry and even the news of the world all falls by the wayside. It's about being ready physically and emotionally prepared for whatever moment may present itself in the theatre. I learn my lines as soon as I can possibly cram them in my head, read and re-read the script, research for the role, cook healthy and easily digestible meals, work out, sleep and think, think, think about

my part. It sounds a bit monastic, but it makes me a ferocious actor full of concentration and stamina. Such single-mindedness is not for everyone but it's usually for only about three or four weeks and it's a huge boost in confidence to know you gave it your utmost. Plus, such focus can be easily recalled when you are actually running the show. (I have also found that over time, you can train your friends and family to give you some space, at least during tech week!)

—Kate Eastwood Norris, actress

Really hear her

An instance I recall where I felt that a major breakthrough came in rehearsal that solidified a personal and unique character, happened in a production of Shakespeare's *The Taming of the Shrew,* in which I played Petruchio at Arena Stage in Washington D.C. First, in the early days of rehearsal, I was fortunate enough to be at a restaurant with the famed English director Jonathan Miller who had recently directed John Cleese in the same role for the BBC. He said to me, "You must remember, dear boy, that they are desperately in love with each other." Meaning Kate and Petruchio. It was a revelation and colored my whole interpretation.

Last, when Kate has the page long speech at the end of the play. The "hand under the foot" speech and Petruchio responds with only, "Why there's a wench, Come and kiss me Kate." At one run through, the actress playing Kate found such love and devotion in the way she played the speech, and I was able to leave myself alone enough to really hear her. I found that I was completely choked up and could barely speak. The director came rushing down after to say, "Every night. You have to play it that way every night!" It was an instance of the actor being open and relaxed enough to respond absolutely truthfully, which supported the vision and the storytelling.

—Casey Biggs, actor

As you smell it

Whenever I work on a character, I have to figure out a lot of things about her—but one thing that is powerful for me is figuring out how a character smells. Sometimes it's what perfume she wears (when I played the Doctor in *Agnes of God,* I wore Chanel 19) or sometimes it's more metaphorical—when I was doing Angels, I felt that Harper had to smell, in some way, biblical, to Joe; so though Harper is not wearing perfume at all, I wore this honey and almond lotion that just seemed old testament—it was just a really strong feeling I had about her, that I can't really explain. But I would come to the theatre, put this particular lotion on, and I just felt like Harper. I do this for all of my characters and it's just this strange thing I do. I don't really ever tell anyone about it, but sometimes other actors notice.

—Melissa Flaim, actress

On my own

Breakthroughs have occurred for me when I've taken concentrated time on my own to rehearse a scene, monologue or bit of business away from the group rehearsal. This is much like doodling a sketch on a bar napkin before moving to a "first draft" that you then work on with the director and team. Being able to rehearse unwatched, undirected, and then mentally process for yourself what is taking place, is of great value. This is part of the actor's great responsibility to come into rehearsal prepared. I believe solo, private rehearsals are invaluable.

—Rick Foucheux, actor

Anything goes

The only thing that has kept me in the job has been a sincere communication to the director that I am willing to try anything. We have all known others being fired from projects. One time, I had a horrid time with a director. I even went so far as to offer him "off the books" rehearsal time … and I came in for two hours a day for a whole week to work with him. I guess it demonstrated a lack of resistance on my part.

—Lawrence Redmond, actor

Music locked it in

I've been rewarded with the last inner flicker of a character by pushing myself to search for it … anywhere. "Therese Raquin" was just such a character. The deepest, most emotional character I believe I've portrayed, and yet I felt there was an integral piece of her that I hadn't quite locked into. Instinctively I picked up a tape I'd recently been given and started playing it while I drove. It was KD Lang's *Ingénue* album and the cut "Outside Myself"—"I've been outside myself for so long, every feeling I've had is close to gone … " … wham … there she was … Therese was locked in. I've found music to be a good entryway to complete immersion into a character.

—Valerie Leonard, actress

The moment before

Many years ago, I was fortunate enough to land a plum job straight out of school—three roles in rep at the Oregon Shakespeare Festival. While rehearsing for the third—Berthe in *The Father*—I felt stuck. I was doing everything I knew how to do and still felt "at sea" in the first scene. I had done all my research, I had examined the given circumstances, and I had chosen my objective and actions. I discussed the scene with actor friends and I talked to the director. Still, I felt like it wasn't quite working.

Finally—I don't remember how this came to me—it occurred to me to examine the very moment before I entered the room. Not what was happening to the actor—am I relaxed, am I breathing—right before I came on stage, but what had happened to Berthe in the moment right before she came into the room? I can no longer remember the scene well, nor whether my choice was exactly appropriate to it, but I do remember that I decided that Berthe, 14, had slapped her grandmother in a childish fit of pique. It had scared her and upset her and she wanted her father. So I would physically make the action back stage and then enter. It propelled me into the room, raised the stakes and made all that followed more specific for me. Ever since then I examine all my "moments before" and encourage everyone I coach to do the same. The power of the very moment before is strong.

—Gloria Biegler, actress

The doctor's Hush Puppies

I once played the role of Walter in Arthur Miller's *The Price*—an arrogant, tightly wrapped, highly successful surgeon whose attire reflects very expensive tastes (in the text he is described as wearing a camel hair coat).When I saw my wardrobe, I found it to be suitably elegant with the exception of my shoes. The costume designer had decided to go somewhat casual and put me in Hush Puppies. Despite my opinion that I should wear "surgeon shoes"—Italian loafers or something of the sort—the end result was that I found myself wearing an expensive suit, an elegant camel hair coat, and shoes which—especially after they had been distressed—I considered to be downright shabby looking! I appealed to the director but she didn't see a problem.

Once we were in performance I actually found the shoes to be distracting. Walter would never wear these ugly things! Especially today, seeing his brother for the first time in sixteen years. Every time I happened to see my own feet I would experience a wave of anger and exasperation that broke my concentration and pulled me right out of the play. Since my opinion about the shoes was not going to change, I decided to make a slight adjustment to my back story—to the imaginary circumstances that brought me to my first entrance. The new story was this:

Last week Walter dropped off his favorite pair of shoes—the ox blood Italian loafers—at the shoe repair shop. They should have been ready two or three days ago. This afternoon he was running late and on his way to meet his brother (where the play begins), he stopped at the shoe repair shop only to discover that his loafers still weren't ready! Forcing him to wear the shabby, knockarounds he happened to throw on as he was leaving home. …

It worked like a charm! Now, every time I looked at my feet I still felt a wave of anger—at that idiot who ran the shoe repair shop (who happened to look an awful lot like my costume designer).

—Sherman Howard, actor

I'm not Liza Minnelli, I'm Sally Bowles

After three callbacks, I landed one of my first major leading roles in the Chicago theater scene, Sally Bowles in *Cabaret*. Naturally I was thrilled but a little apprehensive about approaching such an iconic role so identified with Liza Minnelli, who also won an Academy Award for her portrayal in the film.

I prepared for the role and had done my research, but throughout the rehearsal process I found I was constantly being compared to and criticized against Liza Minnelli's Sally. Of course my belief was that I wasn't playing Liza Minnelli, I was playing Sally Bowles. I had support from my director but the pressure continued, particularly from the producer and artistic staff of the theater, and the pre-show press articles that were coming out. I thought I was going mad. I started to lose confidence in my judgment. I became confused, insecure and doubtful. Worst of all, I found myself trying to accommodate and please the powers that be who had hired me. I received words of encouragement from my director but with opening night imminent, I knew that the only person who could salvage this performance was myself.

I decided to go back to the original research I had done. I found myself focusing on the original creator of Sally Bowles, Christopher Isherwood. In *Berlin Stories*, Isherwood beautifully paints a detailed picture of Sally. Her physical quirks and idiosyncrasies, the unique manner of her speech, the small, fragile girl within the woman. Then, I came across a small phrase describing how she curled herself up on the couch like a small, black cat. It all came back to me, but even more so.

That small description gave me a completely identifiable image that I could hold onto for Sally. I felt I knew once more who my Sally was.

I wasn't trying to be Liza Minnelli, I was trying to be Sally Bowles. …

—Leisa Mather, actress

Ignored

The show had seven roles, and the director spent almost zero time with anyone but the New York actors … it was as though the only ones included in the process were the director, playwright and the two NY actors—we "others" got no notes, no time aside from blocking, and were generally treated the way "extras" are in film … to be moved around and not heard.

Fortunately for me, I was comfortable within the scope of my talent to make the decision to self-direct, and serve the play, and get as much substance from my character as I could. I went back to the text and worked from the point of what the function of my character was in the play, and the history and present state of his various relationships. I determined my arc, and found a way to make my character grow from the beginning to the end. Ultimately, it was my goal to serve the play that made my choices most evident; that may sound like an obvious concept, but I have met too many actors who try and twist the play to serve their choices.

—Michael Willis, actor

Quite by accident

I was doing the U.S. premiere of a Peter Whelan play called *The Bright and Bold Design,* directed by Joy Zinoman. It takes place in the North Staffordshire potteries district in the 1930s. My character, Grace Rhys … she's an odd mix: she's a socialist, and devoted to the ultra-glamorous American movie stars of the time. As rehearsals progressed, I couldn't make it all fit together.

I think it was the first preview when it happened, the change. We had gathered onstage before the show, partly because it was a tricky set and it was a good idea to walk it, work out business, etc., and partly because we just liked being with each other and playing around. I was goofing off with the actresses playing Jesse and her roommate, doing a take-off on the gym teacher character played by British comedienne, Joyce Grenfell. Joy (the director) came to the edge of the stage and said, "Try that." "With Grace? What the heck." I did a less over-the-top version that night, giving Grace an awkward gusto. There she was: she became the unloved outsider. Now I had someone complex, someone who could truly live the life of that play. She went from someone I knew about to someone I knew."

—Helen Hedman, actress

Playwright's note

At the Guthrie Theatre during M Butterfly, Randy Reyes and I received a great note from the playwright David Henry Hwang. "You need to trust that all the layers: political, cultural, gender, etc., were all playing fine; but the play won't work unless they see a love story between two people who can't keep their hands off each other." And suddenly the play became much easier to do. And the playwright was thrilled with our adjustment that night. A very simple, human note opened the play up for us.

—Andrew Long, actor

Use it

I was working on a play with very demanding fight choreography for much of the cast. We had a leading lady who was very narcissistic. A real diva with serious entitlement issues. She was not respectful of the costume staff … of the actors, director, etc. I was working on lines after I had put my really little children to bed, one night after rehearsal, and my baby monitor picked up on a phone conversation between the leading lady and the fight director. We were all staying in the actor housing of the theater and somehow the cordless phone reception crossed. They were bad-mouthing the project, all of us, the director, other actors, the theatre, etc. They were discussing how they could get the scene to be the way they wanted it to be in the rehearsal the next day if they did certain things to direct the scene themselves, etc. I was so upset. I could barely sleep that night.

I went in to rehearsal the next day and watched the entire plan that I heard over the phone play out before my very eyes. I was furious and had a very hard time maintaining professional behavior. I learned more than ever that day, that no matter what difficulty you have with one of your colleagues, your job is to come in every day and be a good actor. Do your job. Explore and rehearse your role. Concentrate and focus on your own work and no matter what the circumstances may be, you have to find a way to get along for the good of the ensemble … I found a way to manage it by using the ire that I felt toward this kind of behavior in the play, in terms of the emotional struggle my character was having.

> It fueled me every day and allowed me to play moments with more energy and authenticity … Focus on the work.
>
> —Ellen Karas, actress

It's in the text

> Some years ago, rehearsing Prospero in *The Tempest*, I was struggling to resolve how this angry, vengeful man eventually forgives his enemies … [until] late in rehearsals during a run through, just before the wedding, when the play within the play is presented, Prospero asks Ariel if everything is ready, and Ariel replies "Before you can say 'come' and 'go,'" and ends with "Do you love me, master? No?" Suddenly for me, this question resonated hugely. Ariel, a spirit, asking, needing to be loved? Prospero—me—had buried love. I fell apart. I realized I loved no one—yes my daughter, as a father, who I was using, not nurturing, for my own selfish ends. This moment, for me, answered why I abruptly end the wedding; forgot about Caliban, Trinculo, and Stephano; want to really punish them and let them off lightly and eventually give up my power.
>
> —Michael Tolaydo, actor

Playing an icon

Otto Frank, from the life and the play *The Diary of Anne Frank*, is an iconic character. He is overwhelming in his story and historical significance. Nevertheless, he's a simple Jewish businessman living during extraordinarily tragic circumstances. I was intimidated with how to portray him, before and after his experiences in the death camp, where he lost everyone in his family. I certainly felt that my own life history paled by comparison and my imagination was struggling with the enormity of his story. Finally, after doing research of the historic events and his person, I found the answer in the rehearsal room. Lea Michele was playing Anne, Bess Rous was playing Margot, and Kathryn Kelley was my wife, Edith. They were my answer. All I had to do was to *care* for them, to find ways to love *them*, worry about them, and respond to *their* concerns. When I worked at keeping them safe, Otto Frank appeared.

19 Rehearsing life

Fake it 'til you make it

All the world's a stage and most of us are desperately unrehearsed.
—Sean O'Casey, playwright

Committing to an action can jump-start the reality of the moment. This is a tried and true methodology during rehearsal. It works in everyday life, too.

Take your skills outside your art, and improve the way you handle your life. In Chapter 6 "Living Rehearsal," I wrote that:

> the rehearsal room is as big as your life. Being an actor is full alert to the small and the significant everyday moments. Every relationship, every job, every broken heart, every memory, every mistake and everyone has the potential to become an inspiration.

The other side of that coin is that your life is one big rehearsal room. Every technique and role you've played has the potential to become an inspiration for you in everyday life as well.

Acting teacher Sanford Meisner said to "live truthfully in the imaginary circumstances of the material." Try living imaginatively in the truthful circumstances of your life!

Characterization technique

I work at a university, and faculty meetings can be places of extreme ideological disagreement and egotistic confrontations. Like many professions and situations, it can get territorial when determining the direction of the department or handling student affairs.

Sometimes personalities clash and create problems on top of the problem you are trying to resolve. Sometimes we just wish the people with whom we oppose would change their way of working or better yet, change jobs!

There used to be a professor in our drama department who could infuriate me. At most every faculty meeting, he would (in my opinion) filibuster during a conversation to the point of exasperation, and I would lose my temper. This invariably required an apology to the entire faculty on my part. This became a double-losing proposition, and yet I couldn't seem to control my response.

My wife, Christie, offered me advice that changed my approach entirely. As I remember it, she said:

> This is the most important person in the room for you. You don't get along and he is challenging you to become better and learn how to handle a difficult situation. I don't know why you expect him to behave differently than he always does. Just expect him to do what he always does, but be ready for it. You're an actor, isn't there some character that you can assume, who would deal with people like him the way you ultimately want to?

I had used acting skills in life situations before, but they were on the lighter side. For instance, one time I couldn't get help buying women's lingerie, so I adopted a French accent, pretending not to speak English very well, and got all the help I needed. I never thought to try my hand at acting my way out of a faculty meeting! I did know several people whom I considered less of a hothead than I who would likely respond better than I toward my colleague.

I chose Nigel, whom I believe to be a very kind man who cares more about the offender than the offense. I began to assume characteristics of my muse and was determined not to be angered and surprised when the disagreement inevitably erupted. Like putting on a hat, I assumed my character's demeanor and his imagined response to my irritating colleague.

If I was to recall the differences, I would say that I spoke softer, slower, making sure that I understood what he had just expressed and then stated my opinion while acknowledging his. It gave me the necessary *distance* I needed to handle it the way I ultimately wanted to. I had to drop "Nigel's" native British accent, but I kept his eccentric clothing.

There are many other approaches to resolving conflicts with people, but I used characterization. I tried to think and behave and costume my guy in a manner that facilitated the cover. In fact, I liked this new guy, with whom I discovered *faking it 'til I could make it*.

> The shortest and surest way to live with honor in the world is to be in reality what we would appear to be; and if we observe, we shall

> find that all human virtues increase and strengthen themselves by the practice and experience of them.
>
> —Socrates

Do a character sketch: learn from it!

Actor Ted Van Griethuysen recommends another characterization technique that you can try under difficult situations:

> I was doing Laertes in a production of *Hamlet* with the Phoenix Company in New York, in 1960 I guess, and there was a fellow in the cast I really didn't like. And Eli Siegel said I should do what I would do in looking at a character in the play: write a character sketch about this actor. Describe him. Talk about him. It's the principal of acting, really. Look through his eyes. How does he see the world? Learn from it. And then there's the director whose criticism you don't like or the bad review. Just pull up your socks and do what Eli Siegel once suggested to a girl complaining about a criticism that she didn't like: "Take the 5%." If there's anything in it, find it. You'll learn something from it.
>
> So whatever the experience, you come out of it having grown.

Character escape

A more entertaining example of using your acting skills to overcome a situation is one that actor Peter Gallagher told me about how he avoided a mugging in New York City. As I remember, he was in the Broadway revival of *Grease* and, as he was walking up Ninth Avenue, a group of young men surrounded him and asked him for money. Quickly, Peter said that he started speaking to them in gibberish, animated and pretending to be confused. Finally, one of the would-be muggers said, "Hey, this guy doesn't even speak English, where you from, man?"

Peter said that he thought and let slip the word, "Bulgaria." They left him alone and went on their way.

Everyday fire drills

You can rehearse everyday life situations and conversations that you want to go well. You can rehearse your reactions to events that have not even happened yet! For instance, I am basically a patient driver but can be outraged by what I consider to be obnoxious driving. I sometimes rehearse how I want to behave when I'm following a bad driver, or someone pulls in front of me, takes my parking space, or honks at me impatiently from behind. I speak to them like the person I want to be. Gregory Peck! How would Atticus Finch respond?!

As actors, we are constantly giving ourselves permission to emotionally "go there" in a scene. We have learned to wear emotions on our sleeve to have them at the ready but, in real life, that can be disastrous. For instance:

Pre-emptive rehearsal

There was a rash of car-jacking incidents in our city a few years ago, and my wife made me promise not to fight anyone over our car. There was also an upswing in muggings and unpredictable shootings, and I agreed that I would come home without my wallet than lie out on a street wondering whether anyone would find me before I was vanquished. However, it was something I had to begin practicing, aloud, to myself. My instincts and emotional reactions to "what I would do" if someone tried to take my wallet had been practiced many times in my imagination, and I had to *re-rehearse* the heroic scenario that I had often seen in my head. I could clearly see myself tackling and disarming a would-be mugger and holding him down until the police arrived. I have nothing against formal training to accomplish this, but I haven't had it yet. My new rehearsal has started to consist of *" ... Take it."* (Of course, I started carrying two wallets, one with cash but without credit cards or identity.) However, "take it" is now in my script.

The point is that every instinct in my body wants to pummel someone who would try to threaten me into doing something that I don't want to do, but I really don't want to go around pummeling people, even with good reason. I know that even if I could pummel someone, there goes my day, because now I've got to call 911 and wait for an emergency unit and the police to arrive. I mean, I know myself. As soon as I pummel someone, I'll have to get them to a hospital, apologize to their mother and children who come to the hospital and see their dear old pummeled dad. It'll break my heart, so, I think I'll avoid all that and just say, "Take it."

Besides, I'm an actor and if *I* get pummeled instead, I could be playing Scarface parts the rest of my career. I know this because I was mugged on the New York City subway by about eight guys. They started by pulling on my watch, so when I fought against letting them take it, I got punched out just before the subway doors opened. The watch band broke anyway, which they took as they left. I consider it a warning, and I'm not about to become Charles Bronson in *Death Wish* 5. So, I practice the alternative, aloud, to myself, under imagined circumstances.

Recently, an opportunity presented itself to perform what I've practiced. A driver thought that I cut him off and angrily sped around me in the opposite lane to pull in front of me and stop at the next light.

When it changed to green, he didn't move, he just kept looking at me in his rearview mirror.

I knew that a confrontation was coming. He was angry. I was ready. I had been practicing.

I waited, looked at him looking at me in his rear view mirror, until I finally motioned with my hand: "after you."

His hands flew up in exasperation, and he jumped out of his car heading toward mine.

Usually, my Irish temper would have faced him off in the middle of the road, telling him to get back in his car if he didn't want to get smashed. However, I have a two-year-old and a wife to go home to, so my actions have repercussions for more people than myself.

I rolled down my window and said, "Hey, I'm sorry about that, I wasn't trying to cut you off." His expletive is deleted; he got back in his car and drove ahead.

Guns in Washington, D.C. are being used at an alarming rate and over nothing. Rehearsal may have saved my life that day.

The living's the thing

You're an actor. You know how to rehearse situations where you need to succeed. Expand your experience to conversations, speeches, presentations, and introductions.

Yes, spontaneity can be the lifeblood of truthful actions and a sense of immediacy, but most every experienced actor agrees that it's better to prepare for rehearsal and then stay open to what could happen. It's a muscle, strengthened with use anywhere.

My brother, Robert Sloan, is the president and CEO of Sibley Memorial Hospital in Washington, D.C. He tells me that he is often required to deliver reports to his board of trustees and that he runs through every report he has to deliver.

> I read my report out loud to listen to the flow and to see if there are any tongue twisters. If the flow is not good then I edit the report as I am reading it. I also look for natural breaks, breathing points and transitions from one topic to another. I review the report for content and delivery. After I have a final copy I read it again the morning of the meeting to identify the key words. I try not to "over prepare" because it loses its spark if I become too familiar with it. I try to keep my voice enthusiastic, optimistic and filled with confidence. It is important for the Trustees to hear and feel my confidence as I give my report. I practice the presentation with that in mind.

Simple, basic, mindful repetition prepares him, readying both his mind with what he's about to do and the muscles in his mouth to say what he wants to say. As a result, the practice gives him the confidence that he *knows it* and, therefore, the freedom to vary from the text and be spontaneous wherever his instincts in the moment lead him.

Living is the actor's work

You are constantly using and improving your observation skills, your imagination skills, your patience for repetition and review, personal independence, and a soulful response to life. When life sucks, your artistry has the chance to deepen.

Creative process every day

My premise is that the more creative and inventive we become in real life, the more our rehearsal process becomes independent and creative, too. We don't leave ourselves at the door of rehearsal. Enlivening our creativity every day will increase our potential as actors every time. Becoming a problem solver is much of what living is about. As you practice employing creative methods every day, those practiced methods enter the rehearsal room with you too.

- Fluency: lots of different answers for a solution
- Flexibility: looking at a problem from different perspectives
- Originality: trainable through practice, pushing oneself beyond the "expected."

You don't need to be in a play to develop this creative muscle. Every day presents opportunities to exercise your abilities to respond with brainstorming techniques and thinking outside of the norm.

Permission, power, and protection

As in rehearsal, and regardless of whether your parents, teachers, spouses, or partners have or haven't given it to you, you must give yourself the permission, the power, and the protection to live your life the way you want to live it. This is the strength that will maximize your rehearsal process and daily existence. It takes practice.

Staying serious in your life

Take your normal everyday existence more s.e.r.i.o.u.s.ly, too. Try *studying* a particular issue in society for a change, out of mere interest, without assignment. Stretch your exploration muscle by *exploring* a new area of town or musical instrument that you've always wanted to play. Find your way somewhere without a map or at least take a different route somewhere. As you travel, it's not always about getting there as fast as you can but enjoying the trip itself. Get off the highway and visit Radiator Springs (*Cars*; I have a two-year-old).

Employ the *repetition* technique by practicing something you've just learned such as a language, a new poem, monologue, song, or tennis shot. Rehearse different ways of approaching a difficult conversation. It can prepare you for the unexpected. *Independence* is about creating your own future: finding your own apartment, car, or relationship and living the best day you can come up with. Then, take *ownership and responsibility* for whatever happens. An *uninhibited* existence is simply not holding back on your instincts and your passions. It is acting on the truth as you see it in every situation. It takes practice. Just do it. Living with a *spiritual* mind-set is obviously a very personal and self-identified journey, whatever it means to you—be it a moment of awe in front of a beautiful painting or standing amazed at the crib of your newborn baby. It is incorporating your belief in God, life, the secret of positive energy, mysticism, or simply *love* itself into your existence. Practice it every day that it may infuse your work and your life with that spark that Stanislavski describes: " … So long as your spirit is always in a state of exhilaration, so that the ordinary everyday life that surrounds you has always the power to light a spark in you."

Life is a work-out and a high-flying balloon ride for an artist and, in my opinion, the actor in today's world has become digitally distracted and lazy, not engaged in the rigors of sharpening skills, memorizing texts (whether in a show or otherwise), and maintaining the physical, vocal, and mental requirements that an actor needs to be ready when opportunity calls. Walk up the streets of New York City and you'll see a frightening number of people with their heads buried into their cell phones, either texting, e-mailing, or speaking to someone nowhere near their field of vision. They appear to be totally oblivious to the sights, smells, and the classroom of events and characters in front of them. The actor needs to walk through life ready to be amazed and inspired. You'll need it in rehearsal.

> Excellence is an art won by training and habituation. We do not act rightly because we have virtue or excellence, but we rather have those because we have acted rightly. *We are what we repeatedly do*. Excellence, then, is not an act, but a habit.
>
> —Aristotle

Epilogue

> Now cracks a noble heart. Good-night, sweet prince;
> And flights of angels sing thee to thy rest.
>
> —William Shakespeare, *Hamlet*

Gregg Mitchell was a well-known Broadway actor and dancer and my best friend for twenty years. Gregg was a true gypsy and an Italian through and through. He would slap his hand into yours, put his other hand on your shoulder, look you straight in the eye, smile, and say, "How ya doin, buddy boy, you look like a million bucks." One of his life mottos had to be something he often said: "You gotta go for it … full tilt." Gregg did. He gave 100 percent whether he was building a sand box for my daughter or in a Broadway show.

He appeared in *The Phantom of the Opera*, *Merlin*, and *Kiss of the Spider Woman* with Chita Rivera*; Song and Dance* with Bernadette Peters; *Aspects of Love* with John Cullum*; Dangerous Games* directed by Graciela Danielle; *Chicago* with Bebe Neuwirth and Ann Reinking; *Man of La Mancha* with Raul Julia and, many years later, Brian Stokes Mitchell. Broadway was his block, and he wore the gypsy robe.

While on tour in Washington, D.C. at the Kennedy Center in a production of *Forbidden Christmas or The Doctor and The Patient*, Gregg had a heart attack. He was in a scene with Mikhail Baryshnikov when he opened his arms wide and, according to witnesses, floated backward onto the stage, never to recover. People flew in from all over the country to be with him, but Gregg left us during a glorious moment on stage with one of the greatest dancers in the world. He was 52 years old.

Celebrating Gregg's life in New York was like a Broadway show itself, thanks to actor-dancer Robert Montano, who put together the memorial. Bebe Neuwirth and Ann Reinking did a number from *Chicago*, Vanessa Williams sang, as did Bernadette Peters, Debra Monk, Ann Runolfson, and

Brian Stokes Mitchell. Brian sang Gregg's favorite, *The Impossible Dream*. Dozens of Broadway dancers performed and told personal stories about one of their leading macho men in the Broadway dance world.

Chita Rivera said this to me about him:

> When I would work with Gregg I knew I was okay. That's exactly what I meant about being encouraged and being supported and trusting your company. He is the perfect example; I knew that whenever I was dancing with him, it was going to be absolutely fantastic. It's like having good company, it's like having best friends, it's the company you keep—and it all rubs off, you look good and you work together because he gives, gives, gives … listen to me talking about him in present tense—I do that because he's still very much alive, he's a part of my memory, he's a part of my tapestry.

In an article for New Jersey's *Star-Ledger*, Michael Sommers wrote,

> Many performers develop characters from the inside out, but according to the stars and the choreographers with whom he worked in a 30-year Broadway career, actor-dancer Gregory Steven Mitchell was an artist who worked from the outside in.
>
> Mr. Mitchell created his characters through their appearance, agrees chorographer Graciela Daniele … "It was the tilt of the hat, the look of his coat, the way the scarf fell that helped him find those people."

And Sommers quotes Chita Rivera saying, "Gregg carried the entire male gender on his shoulders."

The day of Gregg's memorial fell on me like a tank. I had spent months grieving and then thinking about what I would possibly be able to say. Gregg was godfather to my daughter, and I am godfather to his oldest son, Garrett. Gregg considered himself my "second," the guy who stands beside you during your duel. I was his. And on this day, it honestly felt as if I were holding the coat of my friend after he perished on the field of honor.

I had written down my thoughts and aimed to keep it as light and purposeful as possible, but while watching a run-through of Broadway dancers working on a tango tribute to Gregg, the weight of reality was about to overwhelm me when my wife, Christie, said, "Go rehearse." I knew she was right, but I felt numb.

I found an unoccupied dressing room and stammered through my remarks, without any purpose or presence. To my ear, they just sounded depressed. I thought, "Great, this will add to the experience for everybody. His best friend gets up and can't even put two sentences together. Bum everybody out, why don't you? How selfish is that? Take center stage and start to cry. This is pitiful." I've spent an entire career learning how to cry at a moment's notice but obviously not enough time practicing how not to. "Go over it again."

Again and again I went through it until the words finally hit me—what I was saying really hit me and lifted me into their meaning, their history, and the reason I was asked to say them. Twenty years started to creep into those words and they started to say themselves, with passion, love, purpose, and appreciation. I was the one close enough to bring this man back into the theatre for a minute. It wasn't about me anymore but about what he meant to all of us. I had a few stories that I knew would remind everyone of the unique person who was Gregg Mitchell. I had a chance to celebrate my friend in the one place he loved the most, a theater surrounded by his artist *famille*. I was his best friend, *cast* in this moment *to celebrate* his life.

My "character" became clear in the moments just before I spoke, alone, practicing words, thinking out loud. The time came, and it was no longer about my grief or my sense of responsibility in the moment but, instead, a shared experience between all of us. One of us was on stage, and the rest were watching, but I knew that they were co-directing, co-writing, and filling in their own stories with mine.

Rehearsing the words brought me home, showed me the way through what seemed to be an emotionally impossible situation. It's what actors do, especially when the stakes are high.

James Lipton, on *Inside the Actor's Studio*, asked Al Pacino, "If Heaven exits, what would you like to hear God say when you arrive at the pearly gates?"

To which Al replied, "Rehearsal is tomorrow at three."

Bibliography

Books

Abraham, F. Murray, 2005, *Actors On Shakespeare, A Midsummer Night's Dream*, Faber and Faber, London, England.

Barton, John, 1984, *Playing Shakespeare*, Methuen, London and New York.

Barton, Robert, 2009, *Acting Onstage and Off*, 5th ed., Wadsworth Cengage Learning, Boston, MA.

Boleslavsky, Richard, 1987, *Acting, the First Six Lessons*, A Theatre Arts Book (1933), Routledge, 2005.

Brook, Peter, 1968, *The Empty Space*, Macmillan, New York.

Chekov, Michael, 1953, *To the Actor on the Technique of Acting*, Harper & Row, New York.

Chinoy, Helen Krich and Cole, Toby, 1963, *Directors on Directing*, Macmillan Publishing Company, New York.

Cole, Susan, 1992, *Directors in Rehearsal—A Hidden World*, Routledge, New York and London.

Daw, Kurt, 1998, *Acting Shakespeare and His Contemporaries*, Heinemann, Portsmouth, NH.

Doyle, Arthur Conan, 1894, *The Memoirs of Sherlock Holmes*, *The Adventure of the Crooked Man*, IndyPublish.com, Boston, MA.

Gabriadze, Rezo, 2004, *Forbidden Christmas or The Doctor and the Patient.*

Gladwell, Malcolm, 2005, *Blink*, Little, Brown, Time Warner Book Group, New York.

Gladwell, Malcolm, 2008, *Outliars*, Little, Brown, Time Warner Book Group, New York.

von Goethe, Johann Wolfgang, 1998, *Scientific Studies*, ed. Douglas Miller, Princeton University Press, Princeton, NJ.

Hagen, Uta, 1973, *Respect for Acting*, Macmillan, New York.

Hlavsa, David, 2006, *An Actor Rehearses*, Allworth Press, New York.

Keirsey, David and Bates, Marilyn, 1984, *Please Understand Me—Character and Temperament Types*, Prometheus Nemesis, Del Mar, CA.

Merriam-Webster Online Dictionary, 2011, http://www.merriam-webster.com

Miller, Arthur, 1987, *Timebends: A life*, Grove Press, New York.
Olivier, Laurence, 1982, *Confessions of an Actor*, Penguin Books, Middlesex, England.
Olivier, Laurence, 1986, *On Acting*, Simon and Schuster, New York.
Powers, William, 2010, *Hamlet's BlackBerry*, Harper/Collins, New York.
Rilke, Rainer Maria, 1929, *Letters To A Young Poet*, W. W. Norton, New York.
Ruggles, Eleanor, 1953, *Prince of Players*, W. W. Norton, New York.
Ruiz, don Miguel, 1997, *The Four Agreements—A Practical Guide to Personal Freedom*, Amber-Allen Publishing, San Rafael, CA.
Shakespeare, William, 1997, *Hamlet*, *Julius Caesar*, *A Midsummer Night's Dream*, *Romeo and Juliet*, *Cymbeline*, *King Lear*, *Love's Labor's Lost*, *Richard III*, The Riverside Shakespeare, 2nd ed., Houghton Mifflin Co., Boston, MA.
Silverberg, Larry, 1994, *The Sanford Meisner Approach—An Actor's Workbook*, Smith and Kraus, Lyme, NH.
Spivak, Alice, 2007, *How to Rehearse When there is No Rehearsal—Acting and the Media*, Limelight, New York.
Toporkov, Vasili, 2004, *Stanislavski in Rehearsal*, Routledge, London and New York.

Television/radio/film

Charlie Rose. A Conversation with actor Peter O'Toole. Public Broadcasting network (PBS) WETA channel 26. March 24, 2008.
Hoosiers. Directed by David Anspaugh, writer Angelo Pizzo. DeHaven Production. Hemdale Film. 1986.
Iconoclasts. Cate Blanchett and Tim Flannerey. Sundance channel. October 2010.
Inside the Actor's Studio. An interview with Robert DeNiro. Bravo channel. Jan. 31, 1999.
Inside the Actor's Studio. An interview with Dustin Hoffman. Bravo channel. June 18, 2006.
Inside the Actor's Studio. An interview with Al Pacino. Bravo channel. Oct. 2, 2006.
Looking For Richard. 1996. Directed by and starring Al Pacino, written by Ron Kerrigan. Chal Productions. Jam Productions. Twentieth Century Fox Film Corporation.
60 Minutes. Hilary Swank–Oscar Gold. CBS Network. August, 2005.
Studio 360. Stephen Soderbergh Says Goodbye to Hollywood. NPR. March 3, 2011.
Ted Talks. Elizabeth Gilbert on Nurturing Creativity. Ted.com. February 2009.
The Diane Rehm Show. Interviewing Cate Blanchett. National Public Radio. November 17, 2009.
The Diane Rehm Show. Interviewing A.E. Hotchner. Paul and Me. National Public Radio. March 29, 2010.
The News Hour. Teen Brains on Technology by Miles O'Brien. PBS. January 5, 2011.

Articles

Allen, Colin. October 1, 2003. Sleep Boosts Memory. *Psychology Today.*

Biodrowski, Steve. 2004/2005. Lost Highway, Film Review. *Hollywood Gothique.*

Carney, John. March/April 1993. Drama: Reflections of the Truth, *The Wittenburg Door*, 128, pp. 14–17.

Chaney, Jen. October 17, 2010. Finding a script with the 'zeitgeist in it.' *New York Times*, p. E8.

D'Amboise, Jacques. 2006. The Mind in Dance. *Daedalus*, MIT Press 153(3 Summer):76–77.

Fichandler, Zelda. n.d. Preparing to Rehearse. Tisch School of the Arts at New York University, New York. *MFA Graduate Acting Program.*

Gerson, Michael. August 8, 2007. Ourselves in Shakespeare [Editorial]. *Washington Post.*

Grobel, Lawrence. December 1979. *Playboy* interview: Al Pacino. *Playboy Magazine.*

Itzkoff, Dave. November 22, 2009. Opening Wide His Heart, Now Repaired. *New York Times*, p. 9.

Lahr, John. August 28, 2006. Petrified. *The New Yorker*, p. 35.

Lectio Divina. January 2011. *Wikepedia*. en.wikipedia.org/wiki/LectioDivina.

Sommers, Michael. November 20, 2004. Gregory Mitchell, Masterful Actor. *Star Ledger*.

Stickgold, Robert. December 2007. Sleep, Learning and Memory. *Healthy Sleep. med.Harvard.*

The Four Agreements [Summary]. http://humanpotentialunlimited.com/ *Human Potential Unlimited.*

Wetzel, Dan. January 8, 2010. Agonizing Night for Texas QBs, *Yahoo Sports.*

Photograph courtesy of Keith Hamilton Cobb

About the author

Gary Sloan has been a professional actor for thirty years and has performed leading roles in New York, Los Angeles, and the most prestigious regional theaters in the United States. Recent performances include: a world premiere of a new play for young audiences by Ken Ludwig at Adventure Theatre in D.C.; narrations in *Defiant Requiem: Verdi at Terezin* for the Prague Music Festival as well as the Kennedy Center in Washington, D.C., and *Enoch Arden* by Alfred Lord Tennyson for the Virginia Chamber Orchestra. In 2009, he traveled to the English Theatre of Vienna to perform the role of Walter in Arthur Miller's *The Price*, directed by the late Robert Prosky. He co-authored and continues to perform the role of Edwin Booth in a one-person show, which he did at the National Portrait Gallery as part of the Kennedy Center's Shakespeare in Washington Festival.

Favorite stage roles include Shakespeare's Hamlet, Mercutio, Mark Antony, Berowne, and Edgar at The Shakespeare Theatre in Washington, D.C.; Rakitan in *A Month In the Country* and Kurt in *The Dance of Death* at Arena Stage; Macbeth at the Folger; Walter in *The Price* at Theatre J; Doc Holliday in *Dark Paradise*: *The Legend of the Five Pointed Star* at Cincinnati Playhouse; Moe Axelrod in *Awake & Sing* at the Huntington Theatre in Boston; Otto Frank in *The Diary of Anne Frank* at the Round House theatre; Serge in *Art* at Syracuse Stage; Judge Brock in *Hedda Gabler* at the Hudson Guild in Los Angeles; Jack Rover in *Wild Oats*; and Faust in Goethe's *Faust* off-Broadway at the CSC Repertory; and a production of *King Lear* with Hal Holbrook at the Roundabout Theatre in New York.

Television includes recurring roles on *The Guiding Light*, *As the World Turns* and *General Hospital.*

Onstage, Sloan has appeared opposite such recognizable names as Tom Hulce, Peter Gallagher, Sigourney Weaver, Pat Carroll, Keith Hamilton Cobb, Mary Beth Hurt, J.T. Walsh, Stacy Keach, Fritz Weaver, Michael Learned, Stephen Spinella, Marsha Mason, Kathleen Chalfant, JoAnna Going, Lynn Redgrave, Lea Michele, Robert Prosky, and Hal Holbrook.

Sloan is a graduate of Wheaton College and obtained his MFA in acting at The Southern Methodist University in Dallas, TX.

Index